An Introduction to the Theory of Knowledge

Epistemology, or the theory of knowledge, is one of the cornerstones of analytic philosophy, and this book provides a clear and accessible introduction to the subject. It discusses some of the main theories of justification, including foundationalism, coherentism, reliabilism, and virtue epistemology. Other topics include the Gettier problem, internalism and externalism, skepticism, the problem of epistemic circularity, the problem of the criterion, *a priori* knowledge, and naturalized epistemology. Intended primarily for students taking a first class in epistemology, this lucid and well-written text would also provide an excellent introduction for anyone interested in knowing more about this important area of philosophy.

NOAH LEMOS is Professor at the College of William and Mary. He is author of *Intrinsic Value* (1994) and *Common Sense* (2004).

An Introduction to the Theory of Knowledge

NOAH LEMOS

The College of William and Mary

CAMBRIDGE
UNIVERSITY PRESS

CAMBRIDGE UNIVERSITY PRESS
Cambridge, New York, Melbourne, Madrid, Cape Town,
Singapore, São Paulo

Cambridge University Press
The Edinburgh Building, Cambridge CB2 8RU, UK
Published in the United States of America by Cambridge
University Press, New York

www.cambridge.org
Information on this title: www.cambridge.org/9780521603096

First published 2007

Printed in the United Kingdom at the University Press, Cambridge

A catalogue record for this publication is available from the British Library

Library of Congress Cataloging-in-Publication Data

Lemos, Noah Marcelino, 1956-
   An introduction to the theory of knowledge / Noah Lemos.
      p. cm. -- (Cambridge introductions to philosophy)
   Includes bibliographical references and index.
   ISBN-13: 978-0-521-84213-6 (hardback : alk. paper)
   ISBN-10: 0-521-84213-1 (hardback : alk. paper)
   ISBN-13: 978-0-521-60309-6 (pbk. : alk. paper)
   ISBN-10: 0-521-60309-9 (pbk. : alk. paper)
   1. Knowledge, Theory of. I. Title. II. Series.

   BD161.L375 2007
   121--dc22

                                                        2006038544

ISBN   978-0-521-84213-6 hardback
ISBN   978-0-521-60309-6 paperback

For my sons, Christopher and Adam

Contents

Preface

The theory of knowledge, or epistemology, is one of the main areas of philosophy. Some of the problems are as old as Plato, yet they remain alive and interesting today. This book is intended to introduce the reader to some of the main problems in epistemology and to some proposed solutions. It is primarily intended for students taking their first course in the theory of knowledge, but it should also be useful to the generally educated reader interested in learning something about epistemology. I do not assume that the reader has an extensive background in philosophy.

In writing an introductory text, one must balance many things. I have sought to strike a balance between impartial presentation and advocacy. In general, I have tried to be fair and neutral between competing positions, yet in some places I defend some views. I have also sought to hit the mean between breadth and depth of coverage. I have not tried to cover every important or recent position or to cover every development within the views I discuss. I have tried to focus with clarity on some main features of a few major positions. I hope this approach will be helpful to the reader seeking an introduction to epistemology. I have tried to hit the mean, but as Aristotle says, the mean rests with perception. I apologize for my blindspots.

In chapter 1, I distinguish between some senses of "knows" and note that our primary focus will be on propositional knowledge. I introduce the traditional view that propositional knowledge is justified true belief and discuss in a general way the concepts of belief, truth, and justification. In chapter 2, we consider some problems for this traditional view, problems made prominent in a brief essay by Edmund Gettier. Much of chapter 2 is devoted to considering some simple ways of analyzing or defining knowledge that avoid the problems to which Gettier calls our attention. Unfortunately, none of these are successful, but they represent some basic attempts upon which others have tried to improve. In chapters 3, 4, and 5, we explore some views about what makes beliefs justified. In these chapters we will look at versions of foundationalism, coherentism, reliabilism, and virtue epistemology. I have tried not to discuss every version or nuance of these views. Most likely, too much detail would overwhelm the reader and prevent one from understanding the main points of the theory. In chapter 6, I discuss briefly the debate between internalism and externalism about justification before turning to the problem of epistemic circularity. The problem of epistemic circularity arises when we consider how we can know that our ways of forming beliefs are reliable. Can one use a way of forming beliefs to support the belief that that way of forming beliefs is reliable? Can one use memory, for example, to support the belief that memory is a reliable way of forming beliefs? Chapter 7 addresses the problem of skepticism. We consider several skeptical arguments and consider some main responses to them. These include the Moorean response, the relevant alternatives response, the contextualist response, and the inference to the best explanation response. In chapter 8, we turn to the problem of the criterion. We focus on Roderick Chisholm's formulation of the problem and his favored position, "particularism." Throughout much of this book we will appeal to particular examples of knowledge and justification in assessing criteria of knowledge and justification. Is this an epistemically unsatisfactory procedure? In chapter 9, we will explore some views about *a priori* knowledge and justification and consider whether our *a priori* knowledge and justification is confined to what is "analytic." Chapter 10 concludes with a brief discussion of some central themes in naturalistic epistemology.

Again, I have tried to balance breadth with depth and always with an eye to providing a clear and useful introduction to epistemology. I would recommend that anyone seriously interested in studying the subject read this book in conjunction with a good anthology of contemporary essays in the field. In that way the reader will be exposed to more sophisticated and detailed versions of the views considered here.

I wish to thank Hilary Gaskin of Cambridge University Press for her support and patience. I wish to thank several people who read and commented on parts of the manuscript: Erik Wielenberg, Girrard Brenneman, Luke M. Davis, and most especially James Beebe. I wish to thank my wife, Lisa, for her patience and for putting so much on hold while I completed this project. I also thank her for my sons, Christopher and Adam, to whom this book is dedicated.

1   Knowledge, truth, and justification

Epistemology, or the theory of knowledge, is concerned with a variety of questions about knowledge and related topics. Certainly one of the most important questions is "What is the extent of our knowledge?" Some philosophers, especially those in the "common sense" tradition, would say that we know pretty much those things that we ordinarily think we know. They would tell us, for example, that we know that there are other people, that they think and feel, that we were alive yesterday, that there are cars and dogs, and so on. They would tell us that we know a lot about our immediate physical surroundings, other people, and the past. Others would add that we know various ethical and moral truths and some would also say that they know various truths about God and God's attitude toward mankind. Still other philosophers, influenced by various forms of skepticism, would say that we know much less than any of this, and the most extreme skeptics would say that we really know nothing at all.

Evaluating these views is no easy matter, and when we reflect on them, and the reasons advanced in favor of them, we are soon led to other questions about knowledge. Such reflection might naturally lead us to ask one of the most important and oldest epistemological questions, "What is knowledge?" Over two millennia ago, Plato wrestled with it in his dialogue, *Theaetetus*. Plato sought a definition of knowledge, but came to no clear answer and the dialogue ended inconclusively.

The primary aim of this chapter is to introduce the traditional account of propositional knowledge as epistemically justified true belief. In the first section, propositional knowledge will be distinguished from other sorts of knowledge. In the second section, the traditional account of knowledge will be introduced. Next, I shall make some general remarks about the main components of the traditional account, about belief, truth, and epistemic justification. Finally, I will make some general comments about justification and evidence, and introduce the concept of evidential defeat.

Three senses of "knows"

In ordinary language when we say that someone knows something, we can mean different things by "knows." There are different senses of "knowledge" or, we may say, different kinds of knowledge. Among the three most significant are (1) propositional knowledge, (2) acquaintance knowledge, and (3) "how to" knowledge. Let us begin with propositional knowledge.

Propositional knowledge is knowledge of facts or true propositions. So, consider the following examples of propositional knowledge:

(1) John knows that Caesar was assassinated.
(2) John knows that the sky is blue.

In these examples, the objects of knowledge, or *what* is known, are, respectively, the true propositions that Caesar was assassinated and that the sky is blue.

It is important to distinguish between sentences and propositions. Consider two people, Paul and Pierre. Let's suppose that each believes that the sky is blue. Paul, however, speaks only English and Pierre speaks only French. In expressing his belief, Paul would say, "The sky is blue," and Pierre would say, "Le ciel est bleu." Though each expresses his belief by a different sentence, each believes the same proposition. Similarly, since each knows that the sky is blue, each knows the same proposition.

We may think of belief as a relation between a subject and a proposition. If the proposition one believes is true, then one's belief is true and if the proposition one believes is false, then one's belief is false. We may also think of propositional knowledge as a relation between a subject and a proposition. More precisely, propositional knowledge is a relation between a subject and a *true* proposition.

Propositional knowledge is not the only sort of knowledge. Suppose, for example, someone made the following claims:

(3) John knows the President of the United States.
(4) John knows the Pope.

We might naturally take these claims to imply that John is acquainted with the President of the United States and that he is acquainted with the Pope. We might naturally take (3) and (4) to imply that John has met them. If we *do* take (3) and (4) in this way, then we are attributing acquaintance knowledge to John. To say that John has acquaintance knowledge of someone is to imply that he is acquainted with him or that he has met him.

Acquaintance knowledge needs to be distinguished from propositional knowledge. Obviously, one can have a great deal of propositional knowledge about someone without having acquaintance knowledge of him. I might have, for example, a great deal of propositional knowledge about the President. I might know that he was born on such and such a date and that he attended such and such a university. I might know a great many similar true propositions about him. But though I might have a great deal of propositional knowledge about the President, it would not follow that I have acquaintance knowledge of him since I am not acquainted with him and have not met him.

In ordinary language, when we say "A knows B," we are sometimes using "know" in the propositional sense and sometimes in the acquaintance sense. Suppose, for example, a detective says grimly, "I know this killer. He'll strike again—and soon." Our detective need not be taken to mean that he has actually met the killer or that he is acquainted with him. He might mean simply that he knows that the killer is the sort that will soon strike again. He has a certain sort of propositional knowledge about the killer. Similarly, if I am impressed with John's vast knowledge about Caesar, I might say, "John *really* knows Caesar." Clearly, I am implying that John has a lot of propositional knowledge about Caesar and not that John has met him.

One can have acquaintance knowledge of things other than people. One can have, for example, acquaintance knowledge of Paris or the taste of a mango. If one has such knowledge of Paris, then one has been there and if one has such knowledge of the taste of a mango, then one has tasted a mango. Again, we need to distinguish knowledge of this sort from propositional knowledge. One might have much in the way of propositional knowledge about Paris, knowing what the main boulevards are, when the city was founded, knowing where various landmarks are, without having the sort of acquaintance knowledge that implies actually having been there.

In addition to propositional knowledge and acquaintance knowledge, let us consider "how to" knowledge. Sometimes when we say, "A knows how to X," we mean or imply that A has the ability to X. In other cases, however, when we say that "A knows how to X" we do *not* mean or imply that A has the ability to X. There is, then, one sense of "knowing how to X" which implies that one has the ability to X and another sense that doesn't. According to the first sense of "knowing how,"

(5) John knows how to play a piano sonata

implies

(6) John has the ability to play a piano sonata.

But, again, there is another sense of knowing how to X that does not imply that one has the ability to X. To appreciate this second sense suppose that John is a talented violinist who reads music well, but can't play the piano at all. Imagine that he has a lot of knowledge about how to play a particular piano sonata. He might know, for example, that the right index finger should play this note and the right thumb should play that note, and so forth. Indeed, John might be able to describe precisely how to play the piece, even though he cannot play it himself. In this case, we may say that John knows how to play the sonata, even though he does not have the ability to play. In this sense of "knowing how," (5) does *not* imply (6). There is, then, a sense of "knowing how" to do something which is simply a matter of having propositional knowledge about how to do it. John the violinist, for example, has a great deal propositional knowledge about how to play a piano sonata. But in another sense of "knowing how," he does *not* know how to play a piano sonata because he lacks the ability to do so.

As the previous case illustrates, one can have a lot of propositional knowledge about how to do something without having the ability to do it. Conversely, one can have the ability to do something without having much propositional knowledge about it. To see this, imagine a physiologist who has a lot of propositional knowledge about how to walk. He has studied how one needs to transfer weight from one foot to another, how the knees should bend, how the foot should bend, what muscles are involved, etc. Our expert might have a great deal of propositional knowledge about walking. But now consider young Mary. Mary is ten months old and has just learned to walk. She knows how to walk, but we can easily imagine that she lacks the propositional knowledge about how to walk enjoyed by the expert. Mary's propositional knowledge about how to walk is probably quite meager, if, indeed, she has any at all.

We have distinguished propositional knowledge from both acquaintance knowledge and knowing how to do something. Traditionally, philosophers have been most concerned with propositional knowledge. One reason for this is that philosophers are typically concerned with what is true. They want to know what is true and they want to evaluate and assess their own claims, and those of others, to know the truth. When philosophers ask, for example, about the extent of our knowledge, they are typically concerned with the extent of our propositional knowledge, with the extent of the truths that we know. When one philosopher says he knows that there are external objects and another philosopher denies this, they are disagreeing about whether there is propositional knowledge of a certain sort. They are disagreeing about whether truths of a certain kind are known. Acquaintance knowledge and "how to" knowledge are not in the same way "truth focused." So let us consider the concept of propositional knowledge more closely.

Propositional knowledge and justified true belief

We noted at the beginning of this chapter that the question, "What is knowledge?", is an ancient one. Since our focus is on propositional knowledge, we might ask, "What is it for someone to have propositional knowledge?" Alternatively we might ask, "What is it for a subject, S, to know that p (where p is some proposition)?"

According to one traditional view, to have propositional knowledge that p is to have epistemically justified true belief that p. Before we consider this traditional view, let us begin by considering the following clearly mistaken view:

D1   S knows that p = Df. S believes that p.

According to D1, believing something is sufficient for knowing it. If D1 were true, then someone who believed a false proposition would know it. If a child, for example, believed that $2 + 3 = 6$, then, according to D1 the child would *know* that $2 + 3 = 6$. But the child does not know that. So, D1 is false.

Now, admittedly, people do sometimes say that they know things that are false. For example, a football fan might be utterly convinced that his team will win the championship. After his team loses, he might say, "I just *knew* they would win. Too bad they didn't." But our fan did not know that his team would win. He was simply confident or convinced that they would. His claim to know is perhaps best understood as a bit of hyperbole, as when one says, "I am just *dying* of hunger" or "I'd just *kill* for a cigarette." Such claims are, usually, not to be taken literally. Strictly speaking, what our fan says is false.

Mere belief, then, is not sufficient for knowledge. Knowledge requires that one's belief be true. So, let us consider the following view:

D2 S knows that $p = $ Df. (1) S believes that p and (2) p is true.

D2 tells us that one knows that p if and only if one has a true belief that p. D2 says that having a true belief that p is *sufficient* for one's knowing that p. But this, too, is clearly mistaken. One might have a true belief that is not knowledge. True beliefs that are mere lucky guesses or mere hunches or based on wild superstitions are not instances of knowledge. Suppose, for example, Bonnie reads her horoscope in the newspaper. It says that she will soon come into money. Bonnie has no evidence to believe that this is true, still she believes what her horoscope says. Later that day she finds fifty dollars in the pocket of her old coat. Bonnie's belief that she would come into money was true, but it was not knowledge. It was a true belief based on no evidence. Consider also Malcomb, an extreme pessimist. Every morning he forms the belief that something *really* bad will happen to him today. Every morning he forms this belief, though he has no reasons or evidence for it and the belief is almost always false. One afternoon he is hit by a bus and killed. On that morning, Malcomb's belief that something really bad would happen to him turned out to be true. But it is false that Malcomb *knew* that something really bad was going to happen to him. His belief, though true, was not an instance of knowledge. Since D2 takes mere true belief to be sufficient for knowledge, it implies incorrectly that Bonnie and Malcomb have knowledge.

If mere true belief is not sufficient for knowledge, then what else is needed? One traditional answer is that S knows that p only if p is *epistemically justified* for S or p is *reasonable* for S to believe. We may formulate this traditional account this way:

D3   S knows that $p =$ Df. (1) S believes that p, (2) p is true, and (3) p is epistemically justified for S.

According to D3, knowledge requires epistemically justified true belief. So, let's say that D3 represents a JTB account of knowledge.[1]

As we have seen, D2 implies incorrectly that Bonnie knows that she will come into money and Malcomb knows that something really bad will happen to him today. But D3 need not be taken to have that flaw. To see why consider Bonnie again. She believes that she will come into money. She believes this because she read it in the newspaper's horoscope and she has no other evidence for believing it. Under these circumstances, the proposition that she will come into money is not one that is justified or reasonable for her. Bonnie's belief does not meet the justification condition in D3. So, D3 does not imply that Bonnie knows. Similar considerations apply to Malcomb's case. The proposition that something really bad will happen to him today is not justified or reasonable for him. He simply accepts it on the basis of an exaggerated pessimism. So, D3 does not imply that Malcomb knows. D3 seems in this respect to be an advance over D2.

D3 seems to be on the right track. In the next chapter, however, we shall consider some serious objections to D3 and the need to add yet further conditions. Still, while almost all philosophers agree that D3 is not adequate as it stands, many agree that knowledge does require epistemically justified true belief. For the moment then, let us turn to consider briefly these components of propositional knowledge. I shall make some general comments about each in the hope that we might get a better understanding of the traditional view about knowledge.

Belief

Whenever we consider a proposition, there are three different attitudes we can take toward it. First, we can believe it or accept it as true. Second, we can

---

[1] Versions of a JTB account of knowledge were held at one time by Roderick M. Chisholm and A. J. Ayer. See Roderick Chisholm, *Perceiving: A Philosophical Study* (Ithaca: Cornell University Press, 1957), p. 16 and A. J. Ayer, *The Problem of Knowledge* (New York: St. Martin's Press, Inc., 1955), pp. 31–35.

disbelieve it, i.e. believe that it is false or believe its negation. Third, we can withhold belief in it or suspend judgment. We may illustrate these attitudes by reflecting on the attitudes of the theist, the atheist, and the agnostic toward the proposition that God exists. The theist accepts the proposition, the atheist disbelieves it, and the agnostic withholds belief in it.

As we noted earlier, we may think of belief as a *propositional attitude*, as a relation between a subject and a proposition. There are, of course, many propositional attitudes in addition to belief. Hope, fear, doubt, and desire are just some ways in which one may be related to a proposition. Consider the proposition that it will rain. In addition to believing that it will rain, one can hope, fear, doubt, or desire that it will rain.

Believing a proposition needs to be distinguished from other propositional attitudes such as entertaining and considering a proposition. To entertain a proposition is merely to "hold it before the mind." To consider a proposition is to entertain it and to study or examine it. One can entertain or consider a proposition without believing it. I can now, for example, entertain and consider the proposition that the earth is a cube without believing it. One can also believe something without entertaining or considering it. This morning, for example, I believed that the earth was round, but I did not entertain or consider that proposition.

We all believe a great many things that we are not entertaining or considering. These beliefs are said to be *dispositional* beliefs. My belief this morning that the earth is round was a dispositional belief. When we believe some proposition that we are entertaining, then our belief is said to be an *occurrent* belief. Since I am now entertaining the proposition that the earth is round, my belief that the earth is round is an occurrent belief.

Having a dispositional belief needs to be distinguished from a disposition to believe something. There are many propositions that we do not now believe, but are such that we *would* believe them *if* we considered them. Someone might never have considered the proposition that no elephant is a neurosurgeon and might not believe that proposition. Still, he might be such that he would believe that proposition if he considered it. He would have a disposition to believe that proposition, even if he did not have a dispositional belief in it.

Let's conclude this brief discussion by making two points. First, according to the traditional JTB account of knowledge, knowledge that *p* requires that one believe that *p*. We may say that knowledge requires either occurrent or dispositional belief. Thus, we can say I knew this morning that the earth was round even though my belief in that proposition was dispositional. Second, belief ranges in intensity or strength from complete and firm conviction to tentative and cautious acceptance. Thus, one might be firmly and strongly convinced that God exists or one might accept it with some weaker degree of conviction. Now, if knowledge requires belief and belief comes in varying degrees of intensity, is there some degree of intensity of belief that is required for knowledge? According to the traditional view, knowledge simply requires justified true belief. As long as one believes that *p* and the other conditions are met, then one knows that *p* whatever the intensity of one's belief.

Truth

There are many theories about the nature of truth and about what makes a proposition or a belief true or false. One of the oldest and perhaps most widely held is the *correspondence theory of truth*. The correspondence theory makes two main claims. First, a proposition is true if and only if it corresponds to the facts. Second, a proposition is false if and only if it fails to correspond to the facts. Advocates of the correspondence theory often add a third claim, that the truth of a proposition or belief is *dependent* on the facts or upon the way the world is. Such a view is suggested by Aristotle, who wrote, "It is not because we think truly that you are pale, that you *are* pale; but because you are pale we who say this have the truth."[2] The proposition that you are pale is true because you *are* pale. The proposition that you are pale is true because of, or in virtue of the fact that you are pale.

According to the correspondence theory of truth, a proposition is not true because of what we believe about it. The truth of the proposition that someone is pale, for example, does not depend on our believing it or on what we believe about it. The proposition is true if and only if someone is pale. It is true, as Aristotle notes, because of the fact that someone is pale.

Moreover, according to the correspondence theory, one and the same proposition cannot be both true and false. The proposition that you are pale cannot be both true and false. Neither can the proposition be

---

[2] Aristotle, *Metaphysics*, bk. IX, ch. 9, 1051b, trans. W. D. Ross, in *The Basic Works of Aristotle*, ed. Richard McKeon (New York: Random House, 1941), p. 833.

"true for you and false for me." The truth is not "relative" in this way. Of course, you might *believe* some proposition that I reject. We might thus disagree about the truth of some proposition. Still, the truth of the proposition is determined by the facts and not by whether you or I believe it. Again, suppose that some ancient culture believed that the earth was a disk floating in an endless sea. Should we say that this proposition was true "for them"? According to the correspondence theory, the answer is "no." They accepted the proposition. They believed it was true. But the proposition they believed was false. It did not correspond to the facts.

Still, let us consider the following objection. "Suppose that Jim is in London talking to his brother, Tom, in New York. Jim looks out his window, sees the rain falling and says, 'It is raining.' Tom looks out his window, sees the sun shining and says, 'It is not raining.' Couldn't they both be right? Isn't this a case where a proposition is both true and false?" Of course, they could both be right. In fact, given our description of the case, each of them *is* right. But this does not show that one and the same proposition is both true and false. We should say that the proposition that Jim accepts is that it is raining in London, and the proposition that Tom accepts is that it is not raining in New York. Each of them accepts a true proposition. But they do not accept *the same* proposition.

The correspondence theory of truth is old and widely held. There are, however, objections to theory. Some object that unless we have some explanation of what it is for a proposition to correspond with the facts, the theory is not very informative. Others object that the theory is uninformative because the notion of a fact is obscure. Yet others would say that one cannot explain what a fact is without making use of the concepts of truth and falsity, and, therefore, the correspondence theory is circular and ultimately unenlightening.

These are important criticisms. Unfortunately, to assess these objections adequately would simply take us too far afield. Still, the basic intuition that the truth of a proposition depends upon the facts has proved stubbornly resistant to criticism. I shall be assuming throughout this book that some version of the correspondence theory of truth is correct. It is worth noting, though, that there are other theories of truth. Let us consider briefly two of them.

One alternative to the correspondence theory is *the pragmatic theory of truth*. A central insight of the pragmatic theory is that true beliefs are generally useful and false beliefs are not. If a doctor wants to cure a patient, it is useful for the doctor to have true beliefs about what will cure the patient. If a man wants to go to Boston, true beliefs about which road to take are generally more useful than false beliefs. Noting this connection, the pragmatic theory tells us that a proposition is true if and only if believing it or acting on it is, or would be, useful (in the long run). Roughly, a belief is true if and only if it is useful or expedient. William James, the great American pragmatist, wrote, "The true is only the expedient in the way of our behaving, expedient in almost any fashion, and expedient in the long run and on the whole course."[3]

Suppose that true beliefs generally provide a good basis for action, that they are generally useful and that false beliefs are generally a bad basis for action. Critics of the pragmatic theory note that even if this is so, it would not follow that we should identify true belief with useful belief. Sometimes a true belief might have very bad consequences and a false belief might have very good ones. Suppose for example the following proposition is true:

(7) Tom will die in old age from a long and painful illness.

Suppose further that if Tom were to believe this, he would be quite distraught. The joy that he now finds in life would be greatly diminished. He would be haunted by the specter of his painful death. Let us suppose that it is not useful for Tom to believe (7). Still, since (7) is true, it seems we should reject the view that a proposition is true if and only if believing it or acting on it would be useful. Similarly, there could be false propositions that *are* useful to believe or act on. Imagine, for example, that when Tom is old and suffering from his painful and fatal illness, he consoles himself with the belief that:

(8) Others in the hospital are suffering more than I am and doing so with courage.

Believing (8) helps Tom face his own suffering calmly and with courage. He thinks that since others are courageously facing suffering greater than his, then at least he can do the same. Believing (8) is very useful for Tom. But suppose (8) is false. Suppose no one in the hospital is suffering worse

---

[3] William James, *Essays in Pragmatism* (New York: Hafner Publishing Co., 1948), p. 170.

than Tom. Again, it seems that what is useful to believe is not always true, and what is true is not always useful to believe.

Another theory of truth is *the coherence theory of truth*. Not surprisingly, the concept of coherence is central to the theory. We shall say more about coherence in chapter 4. For the moment, let us consider the following example that we may take to illustrate the concept. Suppose that I believe the following propositions: (i) I have the sense experience of something white in my hand, (ii) I have the experience of something round in my hand, (iii) I have the experience of something cold in my hand. The proposition, (iv) there is a snowball in my hand, coheres with (i)–(iii). It would seem that (iv) better coheres with (i)–(iii) than some other propositions, e.g. that I have a hot lump of coal in my hand.

Some philosophers take the fact that a proposition coheres or "hangs together" with other propositions one believes to be indicative of its truth or a good reason to believe it's true. In other words, they treat coherence as a source of justification. So, for example, if one believes (i)–(iii), then, other things being equal, it is more reasonable to believe (iv) than that one has a hot lump of coal in one's hand because of (iv)'s greater coherence with (i)–(iii). Proponents of the coherence theory of truth, however, treat coherence not merely as a source of justification; they take coherence to be a *condition* of truth. They hold that for a proposition to be true is nothing more than a matter of its coherence with other propositions. Brand Blanshard, a defender of the coherence theory of truth, wrote "Assume coherence as the test [of truth], and you will be driven by the incoherence of your alternatives to the conclusion that it is also the nature of truth."[4]

Critics of the coherence theory of truth raise a variety of objections. First, they note that the concept of "coherence" is murky. Indeed, some critics claim that the concept of coherence is at least as much in need of explanation as those of "correspondence" and "fact." They would say that the coherence theory has no real advantage in clarity over the correspondence theory. Second, they note that we cannot say simply that a proposition is true if and only if it belongs to a coherent set of propositions. A very realistic piece of fiction might be a coherent set of false propositions. Moreover, the fact that (iv) above coheres with other propositions that I believe such as (i)–(iii) does not guarantee that (iv) is true. I might believe

---

[4] Brand Blanshard, *The Nature of Thought*, vol. 2 (New York: Macmillan, 1940), p. 269.

(i)–(iv) and be merely having an hallucination of a snowball or merely dreaming that I am holding a snowball. Indeed, Descartes raised the possibility of massive deception by an evil demon, deception so massive that most of our sensory experience of the world is illusory. In such a scenario, our beliefs about the world around us would be almost entirely false. Still, they might be quite coherent. In fact, our beliefs might enjoy as much coherence in such a scenario as they do right now. But again, they would be false. Finally, critics argue that we should not confuse a criterion of justification with a condition of truth and we should not assume that because we have a criterion of justification we have *ipso facto* a condition of truth. Even if coherence turns out to be a source of justification, it does not follow that it is what makes a proposition true.

Epistemic justification

According to the traditional JTB account, knowledge that *p* requires that one be epistemically justified in believing that *p*. Much of this book will be concerned with the topic of epistemic justification. Indeed, much of recent epistemology has focused on this topic. For the moment, we may make the following general points.

First, the kind of justification knowledge requires is *epistemic* justification. We must note that there are kinds of justification that are not epistemic. For example, the batter who steps up to the plate might be more likely to get a hit if he believes that he will. Of course, he will probably not get a hit. Even for the best batters the odds of doing so are poor. Still, believing that he will succeed and having a positive attitude will help him. So, we may grant that he has a *practical* justification for his belief even if he has no epistemic justification for it. Again, consider someone facing a life threatening illness, one from which most people do not recover. Even though the evidence is against his recovery, a belief that one will recover might improve one's chances. In such a case, one might have a moral or prudential justification for believing that one will recover even if one has no epistemic justification for it. Unlike prudential or moral justification, epistemic justification seems to be tied in an important way to truth, though it is hard to say in exactly what way it is connected with truth. Perhaps we might say that epistemic justification aims at truth in a way that prudential and moral justification do not. Perhaps we might say that if one is epistemically justified in believing a proposition then one's belief is likely to be true. As we shall see, philosophers differ about the connection between truth and epistemic justification. In any case, our focus will be on epistemic justification, so henceforth when I refer to justification, I shall be referring to epistemic justification.

Second, a proposition can be true and not justified. Consider the propositions: (i) the number of stars is even, and (ii) the number of stars is *not* even. Either (i) or (ii) is true. But clearly neither (i) nor (ii) is justified for us. We have no evidence for either. So, a proposition can be true without being justified for us. Again, the proposition that there is life on Mars might be true, but as of now, given the state of our evidence, it is not something we are justified in believing. With respect to these propositions we might say that one is not justified in believing them. Instead, one is justified in withholding belief in them.

Third, a proposition can be justified and not true. One can be justified in believing a proposition that is false. Suppose, for example, you are justified in believing that it is noon. You are justified because you have just looked at your watch around midday and it says that it is noon. But suppose that, unbeknownst to you, your watch stopped working at noon and it is now 12:30. Given your evidence, your belief is justified but false. Again, I might be justified in believing that the person I see going into the library is Lisa. I am justified because the person I see looks, dresses, and behaves just like Lisa. But suppose that, unbeknownst to me, Lisa has an identical twin and the person I see is not Lisa, but her twin. My belief that the person I saw was Lisa is false, but justified.

Fourth, we need to distinguish a proposition's being justified for a person from *justifying* it. Justifying a proposition is an activity that one engages in, often when one's belief has been challenged. Typically when justifying a proposition one attempts to adduce reasons in its support. In contrast, a proposition's being justified for a person is a state that one is in. Knowledge that p requires that one be justified in believing that p, but it does *not* require that one justify one's belief that p. There are a great many things that each of us knows that we have never attempted to justify.

Fifth, unlike truth, justification is relative in the sense that a proposition can be justified for one person, but not for another. This can happen if one person has evidence that another person lacks. Suppose, for example, that Smith is a thief. The proposition that Smith is a thief might be justified for Smith, but not for anyone else. Smith could have a lot of evidence that he is a thief, though no one else has any. Indeed, many of Smith's friends, we may suppose, are justified in believing that he is not a thief. (Here again we would have an example of a belief that is justified yet false.) Furthermore, a proposition can be justified for a person at one time, but not at another time. After Smith is caught, tried, and convicted his friends who have followed the trial closely are highly justified in believing that he is a thief. They now have evidence that they did not have before. Justification, then, can vary from person to person and it can vary for one person from time to time depending upon the evidence he has.

Sixth, epistemic justification comes in degrees. It ranges from propositions that are *certain* or maximally justified for us to propositions that are just barely justified, that are just barely reasonable to accept. The propositions that $2=2$, that I think, that I exist, are certain for me. In contrast, the proposition that I will be alive in three months is one that it is not certain or maximally justified for me. It is not maximally justified because the proposition that I am alive now is more justified for me than it is. Still, I am justified in believing that I will be alive in three months. I am more justified in believing *that* proposition than I am in believing that there is life on Mars or that the number of stars is even.

If knowledge requires justification, then we might ask, "What degree of justification does knowledge require?" Strictly speaking, D3 does not tell us. It seems reasonable to believe that not just any level of justification will do. The proposition that I will be alive in ten years has some degree of justification for me, but it is not high enough for me to *know* it. Similarly, if I know that 60 out of 100 marbles in an urn are black, then the proposition that I will draw a black marble has some positive justification for me, but I am not sufficiently justified to know that I will. So, some levels of justification are too low for knowledge. Should we say, then, that knowledge that *p* requires that one be certain that *p*? That knowledge requires maximal justification? I think most philosophers who have defended a JTB account would say that knowledge does *not* require certainty. They would hold, reasonably, that we do know, for example, that Washington was the first President of the United States, that Caesar was assassinated, and many similar things. But these propositions are not certain for us, they are not as justified for us as $2=2$ or I exist. I think it is fair to say that most defenders of the JTB account would say that while knowledge does not require certainty, it does require a high degree of justification.

Finally, a proposition can be epistemically justified for a person even if he does not believe it. Consider the confident batter who steps into the batter's box. Again, more often than not, even the best batters fail to get a hit. The proposition that he won't get a hit is epistemically justified for him. But though the proposition is justified for him, he does not believe it. Indeed, he believes its negation. Similarly, the proposition that nothing terrible will happen to him today is justified for pessimistic Malcomb, but he fails to believe it.

Some philosophers draw a distinction between a proposition's being justified for a person and a proposition's being "well-founded" for a person.[5] To say that a proposition, p, is well-founded for a person, S, is to say that (i) p is justified for S, and (ii) S believes that p on the basis of his evidence for p. If a proposition is well-founded for a person, then he believes it and he believes it on the basis of evidence that supports it. If a proposition, p, is well-founded for a person, then he not only has good reasons for believing it, he also believes it on the basis of good reasons. In such a case, we may also say that his belief that p is well-founded or that he justifiably believes that p

To illustrate the distinction between a proposition's being justified and its being well-founded, suppose that Jones is suffering from a serious illness. Though the illness is quite serious, he has excellent evidence that he will fully recover. His doctor, an expert in the field, tells him there are highly effective treatments for his condition and that the recovery rate is over 99 percent. Jones also reads the same information about the effectiveness of treatments in a well-respected medical journal. Under these circumstances we may assume that the proposition that he will recover is justified for Jones. Suppose, however, that Jones does *not* believe that he will recover on the basis of this evidence. Instead, he believes that he will recover on the basis of some very bad reason. Suppose he believes that he will recover because his tea-leaf reader said he would, or he believes he will recover simply on the basis of wishful thinking. The point is that even though Jones has excellent reasons for believing that he will recover, his belief is not *based* on those reasons. Jones's belief that he will recover is not well-founded.

---

[5] Earl Conee and Richard Feldman, "Evidentialism," *Philosophical Studies*, 48, 15–44.

If Jones's belief that he will recover is not based on the evidence that he has for that proposition, but is based instead on wishful thinking or the testimony of his tea-leaf reader, then it seems plausible to think that Jones's belief is not an instance of knowledge. We might think that knowledge requires not simply that one have evidence for one's belief, but that one's belief be based on one's evidence. Given the concept of a proposition's being well-founded for a person, we might modify the account of knowledge to take account of the distinction. We might say:

D3′   S knows that p = Df. (1) S believes that p, (2) p is true, and (3) S's belief that p is well-founded.

On this view, S's knowing that p requires not simply that p be justified for S. It also requires that S believe that p on the basis of evidence that supports p. Such a view seems plausible.

Justification, evidence, and defeat

Whether a belief is justified and the degree to which it is justified is often, if not always, a function of the evidence one has for it. One might think of a person's evidence at a certain time as consisting in all the information or data he has at that time. It is widely and commonly held that sense perception, memory, introspection, and reason are "sources" of evidence. We might think of these sources as providing information or data that serves as evidence for our beliefs. We might think that they provide evidence through such things as memory experiences, sense experiences, introspective experiences, and rational intuitions. Such experiences along with our justified beliefs may be thought to constitute our evidence. Thus, my evidence that there is a cup of coffee on the desk would include my sensory experiences that I see the coffee and that I smell it, that I remember making the coffee and putting the cup there on the desk, and my justified belief that I almost always have a cup of coffee on the desk at this time of day.

We may distinguish between two types of evidence, *conclusive* and *nonconclusive*. Conclusive evidence guarantees the truth of the proposition it supports. If e is conclusive evidence for a proposition, p, then it is impossible for p to be false given e. Perhaps we might illustrate the concept of conclusive evidence by considering the proposition that I think. I am introspectively aware that I think. The introspective awareness that I think is evidence for the proposition that I think. It is also conclusive evidence. It is impossible for the proposition that I think to be false given my introspective awareness that I am thinking. Similarly, my introspective awareness that I think is conclusive evidence for the proposition that I exist. It is impossible for the proposition that I exist to be false given my introspective awareness that I think.

Often, however, our evidence for a proposition is nonconclusive. It is nonconclusive in the sense that it does not guarantee the truth of the proposition that it supports. Suppose that I know that there are 100 marbles in an urn and that 95 of them are black. My evidence supports the proposition that I will draw a black marble, but it does not guarantee it. My evidence is nonconclusive. Suppose, to recall an earlier example, I have the following evidence: I see that my watch says it is noon, I am justified in believing that it is around midday and that my watch has been highly reliable in the past. But, again, suppose that, unbeknownst to me, my watch quit working at noon and that is now 12:30. In this case, my evidence that it is noon is nonconclusive. My evidence supports the proposition that it is noon, but it does not guarantee it.

The evidence for the existence of material objects provided by our sensory experience is nonconclusive evidence. As Descartes famously pointed out, it is possible that my sensory experience is produced, not by material objects, but by a powerful evil demon intent on deceiving me. Thus, even if I am having the sensory experience of a snowball in my hand, that evidence does not guarantee that there is a snowball in my hand. It is logically possible that I have that experience and there be no snowball in my hand.

The term "nonconclusive evidence" can be misleading. To say that *e* is nonconclusive evidence for *p* is *not* to say that *e* does not make it reasonable for us to conclude that *p*. If, for example, I know that 95 of the 100 marbles are black, then it *is* reasonable for me to conclude, to believe or accept, that I will draw a black one. To say that evidence is nonconclusive is not, therefore, to imply that it does not support a particular conclusion, it is rather to note that it does not guarantee that conclusion. Furthermore, as Mathias Steup notes, we should not confuse nonconclusive evidence with "inconclusive" evidence.[6] To say that a body of evidence, *e*, is nonconclusive

---

[6] Matthias Steup, *An Introduction to Contemporary Epistemology* (Upper Saddle River, NJ: Prentice-Hall, 1996), pp. 11–12.

with respect to a proposition, p, is to say that e supports p but does not guarantee it. In contrast, to say that a body of evidence, e, is inconclusive with respect to p is to say that e does not support believing p. In our previous examples, my evidence *does* support my beliefs that it is noon and that I will draw a black marble. My evidence for those propositions is not, therefore, inconclusive.

Given that there is some connection between evidence and justified belief, can we say simply that if someone has evidence for a proposition, then he is justified in believing it? No. Suppose that someone has evidence for believing p *and* equally good evidence for believing that *not-p*. If this is all the evidence one has, then one is epistemically justified in withholding belief that p. Whether one is justified in believing that p depends on one's *total* evidence. A more plausible view, then, is that if one's total evidence on balance supports p, then he is justified in believing that p.

As we noted above, one's justification for believing various propositions can change over time as one acquires additional information. Sometimes our evidence for a proposition can be "defeated" or "overridden." We can lose our justification for believing a proposition when our evidence for it is defeated or overridden. Let us define the concept of "evidential defeat" as follows:

D4 d defeats e as evidence for $p = $ Df. e is evidence for believing that p, but e *and* d is not evidence for believing that p.

Let's consider two examples that illustrate the concept of defeat. Suppose that a certain table looks red to you. Let's call this bit of evidence, a. Now consider the proposition that the table is red. Let's call this proposition, b. We may say that a is evidence for b. We may say that the fact that the table looks red to you offers some support for the proposition that the table is red. Now, suppose that you get some additional information. Suppose that you learn that there is a red light shining on the table. Let's call this additional bit of information, c. Note that a *and* c is *not* evidence for b. In this case, c defeats or overrides a as evidence for b. Speaking somewhat loosely, if your only information about the color of the table were a *and* c, then you would no longer be justified in believing b. Again, we cannot say simply that if one has some evidence for a proposition, then one is justified in believing it. The evidence that one has might be defeated by one's other information.

Let us consider a second example of defeat.[7] Suppose you go to a party and you learn that (*h*): Most of the people in the room are Democrats and John is in the room. We may say that *h* is evidence for (*i*) John is a Democrat. But now suppose you learn that (*j*): Most of the people on the right side of the room are not Democrats and John is on the right side of the room. Even though *h* is evidence for *i*, *h and j* is not evidence for *i*. *j* defeats *h* as evidence for *i*.

It is worth noting that defeaters can themselves be defeated. Again, consider the previous example. Suppose that along with your previous evidence, *h and j*, you also come to learn (*k*) 49 of the 50 people in the room who voted for the trade bill are Democrats and John voted for the trade bill. Even though *h and j* is not evidence for believing *i*, *h and j and k* is evidence for believing *i*. So, along with the concept of evidential defeat, we may add:

D5   *x* defeats *d* as a defeater of evidence *e* for *p* = Df. (i) *e* is evidence for believing that *p*, (ii) *e and d* is not evidence for believing that *p*, and (iii) *e and d and x* is evidence for believing that *p*.

Again, since one can have some evidence for believing a proposition that is defeated by one's other information, it is important to bear in mind that whether one is justified in believing some proposition depends on one's total evidence. A more promising view would be that, if one has evidence for a proposition, *p*, and nothing in his total evidence defeats his evidence for *p*, then *p* is justified for him.

The fact that evidence can be defeated or overridden has an analogy in ethics. Sometimes one feature of a situation ethically requires that one perform an act and certain other features of the situation require that one *not* perform that act. For example, suppose that Jones has promised to meet his friend Smith for lunch at noon. The fact that Jones promised to meet Smith at noon requires that he meet Smith at noon. Suppose we let *p* = Jones's promising to meet Smith at noon and let *q* = Jones's meeting Smith at noon. We may then say that *p* requires *q*. Suppose, however, that on his way to meet Smith, Jones comes across Brown, who has been severely injured in an automobile accident. Jones is the only person present who can

[7] Cf. Roderick Chisholm's *Theory of Knowledge* 2nd edn. (Englewood Cliffs, NJ: Prentice-Hall, Inc., 1977), pp. 71–73.

help the severely injured Brown. Relative to these wider, more inclusive, circumstances, Jones is *not* ethically required to meet Smith at noon. Suppose we let $r =$ Jones's being the only one who can help the severely injured Brown. We might then say that while p requires q, p *and* r does not require q. The ethical requirement for q imposed by p has been overridden or defeated by r.[8] In the epistemological case, what one is justified in believing depends on one's total evidence. So too, it would seem that in the ethical case, the right action depends on one's total circumstances. Just as one's reasons for performing certain actions can be defeated by further considerations, so too one's reasons for believing various things can be defeated by further evidence.

In this chapter, we have distinguished propositional knowledge from acquaintance knowledge and "how to" knowledge. We also introduced the view that propositional knowledge is justified true belief and looked very briefly at some views about belief, truth, and epistemic justification. In later chapters, we shall examine in more detail some important views about the nature of justification. In the next chapter, however, we will look at some objections to the view that knowledge is justified true belief. These objections are important, for they show that the simple view of knowledge introduced here is not quite right. In considering these objections, and the responses to them, we shall be pursuing an answer to the ancient question, "What is knowledge?"

---

[8] Of course, it might be that yet further circumstances restore the requirement that Jones meet Smith at noon. Suppose for example that Brown's injuries, though severe, are not life threatening, and that Jones has promised to meet Smith at noon in order to pay a ransom that will save the lives of several hostages. Thus, if r defeats the requirement for q imposed by p, there might be further features that defeat r as a defeater for the requirement for q.

2　The traditional analysis and the Gettier problem

In the last chapter we considered the view that knowledge is epistemically justified true belief. In this chapter, we shall consider some counter-examples to the justified true belief (JTB) account and consider some attempts to repair the definition of knowledge in light of these examples. The objection we shall first consider was made prominent by Edmund Gettier in his brief, yet famous, 1963 essay "Is Justified True Belief Knowledge." The difficulty for the traditional account to which he calls our attention has become known as "the Gettier Problem." Since 1963, it has received a great deal of attention in epistemological circles and there have been a great many attempts to solve it. It would be fair to say, however, that there remains no widely accepted solution. Many of the attempted solutions are quite ingenious and many are quite complicated and difficult to evaluate. In this chapter we shall have to content ourselves with considering some very simple proposals. The solutions we shall consider are fairly early attempts to solve the problem, solutions that appeared within ten years of Gettier's original essay. None of them are adequate, but the ways in which they fail are instructive and many of the more promising attempted solutions involve refinements and developments of these simple proposals. The three approaches we shall consider are (1) the No False Grounds approach, (2) the Defeasibility approach, and (3) the Causal approach.

The Gettier problem

According to the traditional account of knowledge examined in the last chapter, propositional knowledge is epistemically justified true belief. Recall that in the last chapter, we introduced the following definition:

D3   S knows that p = Df. (1) S believes that p, (2) p is true, and (3) p is epistemically justified for S.

In his brief two and a half page essay, Edmund Gettier presents two counter-examples to the traditional definition. Gettier shows that some cases of justified true belief aren't instances of knowledge. If some instances of justified true belief aren't instances of knowledge, then traditional JTB accounts, such as D3, are mistaken. Let us consider Gettier's counter-examples.[1]

> *Case 1.* Smith and Jones have applied for a certain job. Smith has strong evidence for the following proposition:
>
> (d) Jones is the man who will get the job and Jones has ten coins in his pocket.
>
> Let us suppose that Smith's evidence for (d) is that the company president has assured Smith that Jones will get the job and let us suppose that Smith has only minutes ago counted the coins in Jones's pocket. Let us suppose that from (d), Smith deduces:
>
> (e) The man who will get the job has ten coins in his pocket.
>
> So, Smith is justified in believing (d) and deduces (e) from (d). Smith is therefore justified in believing that (e) is true. But now imagine that unbeknownst to Smith, *he*, not Jones, will get the job, and also, unbeknownst to Smith, *he* has ten coins in *his* pocket. So, (e) is true. In this example, all of the following are true: (i) (e) is true, (ii) Smith believes that (e) is true, and (iii) Smith is justified in believing that (e) is true. But clearly Smith does not *know* that (e) is true. It is a matter of luck or sheer coincidence that Smith is right about (e).
>
> *Case 2.* Suppose that Smith has strong evidence for the following proposition:
>
> (f) Jones owns a Ford.
>
> Let us imagine that Smith's evidence includes that, for as long as Smith can remember, Jones has owned a car, and always a Ford, and has just offered Smith a ride in a Ford. Let us assume that Smith is justified in

---

[1] Edmund Gettier, "Is Justified True Belief Knowledge?," *Analysis*, 23 (1963), 121–23.

believing that (f). Now, suppose that Smith has another friend, Brown, whose whereabouts are unknown to Smith. Smith selects some place names at random and deduces from (f) the following:

(g) Either Jones owns a Ford or Brown is in Boston.

(h) Either Jones owns a Ford or Brown is in Barcelona.

(i) Either Jones owns a Ford or Brown is in Brest-Litovsk.

Since Smith is justified in believing (f) and sees that (f) entails (g)–(i), he is justified in believing each of them. But, suppose that (f) is false. Jones does not own a Ford, but has been recently driving a rented car. Moreover, suppose that by sheer coincidence and utterly unknown to Smith, Brown *is* in Barcelona. In other words, (h) is true. So, again, the following conditions are met: (i) (h) is true, (ii) Smith believes that (h) is true, and (iii) Smith is justified in believing that (h) is true. But Smith does not know (h). It is only by sheer coincidence or mere luck that Smith is right about (h).

In Cases 1 and 2, Smith has evidence for, and is justified in believing, some false proposition. From this falsehood he deduces a true proposition. On the basis of this inference he acquires a justified true belief, but not knowledge. What these cases show is that one can satisfy the requirements of the JTB account of knowledge, that one can meet the requirements laid out in D3, and yet fail to have knowledge.

Gettier notes that the counter-examples he presents presuppose two things about epistemic justification. First, they presuppose that one can be justified in believing a false proposition. In Case 1, Smith is justified in believing the falsehood, (d), Jones is the man who will get the job and Jones has ten coins in his pocket. In Case 2, Smith is justified in believing the falsehood, (f), Jones owns a Ford. As we noted in chapter 1, it is commonly assumed that one can be justified in believing a false proposition. To be justified in believing a proposition on the basis of nonconclusive evidence is to have evidence that does not guarantee the truth of what is believed. As long as we accept that a proposition can be justified for us on the basis of nonconclusive evidence or reasons, we must accept that we can be justified in believing some false proposition.

Second, the examples presuppose the following *Principle of Deductive Closure* (PDC):

Principle of Deductive Closure

If S is justified in believing that p and p entails q and S deduces q from p and accepts q as a result of this deduction, then S is justified in believing q.

The PDC tells us, roughly, that justification is transmitted through deduction from propositions one is justified in believing. In Case 1, Smith is justified in believing (e) because he deduces it from (d). In Case 2, Smith is justified in believing (h) because he deduces it from (f). In these cases, Smith gains justification for believing a true proposition by deducing it from a false proposition that he is justified in believing.

In responding to Gettier's counter-examples, it is tempting to defend the traditional JTB account by calling into question one or both of these presup-positions. One might, for example, deny the PDC. One might hold that in Case 1, Smith is justified in believing (d) and correctly deduces (e) from (d), but deny that Smith is justified in believing that (e). If justification is not transmitted through deduction in Smith's case, then we need not hold that Smith is justified in believing (e) and we need not hold that he has a justified true belief in (e).

Whether the PDC is true is controversial. Some philosophers hold that in some cases justification is not transferred through deduction. But even if that is true in some cases, it is not clear why it would be true in either of these cases. Why would Jones *not* be justified in believing (e) on the basis of (d)? Why would Smith *not* be justified in believing (h) on the basis of (f)? In each case, it seems intuitively plausible that he is justified in believing the one proposition by deducing it from the other. Moreover, as a general strategy for dealing with Gettier cases denying the PDC seems inadequate. This is because there seem to be some Gettier-type cases that do not involve deducing one proposition from another. Suppose, for example, you are visiting your friend in the physics department. As you walk down the hall you look in the doorway and seem to see a man in the room. You form the perceptual belief "There's a man in that room." Your perceptual belief is not formed on the basis of an inference. You simply look in the room and form the belief. Now suppose that what you saw was in fact an extremely realistic holographic image of a man. Still, given the realistic holographic image, it seems that your perceptual belief is justified. But now let's suppose that your belief is also true − there is a man in the room. He's simply not visible to you from the doorway. In this case, your belief that there is a man in the room is true and justified, but it is not an instance of knowledge.

This seems to be another case in which we have a justified true belief that is not knowledge. But note that in this case your justified true belief is not formed by inferring it from some other justified belief. Consequently, it is not clear how denying the PDC would help with this case.

Alternatively, one might respond to the Gettier problem by denying that it is possible for someone to be justified in believing a false proposition. Suppose that one cannot be justified in believing a false proposition. Why would this matter for Gettier's counter-examples? Gettier claims that (e) and (h) are instances of *justified* true belief that are not instances of knowledge. Smith gets his justification for (e) and (h) by deducing them from (d) and (f), falsehoods that he is supposedly justified in believing. But if one can't be justified in believing a falsehood, then Smith isn't justified in believing (d) and (f) and, consequently, he isn't justified in believing (e) and (h). In short, if one can't be justified in believing a falsehood, then Smith doesn't have a justified true belief in either (e) or (h) and Gettier doesn't have an objection to D3.

Unfortunately, this line of response does not seem promising. Again, as we noted in chapter 1, a common assumption about justification is that one can be justified in believing a false proposition. Such an assumption seems quite plausible. I am justified in believing that Lisa went into the library if unbeknownst to me Lisa has an identical twin and the woman I saw enter the library was the twin. Again, suppose I incorrectly predict that the next marble drawn from an urn will be red. Wouldn't such a false belief be reasonable or justified for me if I knew only that the urn contained 1,000 marbles and 998 of them were red? Consider again Smith's position with respect to (f). Suppose that Smith knows that Smith has always owned a car in the past and always a Ford, that Smith has just offered Smith a ride while driving a Ford. Suppose we add to Gettier's original description that Jones shows Smith a cleverly forged title to the car stating that the Ford is Jones's and Jones tells Smith, "This is my Ford. I own it." It seems quite plausible to assume that Smith is justified in believing Jones owns a Ford.

Defending the traditional JTB account of knowledge by rejecting one or both of Gettier's presuppositions about justification does not appear to be a promising approach. The philosophical literature is rich, however, with other sorts of approaches. Some philosophers have focused on the justification requirement for knowledge. They hold that knowledge requires epistemic justification, but, they suggest, it also requires that one's justification be of "the right sort." According to this idea, a Gettier case involves justified true belief, but the subject's justification is in some way "defective" or not the right sort to yield knowledge. Those who take this view hold that knowledge that p requires that one's justification for believing p meet some further condition, e.g. that one's justification does rest on any false grounds. Other philosophers have focused on the idea that knowledge requires that one not be right "by accident." Knowledge requires true belief where one's true belief is not the result of accident or coincidence. This view has led some philosophers to hold that knowledge requires some *causal* connection between the fact that p and one's belief that p.

As we have noted, there are many attempts to solve the Gettier problem. While there is no possibility of surveying them here, let us consider a few fairly straightforward, simple and suggestive approaches.[2] As we noted earlier, the three approaches we shall consider are (1) the No False Grounds Approach, (2) the Defeasibility Approach, and (3) the Causal Approach. Of these three approaches, the first two tend to focus on the role of epistemic justification and develop the idea that one's justification must be of the right sort. The third is an early attempt to use the notion of causal connection to make sense of the idea that knowledge is true belief that is not the result of accident or coincidence.

The no false grounds approach

One approach to solving the Gettier problem begins by noting that in Gettier's examples Smith deduces a true proposition from a falsehood. His justification for believing the true proposition depends upon his being justified in believing a false proposition. Proponents of the No False Grounds approach claim that Smith's justification for believing the true proposition is defective, at least from the standpoint of knowledge, insofar as his grounds for believing the true proposition include one or

[2] For a detailed and acute survey of a wide variety of attempted solutions see Robert Shope, *The Analysis of Knowing: A Decade of Research* (Princeton, NJ: Princeton University Press, 1983) and his "Conditions and Analyses of Knowing," in *The Oxford Handbook of Epistemology*, ed. Paul K. Moser (Oxford: Oxford University Press, 2002).

more falsehoods. This suggests a fairly simple solution, namely, that we modify D3 as follows:

D6   S knows that p = Df. (1) S believes that p, (2) p is true, (3) p is
                      epistemically justified for S, and (4) S's grounds for believing
                      that p do not include any false propositions.

How is D6 supposed to help with the Gettier problem? Consider Case 1. Smith's grounds for believing (e), the man who will get the job has ten coins in his pocket, include the false proposition (d), Jones is the man who will get the job and Jones has ten coins in his pocket. Smith has a justified true belief in (e). According to D6, then, Smith does *not* know (e), since his grounds for believing (e) include the false proposition (d). Smith's belief in (e) does not meet our added fourth condition. Similar considerations would apply to Case 2. In that case, Smith's grounds for believing (h), Jones owns a Ford or Brown is in Barcelona, include the falsehood, (f), Jones owns a Ford. So, Smith's belief in (h) fails to meet the added fourth condition and, thus, we get the right result that Smith does not know (h). When applied to Cases 1 and 2, D6 gives us the right result.

Unfortunately, D6 is not satisfactory. There are two problems with D6. First, it is too weak to rule out some Gettier cases. Second, it is too strong insofar as it rules out some plausible instances of knowledge. Let us consider first the objection that D6 is too weak.[3] Let us consider the following case.

> *Case 3.* Suppose that Smith knows, and is thus justified in believing, the following:

> (j) Jones, who works in my office, has always driven a Ford in the past, has just offered me a ride in a Ford, and says that he owns a Ford.

> From (j), Smith deduces:

> (k) There is someone, who works in my office, who has always driven a Ford in the past, has just offered me a ride in a Ford, and says that he owns a Ford.

---

[3] The following objection was raised by Richard Feldman in "An Alleged Defect in Gettier Counterexamples," *Australasian Journal of Philosophy*, 52 (1974), 68–69. See also Feldman's discussion of the Gettier problem in his *Epistemology* (Upper Saddle River, NJ: Prentice-Hall, 2003), pp. 25–37.

On the basis of (k), Smith believes:

(l) Someone in my office owns a Ford.

Given that Smith is justified in believing both (j) and (k), Smith is justified in believing (l). So, Smith has a justified belief in (l). Now, let us suppose that, as in Gettier's original case, Jones does not own a Ford. Jones has recently been pretending to own a Ford. But let us also suppose that, completely unbeknownst to Smith, someone else in Smith's office, Brown, *does* own a Ford. So, (l) is true. Thus, the following conditions are met: (i) (l) is true, (ii) Smith believes that (l) is true, and (iii) Smith is justified in believing that (l) is true. Still, Smith does not *know* (l). It is only by sheer coincidence or luck that Smith turns out to be right about (l).

In Case 3, as in Gettier's original cases, we have an instance of justified true belief that isn't knowledge. But our amended definition, D6, appears too weak to rule out Smith's belief in (l) as an instance of knowledge. Why? The reason is that D6 requires that one's grounds for believing that *p* do not include any *false* propositions. But in Case 3 Smith's grounds for believing (l) are the propositions (j) and (k) and they are both *true*. Since Smith's grounds for believing (l) are true, his belief in (l) meets the requirements for knowledge laid out in D6. Therefore, D6 is too weak to rule out Smith's belief in (l) as an instance of knowledge. D6 gives us the wrong result in Case 3.

D6 also seems too strong insofar as it rules out some beliefs that are clearly instances of knowledge. Suppose, for example, that you have a lot of evidence for believing some proposition. Most of your grounds consists of truths that you know. But suppose that your grounds include *some* false propositions. In some cases, it seems reasonable to think that you would still have knowledge even if your grounds included some false propositions. Suppose, for example, that Smith wants to know who won last night's basketball game. He sees a group of his friends and asks them who won. Each friend says that he watched the game and that the home team won. It seems reasonable to believe that Smith knows on the basis of their testimony that the home team won. But suppose that one of his friends, Jones, caught up in an uncharacteristic yet pathetic urge to fit in, lies about watching the game. Jones says, "I watched the game. It was great. The home team won." As a result, Smith's grounds for believing that the home team won includes the falsehood that Jones watched the game and said the home team won. Still, this fact would not seem to prevent Smith from knowing that the home team won.

As it stands, D6 is not satisfactory, though, perhaps, some modification of it will be acceptable. Let us consider a different approach, but one that like D6 also focuses on the role of falsehoods. Let us consider:

D7   S knows that $p =$ Df. (1) S believes that p, (2) p is true, (3) p is epistemically justified for S, and (4) S's grounds for believing that p do not justify any false proposition for S.

According to D6, knowledge requires that none of one's grounds are false. In contrast, D7 requires that one's grounds do not justify any false proposition. How would D7 handle Gettier's original examples? Consider Case 1. Smith's grounds for believing (e), the man who will get the job has ten coins in his pocket, *also* justified Smith in believing the false proposition, (d) Jones is the man who will get the job and Jones has ten coins in his pocket. Since Smith's grounds for believing (e) also justify a false proposition for him, D7 gives us the right result that Smith does not know (e). Something similar is true in Case 2. In that case, Smith's grounds for believing (h), Jones owns a Ford or Brown is in Barcelona, *also* justified for Smith the false proposition (f), Jones owns a Ford.

As we have seen, D6 failed to give us the right results in Case 3. Does D7 fare any better? In Case 3, we assumed that Smith had no false grounds for believing (l), someone in my office owns a Ford. However, among Smith's grounds for believing (l) was (j), Jones, who works in my office, has always driven a Ford in the past, has just offered me a ride in a Ford, and says he owns a Ford. We assumed that Smith did in fact know (j). But note that (j) does justify Smith in believing the falsehood (f), Jones owns a Ford. Since Smith's grounds for believing (l) justify him in believing a false proposition, D7 implies that Smith does *not* know (l). D7 seems to yield the right result in Case 3.

Unfortunately, D7 is also too strong. Consider again Case 3. We assume that Smith knows,

(j) Jones, who works in my office, has always driven a Ford in the past, has just offered me a ride in a Ford, and says he owns a Ford.

From (j) Smith deduces,

(k) There is someone, who works in my office, who has always driven a Ford in the past, who has just offered me a ride in a Ford, and says he owns a Ford.

Surely Smith knows (k). But here's the problem with D7. Smith's grounds for (k) include (j) and (j) justifies Smith in believing the falsehood (f), Jones owns a Ford. Since Smith's grounds for believing (k) justify a false proposition for Smith, D7 implies incorrectly that Smith does not know (k). As with D6, it might be that some modification of D7 will prove acceptable.[4]

The defeasibility approach

Another approach to solving the Gettier problem begins with the observation that in Gettier's original cases, there is some true proposition which is such that *if* one were justified in believing it, then one would no longer be justified in believing the spurious instance of knowledge. To illustrate this point, consider again Case 3. Smith knows (j) and (k) and these propositions are evidence for (l), someone in my office owns a Ford. But now consider the true proposition, Jones is just pretending to own a Ford, (m). If Smith were justified in believing (m) or if (m) were added to his evidence, then he would *not* be justified in believing (l). We may say that (m) defeats (j) and (k) as evidence for (l).

According to one version of the Defeasibility approach, one's justification for believing *p* is defective, at least from the standpoint of knowledge, if one's evidence for believing *p* could be defeated by the addition of some true proposition to one's body of evidence. The basic idea here is that if one's justification for believing *p* would be defeated by the addition of some true proposition, then one's justification for believing *p* is not the right sort for knowing that *p*. Given this assumption, perhaps we could say that one knows that *p* only if there is no true proposition that could be added to one's evidence for *p* and defeats one's justification for believing *p*. We might say, roughly, that one knows that *p* only if there is no true proposition which would defeat one's justification for believing that *p*. This is an intriguing idea. Let's consider this view more closely.

[4] Roderick Chisholm writes, "The various Gettier cases also have this feature in common: the proposition involved is made evident by a proposition that makes some *false* proposition evident." *Theory of Knowledge*, 3rd edn. (Englewood Cliffs, NJ: Prentice-Hall, 1989), p. 98. Chisholm's proposed solution may be seen as a sophisticated development of the basic idea that underlies the flawed D7.

One way to develop this idea is as follows:

D8   S knows that p = Df. (1) p is true, (2) S believes that p, (3) p is epistemically justified for S, and (4) there is no true proposition, q, such that if S were justified in believing q, then S would not be justified in believing that p.[5]

How would D8 help us with the Gettier cases? Consider Case 1. Smith's belief in (e), the man who will get the job has ten coins in his pocket, does not meet condition (4) in D8. This is because there is a true proposition which is such that if Smith believed it, then he would not be justified in believing (e). If Smith were justified in believing the true proposition that Jones will not get the job, then he would not be justified in believing the false proposition (d), Jones is the man who will get the job and Jones has ten coins in his pocket, and, consequently, he would not be justified in believing (e). Since Smith's belief in (e) does not meet condition (4) in D8, D8 implies that Smith does not know (e). This is the right result.

Similar considerations apply to Case 2. Smith's belief in (h), either Jones owns a Ford or Brown is in Barcelona, does not meet condition (4) in D8. Again, this is because there is a true proposition which is such that if Smith believed it, then he would not be justified in believing (h). If Smith were justified in believing the true proposition, that Jones is merely pretending to own a Ford, then he would not be justified in believing the false proposition (f), Jones owns a Ford, and, consequently, he would not be justified in believing (h). Since Smith's belief in (h) does not meet condition (4) in D8, D8 implies that Smith does not know (h). Again, this is the right result.

It is important to note that D8 makes use of a subjunctive conditional. A subjunctive conditional is a statement that tells us that if one thing *were* true, then something else *would* be. The statement "If I were to hit my thumb very hard with a hammer, then it would hurt" expresses a subjunctive conditional. People often use such statements and, in many cases, we have no difficulty in assessing whether they are true or false.

---

[5] This definition is similar to one offered by Peter Klein, "A Proposed Definition of Propositional Knowledge," *The Journal of Philosophy*, 68, no. 16 (August 1971), 475. One can find similar definitions discussed in Paul Moser, Dwayne H. Mulder, and J. D. Trout, *The Theory of Knowledge: A Thematic Introduction* (Oxford: Oxford University Press, 1998), p. 98, and Richard Feldman, *Epistemology*, pp. 33–36.

But, sometimes subjunctive conditionals are tricky and they often invite difficulties in definitions. That seems to be the case in D8.

To appreciate the difficulty with D8 let's consider the following example. Stan's wife notices that he is awfully quiet and seems troubled about something. She asks if he is upset or angry with Tom, a co-worker. Suppose that Stan knows that he is not angry at Tom. Stan introspectively reflects and finds that he is not. So, Stan knows and is justified in believing,

(n) I am not angry at Tom.

But suppose that earlier in the day, unbeknownst to Stan, Tom had gotten into a rather nasty squabble with Stan's mother. Suppose that the following proposition is true:

(o) Tom grossly insulted Stan's mother.

If Stan *were* justified in believing (o), then he would not be justified in believing (n). For if Tom were justified in believing (o), then he *would* be very angry at Tom. And, if Stan were very angry at Tom, then Stan would know it and he not be justified in believing (n). Tom's belief in (n) does not meet condition (iv) of D8. According to D8, then, Stan does not know (n). But that is the wrong result.

Let us consider a second example suggested by Richard Feldman. Suppose that Smith is sitting in his study with the radio off. Smith knows that the radio is off. But a radio station, Classic Hits 101, is playing Neil Diamond's "Girl, You'll Be a Woman Soon." If Smith had the radio on and tuned to that station, he would hear the song and know that the radio is on. Now, in this case, Smith knows,

(r) The radio is off.

Still, there is a true proposition such that *if* Smith were justified in believing it, then he would not be justified in believing (r). Such a proposition is:

(s) Classic Hits 101 is now playing "Girl, You'll be a Woman Soon."

If Smith were justified in believing (s), it would probably be because he had the radio on and was listening to the song. So, according to D8, Smith does not know (r). Again, that is the wrong result.

Feldman nicely sums up the basic difficulty with D8. He writes, "...one can know some facts and there can be other facts such that if one knew the other facts, then one would not know the original facts. This is because, if one were in a position to know the latter facts, then one would not be in a position to know the former facts. And, in some cases, if one knew the latter facts, the former facts would not even be true."[6]

There are, however, versions of a defeasibility approach that do not make use of subjunctive conditionals. Let us consider one simple version of such a view. To appreciate this view let's recall our definition of evidential defeat:

D4 d defeats e as evidence for p = Df. e is evidence for believing that p, but c *and* d is not evidence for believing that p.

Following Mathias Steup,[7] let's introduce the concepts of "justificational defeat" and "factual defeat":

Justificational defeat

D9 d justificationally defeats S's evidence for believing that p = Df. (i) S has evidence e for believing that p; (ii) S has also evidence e' for a proposition d that defeats e as evidence for p.

Factual defeat

D10 d factually defeats S's evidence for believing that p = Df. (i) S has evidence e for believing that p; (ii) there is a proposition d such that d is true, S does not have evidence for d, and d defeats e as evidence for p.

There are some significant differences between justificational and factual defeat. First, in order for a proposition to be a factual defeater it must be *true*. Justificational defeaters, however, can be either true or false. So, for example, if Jones, who is honest and usually quite reliable, misinforms me that Brown has been convicted three times for embezzlement, then the proposition that Brown is a thrice convicted embezzler is a justificational defeater for my evidence that Brown is honest. But that proposition cannot be factual defeater because it is not true.

---

[6] Richard Feldman, *Epistemology*, p. 35. Cf. Robert K. Shope, "The Conditional Fallacy in Contemporary Philosophy," *The Journal of Philosophy*, 75, no. 8 (August 1978), 397–413.

[7] Cf. Matthias Steup, *An Introduction to Contemporary Epistemology*, p. 14.

Second, justificational defeat involves propositions for which one has evidence. In order for a proposition d to justificationally defeat S's evidence for believing that p, one must have *evidence* for both d and p. In contrast, if a proposition d factually defeats S's justification for believing that p, then S has *no* evidence for d. Factual defeaters are, in this respect "hidden" defeaters. They are defeaters for which one has no evidence.

Third, justificational defeat matters to one's justification in a way that factual defeat does not. If one's evidence for believing some proposition is justificationally defeated, then one loses one's justification for believing that proposition (assuming that the justificational defeater is not itself defeated). But again, one has *no* evidence for factual defeaters. Factual defeaters are hidden. If one's evidence for believing some proposition is factually defeated, this does not affect one's justification for believing that proposition. A proposition can factually defeat one's evidence for believing a proposition without affecting one's justification for believing it.

Given the concept of factual defeat, let us consider the following defeasibility account.

D11   S knows that p = Df. (1) p is true, (2) S believes that p, (3) p is epistemically justified for S, and (4) there is no proposition d that factually defeats S's evidence for believing that p.[8]

According to D11, knowledge that p requires that there be no factual defeaters for one's evidence for p. Roughly, it requires that there be no hidden truths that defeat one's evidence for believing that p.

What does D11 imply about our Gettier cases? Consider Case 3. Smith has a justified true belief (1), someone who works in my office owns a Ford. Smith's evidence for this is,

(j) Jones, who works in my office, has always driven a Ford in the past, has just offered me a ride in a Ford, and says he owns a Ford, and

(k) There is someone, who works in my office, who has always driven a Ford in the past, who has just offered me a ride in a Ford, and says he owns a Ford.

---

[8] *Ibid.*, pp. 17–18.

Is there some true proposition that factually defeats Smith's evidence for believing (l)? Let's suppose that the following proposition is true and one for which Smith has no evidence,

(t) Jones has been pretending to own a Ford.

It seems clear that the (t) defeats (j) and (k) as evidence for (l). In other words, it seems clear that *j and k and t* is not evidence for believing (l). So, (t) is a factual defeater for Smith's evidence for believing (l). Given D11, then, Smith does not know (l). So, D11 seems to give us the right answer in Case 3. It seems likely that D11 will also give us the right answer in Cases 1 and 2.

There is, however, a serious problem for D11. To understand the problem, let's consider the following case. Suppose that Smith sees his acquaintance Tom Grabit remove a book from the library shelf, stick it under his coat, and walk out of the library with it. Smith sees Tom steal the book. Let's assume that Smith knows that Tom stole the book. But now imagine that, completely unknown to Smith, Tom's mother, when informed of the charges against her son, swears that it wasn't Tom. She swears that Tom was a thousand miles away at the time and that it was his identical twin, John, who stole the book. Sadly, however, Tom's mother is insane and a pathological liar. Tom has no identical twin and John is a figment of the mother's deluded mind.

It seems plausible to many that Smith knows that Tom stole the book. However, it seems that D11 implies the Smith does not know that Tom stole the book. It seems that D11 gives us the wrong answer in this case. Consider the following true proposition,

(u) Tom's mother swears that Tom was miles away and Tom's twin stole the book.

The problem is that (u) seems to be a factual defeater for Smith's evidence that Tom stole the book. Smith has no evidence for (u), (u) is true, and the conjunction of (u) with the other propositions for which Smith has evidence are not evidence for believing that Tom stole the book. If (u) is a factual defeater, then D11 implies that Smith does not know that Tom stole the book.

D11 implies that one does not know that *p* whenever there is a factual defeater for one's evidence that *p*. The Tom Grabit case is intended to show that this is not so and that D11 is too strong, that it rules out some genuine instances of knowledge. One problem for D11, then, is that factual defeaters, or hidden truths, sometimes take away our knowledge and sometime they don't. Proponents of defeasibility accounts need to explain when they do and when they don't.

The causal approach

The final approach we shall consider is the causal approach. A causal theory holds that knowledge that p requires that there be some causal connection between one's belief that p and the fact that makes p true. Such a view seems quite plausible when we reflect on some simple cases of perceptual knowledge. For example, I now know that there is a coffee cup on the desk. I know this because I see the cup. My belief that the cup is on the desk is causally connected through the various causal processes involved in perception to the fact that the cup is on the desk. Similarly, my belief that there was a cup here yesterday is causally connected to the fact that there was one here yesterday. Yesterday I formed that belief on the basis of perception and the belief was retained in my memory. What I now believe is causally connected through perception and memory to the fact that the cup was here then. It seems plausible to think that in many cases of perceptual and memory knowledge there is some causal connection between one's belief that p and the fact that p.

Suppose, then, one were to say that S knows that p if and only if the fact that p is causally connected to S's belief that p. Unfortunately, such a simple and straightforward view won't do. Suppose, for example, that Smith has a brain tumor that causes him to believe many strange things. He believes, for example, that aliens are in his basement, that cats and dogs are joined in a conspiracy against him. Suppose further that as a result of his brain tumor he forms the belief that he has a brain tumor. The fact that he has a brain tumor is causally connected to his belief that he has a brain tumor, but surely Smith's belief isn't an instance of knowledge. Other examples illustrate the same point. Suppose that unbeknownst to him, someone has slipped a drug into Jones's coffee. The drug causes Jones to form some paranoid beliefs. He starts to believe that people are watching him, that they are trying to read his thoughts, and that someone has put a drug in his coffee. The fact that someone has slipped a drug into his coffee is causally connected with his belief that he has been drugged, but again his belief does not seem to be an instance of knowledge.

Recognizing these difficulties, Alvin Goldman proposed the following definition of knowledge in his 1967 essay "A Causal Theory of Knowing":

D12   S knows that p = Df. The fact that p is causally connected in an "appropriate" way with S's believing that p.[9]

D12 requires not just any sort of causal connection between a fact and one's belief, it requires that there be an "appropriate" connection. Presumably, the sort of connection between one's belief that one has a brain tumor and the fact that one does in our previous example is not of the right sort. The same may be said of one's belief that one has been drugged.

But what are the appropriate sorts of connections? Goldman says that the appropriate sorts of causal connections include perception and memory. In addition, one knows that p if one properly reconstructs the causal chain from the fact that p to one's belief that p. A proper reconstruction would involve only true beliefs of the subject about the important causal links. The idea of a proper reconstruction may illustrated by one's belief that there had been a campfire on the beach. Walking on the beach one sees the pile of ashes and burned timbers. One believes that the ashes and the burned timbers were caused by a campfire. One thus properly reconstructs the causal chain from one's belief to the fact of the fire. Since one can properly reconstruct the causal connection between the fact of the campfire and one's belief that there was one, one's belief that there was one is in this case an instance of knowledge. Similarly, one can know that centuries ago a nearby mountain erupted by reconstructing the causal connection between the fact of the eruption, the surrounding lava fields which one now sees, and one's belief that the mountain did once erupt. By allowing such reconstructions, Goldman's theory allows that what we know transcends what we perceive and what we remember. That seems clearly a merit of the theory insofar as we do know things which go beyond perception and memory.

How would D12 deal with the Gettier problem? Consider Case 2 and Smith's belief in (h), Jones owns a Ford or Brown is in Barcelona. Goldman notes that what makes (h) true is the fact that Brown is in Barcelona. But that fact is not causally connected to Smith's belief in (h) in any

[9] Alvin Goldman, "A Causal Theory of Knowing," *The Journal of Philosophy*, 64, no. 12 (June 1967), 369.

appropriate way. Smith does not perceive or remember that Brown is in Barcelona and he cannot properly reconstruct the causal chain from his belief in (h) to the fact that Brown is in Barcelona. So, given D12, Smith does not know (h). Something similar would be said about Case 1. Smith has a justified true belief in (e) the man who will get the job has ten coins in his pocket. But what makes (e) true is the fact that he, Smith, is the man who will get the job and he has ten coins in his pocket. Yet this fact is not connected in any appropriate way to Smith's belief in (e). Therefore, according to D12 Smith does not know (e). Finally, in Case 3 what makes it true that (l), someone in my office owns a Ford, is the fact that Brown owns a Ford. But again the fact that Brown owns a Ford is not connected in any appropriate way with Smith's belief in (l). He cannot give a proper reconstruction from the fact that Brown owns a Ford to his belief in (l). D12 appears to yield the right results in Cases 1, 2, and 3.

In spite of its success in dealing with Gettier's original cases and some variations thereof, D12 faces some rather serious objections. First, D12 seems unable to accommodate our knowledge of various general propositions such as all men are mortal. The fact that all men are mortal does not seem to cause anything. It does not seem to be causally connected to one's belief that all men are mortal and, thus, it is not appropriately connected. If D12 were true, then we would not know such a generalization. But since it seems clear that we do, D12 must be false.

Second, consider those cases where knowledge involves a proper reconstruction of the causal chain. Goldman writes that if one is to know p, one's reconstruction of the chain must contain no mistakes. "Though he need not reconstruct *every* detail of the causal chain, he must reconstruct all the important links."[10] Goldman admits that it is hard to give criteria for what is an "important" detail and he suggests that what is important will vary from case to case. Some philosophers find this requirement unacceptably vague. There is, however, a more serious problem. Consider the following case.[11] Suppose that Omar falls down drunk in the street and

---

[10] *Ibid.*, p. 363.

[11] Brian Skyrms gives an example of this sort in his "The Explication of 'X knows that p'," *The Journal of Philosophy*, 64, no. 12 (June 1967), 385–86; cf. also Gilbert Harman's "Inference to the Best Explanation," *The Theory of Knowledge: Classic and Contemporary Readings*, ed. Louis P. Pojman (Belmont, CA: Wadsworth Publishing Co., 1993), p. 154.

passes out. An hour later he dies of a heart attack. Shortly after that, a mad fiend comes along, sees Omar, and cuts off his head. Still later, Smith comes along and sees poor Omar. Smith sees that Omar's head has been cut off and Smith believes that Omar is dead because he was decapitated. In this case, Smith knows that Omar is dead. But Smith has *not* properly reconstructed the causal chain from the fact that Omar is dead to his belief that Omar is dead. Smith erroneously attributes Omar's death to the fact that he was decapitated. Since Smith has not properly reconstructed the causal chain, D12 implies incorrectly that Smith does not know that Omar is dead.

A third difficulty for the causal theory was raised by Goldman himself several years after the publication of "A Causal Theory of Knowing."[12] Goldman asks us to imagine that Henry is driving through the countryside and sees a barn. He forms the belief "There's a barn." But unbeknownst to Henry, he is driving through a region where the natives have constructed many facsimiles of barns, facsimiles that are really just barn facades without back walls or interiors. The facsimiles are so cleverly constructed that tourists like Henry typically mistake them for barns. Under these circumstances, Henry's true belief that there's a barn seems to be right by luck. Goldman suggests that Henry does not know that there is a barn before him. But, as Goldman points out, D12 seems to give us the wrong answer in this case. Henry's belief *is* causally connected in an appropriate way, i.e. through perception, to the fact that there is a barn before him. So, D12 implies that Henry has knowledge. Goldman, however, thinks this is a mistake and that D12 should be rejected.

In our previous example, Henry does not know that he is in a region filled with barn facsimiles. But consider a slightly different version of the case in which he *does* know this. Imagine that Henry *knows* that he is in such a region. Suppose he has read all about the famous barn facades erected by the locals and that he has on occasion inspected such facades up close. Now suppose that in spite of all the evidence that he is in such a region, Henry just ignores it, and forms the belief that there's a barn. Again, it seems that Henry would not have knowledge even though his belief is correct.

---

[12] Alvin Goldman, "Discrimination and Perceptual Knowledge," *The Journal of Philosophy*, 73, no. 20 (November 1976), 772–73.

But, again, his belief seems formed on the basis of perception, and therefore, according to D12, it is an instance of knowledge. But that seems mistaken.

The causal accounts of knowing that we have considered have been no more successful than the No False Grounds and the Defeasibility accounts. At present, it is hard to see how a simple causal account can be successfully modified to solve the Gettier problem.

Some concluding comments

Gettier's counter-examples show us that a simple and straightforward account of knowledge as epistemically justified true belief is mistaken. We have considered three sorts of approaches to providing a definition of propositional knowledge. The specific proposals we have considered are fairly simple and represent some of the earliest attempts to deal with the Gettier problem. Unfortunately, none of the specific proposals we have considered are successful. Still, we have only skimmed the surface of a vast body of literature on the Gettier problem and while it is true that there is no widely accepted solution, there has been a great deal of constructive work. Many of the more recent developments are refinements of the approaches considered here.

It is possible, I think, that some might exaggerate the significance of our failure to solve the Gettier problem and our not having a satisfactory definition of knowledge. Some might think that if we don't have a satisfactory definition of knowledge, then we can't pick out instances of it or make any headway in the theory of knowledge. "How," they might ask, "can we talk intelligently about knowledge, about its extent and scope, and about its other features without a definition of it?"[13] Some might suggest that without a satisfactory definition, we can simply make no progress in epistemology.

I think that would be a mistake. One does not need a definition of knowledge in order to pick out instances of it. In general, it is not necessary for one to know the definition of X in order to be able to pick out instances of X. One can know that this is a man or that is a table without knowing

---

[13] Cf. Socrates's comment in *Meno*: "If I do not know what something is, how could I know what qualities it possesses?" (71b), Plato, *Meno*, trans. G. M. A. Grube (Indianapolis: Hackett Publishing, 1976), p. 4.

a definition of man or table. It is no easy matter to define the concept of man or table, but we can all pick out instances of each. Young children, for example, can pick out men and tables without knowing a definition of either concept. By the same token, we can, I think, pick out instances of knowledge even without knowing a definition of knowledge. Each of us knows, for example, that we exist and that we think, and we know such things even without being able to define the concept of knowledge. Even without having a definition of knowledge or solving the Gettier problem we know that there are other people who think and feel, who have lived for many years. So, again, it is hardly clear that one needs a definition of knowledge or a solution to the Gettier problem in order to pick out instances of knowledge. Moreover, as we have surveyed various attempts to define the concept of knowledge, we have assumed that we could pick out instances of knowledge. For example, we have sometimes rejected a definition because it implies that someone doesn't have knowledge in a particular case when it seems that he does, or it implies someone has knowledge when it seems clear he doesn't. In examining and assessing various definitions, we have assumed that we can pick out instances of knowledge.

Furthermore, it seems false that we can't talk intelligently about knowledge without having a definition of it. One can talk intelligently about human beings and cars and tables without having a definition of those things. So, why should it be any different for knowledge? Even if we have not solved the Gettier problem, it hardly follows that we know nothing about knowledge. We know, for example, that if someone knows that p, then p is true. We know that knowing that p is not the same as having a mere true belief that p or making a lucky guess that p. We know that poor Smith in Gettier's examples lacks knowledge. Moreover, the idea that there can be no progress in epistemology without a solution to the Gettier problem or a definition of knowledge is mistaken. Consider our rejection of various proposed definitions. Rejecting mistaken views on the basis of sound reasons seems to be a kind of progress in epistemology. To discover that some seemingly plausible views about the nature of knowledge are mistaken is itself a kind of progress. These failures are instructive. To appreciate the difficulties with a defeasibility account that makes use of subjunctive conditionals or to see the problems with a simple causal account is in itself a kind of progress.

If some might exaggerate the significance of our failure to solve the Gettier problem or to have a satisfactory definition of knowledge, some might ask why should we care? Indeed, if we don't need to solve the Gettier problem in order to pick out instances of knowledge, then why bother answering the ancient question "What is knowledge?" One response is simply that some people are motivated by a kind of philosophical or intellectual curiosity. They simply want to know in an especially precise and clear way what knowledge is. Such a curiosity is familiar to the readers of Plato, who asked about the definitions of piety, justice, and virtue. It is an ancient sort of curiosity about the nature of things and curious minds want to know. For now, sadly, such curiosity must remain unsatisfied. We don't have a solution to the Gettier problem. Our brief attempt to answer the question "What is knowledge?" ends, as did Plato's, inconclusively.

3   Foundationalism

In the last two chapters, we have focused mainly on the concept of knowledge. In the next few chapters we shall be concerned primarily with epistemic justification. There are at least two reasons for considering theories about epistemic justification. First, even if a satisfactory and widely accepted solution to the Gettier problem remains elusive, many philosophers hold that there is some important connection between knowledge and justification. Many hold that knowledge requires justification, that S knows that p only if p is epistemically justified for S. Similarly, many hold that if S is justified in believing *not-p*, then S does not know that p. Since it is reasonable to think that there is some connection between knowledge and justification, a better understanding of the nature of justification will help us to understand better the nature of knowledge. Second, just as we are interested in the nature of knowledge, so too we may be interested in the nature of epistemic justification. We might simply be curious about what makes a belief justified or reasonable. Most of us believe that some beliefs are justified or reasonable and others aren't, but we may wonder what makes them so.

In this chapter we shall focus on foundationalism. In the first section, we shall lay out some of the main claims of foundationalism and examine the concept of a justified basic belief. We shall also consider the regress argument for the existence of justified basic beliefs. In the second and third sections, we will examine two versions of foundationalism, classical and modest. In the final sections, we will ask, "What makes justified basic beliefs justified?" and consider critically some answers to this question.

Foundationalism and justified basic beliefs

Some of our beliefs are justified on the basis of our other beliefs. In such cases, our belief is justified in virtue of, or because of, certain other things we believe. Examples of this are not hard to find. Suppose, for example, a detective is justified in believing that Smith is a thief. His belief is justified on the basis of certain other things he believes, e.g. that Smith's fingerprints were found at the crime scene, that witnesses saw Smith in the area at the time of the crime, that the stolen object was found in Smith's room. Many of these latter beliefs are themselves justified by yet further beliefs. Take the detective's belief that Smith's fingerprints were found at the crime scene. We may suppose that this belief derives its justification from other things he believes, e.g. that the police report states that Smith's fingerprints were found at the crime scene, that the report was written by a crime scene investigator competent in the collection of fingerprints. Oversimplifying somewhat, we might say that our detective is justified in one belief, B_1, on the basis of other beliefs, B_2 and B_3, and B_2 and B_3 are in turn justified on the basis of yet further beliefs. B_1 is thus supported by an evidential chain or series that includes B_2 and B_3 as well as all the beliefs that support B_2 and B_3 and all the beliefs that support those beliefs and so on.

Does every justified belief derive its justification from some other belief? Some philosophers would say "no." They hold that some beliefs are justified *basic beliefs*. Let us define the concept of a justified basic belief as follows:

D13   B is a justified basic belief = Df. B has some degree of justification that is independent of the justification, if any, it gets from other beliefs.

D13 does not rule out the possibility that a basic belief might have some support from other beliefs. Still, in order for something to be a justified basic belief it must have some degree of justification that is not dependent on the support it gets from other beliefs. It must have some degree of justification not derived from one's other beliefs. Justified basic beliefs are sometimes referred to as "immediately justified beliefs" or "noninferentially justified beliefs." Justified *nonbasic* beliefs *do* depend entirely for their justification on other beliefs. Justified nonbasic beliefs are sometimes referred to as "mediately justified beliefs" or "inferentially justified beliefs."

What are examples of justified basic beliefs? Traditionally, examples of justified basic beliefs include two kinds, (1) beliefs about simple logical or mathematical truths and (2) beliefs about our own mental states. Consider the propositions that all squares are squares or that if something is red and round, then it's round. One's justification for believing them does not seem to be based on one's believing some other proposition or on inferring them from some other propositions. We don't need an argument for these propositions in order to be justified in accepting them. Such propositions are immediately justified for us. One simply considers them and "sees" intellectually that they are true.

Along with such simple logical and mathematical truths, some beliefs about our own mental states would seem to be immediately justified or justified basic beliefs. Our beliefs that we doubt or believe some proposition are often immediately justified for us. Suppose, for example, that I believe that Paris is the capital of France. If I consider whether I have this belief, I need not infer that I do from my other beliefs. I simply consider whether I believe that Paris is the capital of France and I find that I do. I am immediately justified in believing that I have this belief. Similarly, suppose that I doubt that it will rain today. If I consider whether I do doubt this, I need not infer from some other propositions that I do. I simply consider whether I doubt it and find that I do. My belief that I doubt that it will rain today is immediately justified for me.

Some beliefs about other mental attitudes would seem to be immediately justified. My beliefs about whether I am happy, sad, hopeful, or fearful are often immediately justified for me. For example, my belief that I hope it will rain soon is not based on an inference from other things I believe. It seems to be a justified basic belief. Similarly, my belief that I am sad that a colleague has moved away is not based on an inference. I am immediately justified in believing that I am sad that he moved away.

Finally, some beliefs about my own sensations and perceptual experiences would seem to be justified basic beliefs. My beliefs that I am having a sensation of red or that I am in pain are plausibly thought to be immediately justified beliefs. My belief that I am in pain is not based on or inferred from some other belief of mine. It does not seem to depend upon some other beliefs for its justification. Similarly, beliefs about one's own perceptual experiences seem to be immediately justified. Consider the perceptual experiences of seeming to hear a bell or seeming to see a dog. Of course, one might have such experiences whether or not one is actually hearing a bell or seeing a dog. One might have such experiences even if one is merely having an auditory or visual hallucination. Still, the belief that one is having such experiences, whether or not they are veridical, is often taken to be a justified basic belief.

Given the distinction between justified basic beliefs and justified nonbasic beliefs, we are in position to state the two main theses of foundationalism. First, foundationalism holds that there are some justified basic beliefs. It holds that there are some immediately or noninferentially justified beliefs. Second, foundationalism holds that all justified nonbasic beliefs depend ultimately for their justification on justified basic beliefs. It holds that nonbasic justified beliefs derive their justification by being related in some appropriate way to our justified basic beliefs. According to foundationalism, then, our justified basic beliefs are a kind of "foundation" upon which the superstructure of nonbasic justified beliefs rests. There are different versions of foundationalism, but all versions of foundationalism accept these two general claims.

One historically important argument for the existence of justified basic beliefs is "the regress argument." The regress argument is quite old and Aristotle seems to have given a version of it in his *Posterior Analytics*.[1] In order to understand the argument, let's consider again nonbasic justified beliefs. Suppose we assume that if any belief, say B_1, is justified on the basis of other beliefs, then there is an evidential or justificational chain or series that supports B_1. The links in this chain are the beliefs that support B_1. Often when a belief enjoys nonbasic justification, it will be supported by several beliefs and each of these supporting beliefs will be in turn supported by several other beliefs. Our evidential chains will often consist of multiple widening branches. Still, when we consider evidential chains and trace out the lines of support for any particular belief, such as B_1, there seem to be only four options: (i) the series terminates in a belief that is not justified, (ii) the series does not terminate, but contains an infinite number of supporting beliefs, (iii) the series is circular, (iv) the justificational series terminates or ends in a justified basic belief. Given these four alternatives, we can state the regress argument as follows:

The regress argument

(1) Some beliefs have nonbasic justification. Some beliefs are justified on the basis of other beliefs.

---

[1] Aristotle, *Posterior Analytics*, Book 1, chs. 1 and 2.

(2) All beliefs that have nonbasic justification are supported by an evidential or justificational chain.

(3) All justificational chains must either: (i) terminate in a belief that is not justified, (ii) be infinitely long, (iii) be circular, or (iv) terminate in a justified basic belief.

(4) Options (i), (ii), and (iii) are impossible.

(5) Therefore, option (iv) is true — some justificational chains terminate in justified basic beliefs.

The regress argument is an argument by elimination. It holds that there are only four conceivable ways in which evidential or justificational chains can be structured. But since three of the options are impossible, the fourth option, which implies that there are justified basic beliefs, must be correct.

Let us consider more closely premise 4. Why should we think that options (i), (ii), and (iii) are impossible? Option (i) tells us that the evidential chain can terminate in a belief that is not justified. So, for example, option (i) allows that B_1 may be supported by an evidential chain of the following sort: $B_1 \longleftarrow B_2 \longleftarrow B_3 \longleftarrow B_4$, where B_4 is itself an unjustified belief. To many philosophers this option seems implausible. How can a belief which not itself justified confer justification on other beliefs? How can an unjustified belief be a source of justification for other beliefs? Suppose, for example, that our police detective believed that Smith was a thief on the basis of the detective's beliefs that (a) Smith's fingerprints were found at the scene and (b) the stolen object was found in Smith's room. But suppose that the detective was *not* justified in believing (a) and (b). Suppose that he believed (a) and (b) on the basis of a mere hunch. In that case, it seems that he would *not* be justified in believing that Smith was a thief.

Option (ii) tells us that evidential chains can be infinitely long, and so they need not terminate. Option (ii) allows that B_1 can be supported by an evidential chain that has an infinite number of supporting links, such as $B_1 \longleftarrow B_2 \longleftarrow B_3 \longleftarrow \ldots$ and so on. Such an infinite chain would have no final or terminating link. One difficulty with this option is that it seems psychologically impossible for us to have an infinite number of beliefs. If it is psychologically impossible for us to have an infinite number of beliefs, then none of our beliefs can be supported by an infinite evidential chain.

Option (iii) holds that an evidential or justificational chain can be circular. It would permit justificational chains such as: $B_1 \longleftarrow B_2 \longleftarrow B_3 \longleftarrow B_1$. Proponents of the regress argument would say that it is impossible for a belief to confer justification on itself. But in order for B_1 to be supported by a circular evidential chain, it would have to confer justification on itself, if only through the other links of the chain, and this, say the supporters of the regress argument, is impossible. Suppose, for example, our police detective believes that (a) Brown is honest on the basis of his beliefs that (b) Jones is honest and (c) Jones swears that Brown is honest, and he believes that (b) Jones is honest on the basis of his beliefs that (d) Brown swears that Jones is honest and (a) Brown is honest. Given that our detective's justification for believing (a) is based, at least in part, on his belief that (a), it would seem that he is *not* justified in believing that (a).

Proponents of the regress argument claim that option (iv) is the only acceptable option, and therefore, there are justified basic beliefs. They conclude that since some beliefs enjoy nonbasic justification, there must be some beliefs that are justified basic beliefs.

The regress argument is an important argument. Still, it remains controversial. One line of criticism comes from proponents of the coherence theory of justification. The coherence theory of justification, which we shall consider in the next chapter, is an alternative to foundationalism. Proponents of the coherence theory hold, roughly, that a belief is justified in virtue of belonging to a (sufficiently comprehensive) coherent body of beliefs. Coherentists might challenge the *linear* conception of justification which the regress argument presupposes. A linear conception of justification assumes that justified nonbasic beliefs owe their justification to other beliefs and these beliefs owe their justification to still others and so on. A linear conception of justification assumes that justification is transmitted to nonbasic beliefs through the links of an evidential chain of some sort. In contrast, a proponent of the coherence theory might hold a *holistic* conception of justification. A holistic conception of justification sees the justification of a belief as a matter of its relation to one's whole body of belief. On this view, if one's beliefs, B_1, B_2, $B_3 \ldots B_n$, form a (sufficiently comprehensive) coherent body of beliefs, then B_1 is justified. Coherentists might thus reject the view of nonbasic justification embodied in premise 2, that justification must be transmitted to nonbasic beliefs through an evidential chain.

Coherentists might also challenge the notion that no belief can support or confer justification on itself. Suppose, for example, that some of one's beliefs are *mutually* supporting. Suppose, for example, one believes that it is raining, that there is water on the window, that people are carrying umbrellas, and that the cars have their wipers on. These beliefs mutually support one another. But if they mutually support one another so that, for example, the belief that it is raining supports the belief that the cars have their wipers on and *vice versa*, then, the coherentist might ask, is there not some respect in which each of these beliefs indirectly supports itself? Could not one belief support a second belief which in turn supports the first? Coherentists illustrate the notion of mutual support with the example of rifles stacked against one another or a house of cards in which the cards lean against one another. If we grant that beliefs can be mutually supporting and that they can, in this respect, indirectly support themselves, then, the coherentist might suggest, we should reconsider our rejection of option (iii).

Finally, in addition to the responses considered so far, we should note that many philosophers argue that option (iv) and the view that there are justified basic beliefs are also problematic. As we shall see, some philosophers argue that there can be no immediately or non-inferentially justified beliefs. Of course, whether there are, in fact, cogent arguments against the existence of justified basic beliefs remains to be seen. Still, advocates of the coherence theory would deny that there are justified basic beliefs and, therefore, we should reject foundationalism in favor of the coherence theory.

It is safe to say that the regress argument has not been universally accepted and remains controversial. The regress argument, as we noted, is an argument by elimination and in assessing any such argument it is always important to consider all the alternatives. Perhaps, then, it would be wise to consider the coherence theory and arguments against the existence of basic beliefs before passing a verdict on the regress argument or foundationalism. For the moment, however, we shall keep our focus on foundationalism and consider some of its main forms. In the next sections we shall examine two versions of foundationalism, classical and modest foundationalism.

Classical foundationalism

As we have seen, foundationalism, in general, holds that (i) there are some justified basic beliefs, and (ii) that all nonbasic justified beliefs depend ultimately for their justification on justified basic beliefs. Classical foundationalism accepts both of these claims. However, classical foundationalism goes beyond these general tenets in two important ways. First, classical foundationalism holds that basic beliefs must be *infallible*. It holds that S has a justified basic belief that p only if S is infallible about p. We shall say that one is infallible about p just in case one cannot be mistaken about p. One is infallible about p just in case it is impossible for one to be wrong about p. Second, classical foundationalism holds that the only way justification can be transmitted from one belief to another is through *deduction*. If S's belief that q is a nonbasic belief, then the only way for S to be justified in believing that q is by S's deducing q from some other proposition that S is justified in believing. Ultimately, if S is justified in believing that q, then q must follow from, or be implied by, one or more propositions for which S has basic justification. Given these two views, we may say that classical foundationalism accepts:

CF S is justified in believing that p only if (i) S is infallible about p or (ii) S deduces that p from one or more propositions which he infallibly believes.

In short, according to classical foundationalism, epistemic justification requires either infallible belief or deduction from what is infallibly believed.

Let us consider the requirement that justified basic beliefs be infallible. This is a very high standard. Indeed, since infallibility requires the *impossibility* of error, it is clear that very few of our beliefs can meet it. Consider our ordinary perceptual beliefs. Take, for example, my perceptual belief that there is a cup on the table. I take this belief to be true, but is it infallible? In his *Meditations*, Descartes argued that such perceptual beliefs were not infallible. He suggested that it was *possible* that one is deceived in one's perceptual beliefs by a powerful evil demon. Given the possibility of such deception, we cannot hold that our perceptual beliefs are infallible. In the popular movie *The Matrix* we are also presented with the possibility of massive perceptual deception by a computer that stimulates our central nervous system. Such a scenario, though far fetched and entertaining, seems a possibility. If so, then again, it seems that our perceptual beliefs are not infallible. Similar considerations apply to our memory beliefs. I take myself to remember that I was in this room yesterday. But is this memory belief infallible? It would seem not since it is *possible* that I am mistaken.

It is possible that I am deceived by Descartes's demon or a powerful computer or that I am simply mistaken because I am just very absent-minded and forgetful. It seems, then, that we should concede that neither our perceptual nor memory beliefs are infallible. So, if justified basic beliefs must be infallible, then neither perceptual beliefs nor memory beliefs are justified basic beliefs.

Are *any* beliefs infallible? There do seem to be some things about which we are infallible. The proposition that I exist is one that is infallible for me. It is impossible for me to be mistaken in believing that I exist. Similarly, the proposition that I think is infallible for me. It is impossible for me to be mistaken in believing that I think. Neither Descartes's demon nor some powerful computer could deceive me about such things. My beliefs that I think and I exist, then, meet the standard of infallibility. Moreover, each seems to be immediately justified insofar as our justification for believing them does not depend on our inferring them from some other beliefs. Still, if these are the only infallible beliefs, then classical foundationalism's set of basic beliefs would be terribly meager.

Many classical foundationalists, however, also hold that we are infallible about some simple logical and mathematical truths and some propositions about our own mental states. Consider the propositions that all square are squares and that if something is red and round, then it is red. It is reasonable to think that one's belief in such propositions is infallible. It is hard to see how one could be mistaken in believing, for example, that all squares are squares. Consider next propositions about my own mental states, e.g. that I believe that Paris is the capital of France, that I am in pain, that I am having a sensation of red. Classical foundationalists would typically hold that I am infallible about such things. If Descartes's demon can deceive me about what is actually the capital of France, or even that there is such a place as France, he cannot deceive me about the fact that I believe that Paris is the capital of France. He cannot deceive me about what I believe to be the case. Again, it seems plausible that I cannot be mistaken about whether I am in pain, at least severe pain. Not even Descartes's demon can deceive me about whether I am having a sensation of pain. Again, the demon might be able to deceive me about whether there is actually something red before me, say a ripe apple or tomato. But, one might hold, he cannot deceive me about the fact that I have the sensation of red. That I have such a sensation is something about which I cannot be mistaken.

In sum, classical foundationalism requires that justified basic beliefs be infallible, and, given that standard, perceptual and memory beliefs don't qualify. Still, classical foundationalism typically allows that we are infallible about some simple logical and mathematical truths and about some of own mental states. In general, classical foundationalism restricts the sphere of justified basic beliefs to the testimony of introspection and reason or rational intuition.

There are many serious objections to classical foundationalism. Perhaps the most serious objection is that we are justified in believing far more than classical foundationalism allows. Consider some ordinary proposition that it seems reasonable to think I am justified in believing. Suppose, for example, I am looking at my desk in good light and I see plainly that there is a cup on my desk. Under these circumstances it seems reasonable to think that I am justified in believing:

(d)   There is a cup on the desk.

But as we have seen, classical foundationalism holds:

CF S is justified in believing that p only if (i) S is infallible about p or (ii) S deduces that p from one or more propositions which he infallibly believes.

The problem is that my perceptual belief that (d) is true is neither infallible nor does it appear to follow deductively from anything I infallibly believe. So, given CF, classical foundationalism appears to imply that I am not justified in believing (d). But, the objection goes, surely I am justified in believing (d). Therefore, classical foundationalism and CF must be mistaken.

Let us consider this objection more closely. CF and classical foundationalism lay down two conditions for a belief to be justified. The first condition is clearly not met. I am not infallible about (d) and so, according to classical foundationalism, my belief that (d) cannot be a justified basic belief. But what about the second condition? Does my belief that there is a cup on the desk enjoy nonbasic justification because I have deduced it from propositions that I am basically justified in believing?

Unfortunately, this condition is not met for several reasons. First, I do not deduce (d) from other propositions I believe. When I form the belief that there is a cup on the desk, it is not formed on the basis of any inference. I simply look at the desk and form the belief that there is a cup on the desk.

My belief is not formed on the basis of reasoning. It is cognitively spontaneous. Our perceptual beliefs are typically cognitively spontaneous. The same, of course, is also true for our memory beliefs. When I remember that I drove to work today or that I had eggs for breakfast or that my telephone number is so and so, those beliefs are not formed on the basis of inference or reasoning. I do not deduce my telephone number from other propositions that I believe. I simply remember it. Since perceptual and memory beliefs are typically not the result of deduction or inference, they do not satisfy the requirements for justification laid out in CF.

Second, it is doubtful that we have, at any given moment, the right kind of introspective beliefs about our sensations to justify our perceptual beliefs. Consider again my belief that there is a cup on the desk, (d). From what justified basic beliefs is (d) to be inferred? A defender of classical foundationalism might suggest that I deduce (d) from my introspective belief that there appears to be a cup on the table. This belief would be an introspective belief about how things appear to me and it would be, arguably, infallible. Unfortunately, one problem with this response is that when we form perceptual beliefs we typically do *not* also form such introspective beliefs about our mental states. When I formed the perceptual belief that there is a cup on the desk, I did not *also* form the introspective belief about my own mental state, about the way I am appeared to. I simply formed the belief that there is a cup on the desk. No doubt I do have various sensations and I am appeared to in various ways when I see there is a cup on the desk, but in forming perceptual beliefs I do not typically form beliefs about my own sensations and the ways I am appeared to. If this is right, then it is a mistake to think that our perceptual beliefs are deduced from infallible introspective beliefs about our own sensations and the ways we are appeared to. In the typical perceptual case, we simply do not have or form such beliefs.

Third, even if we grant that we do have a rich stock of justified basic beliefs about our own sensations and the ways we are appeared to, nothing follows logically about the existence or nature of external objects. Suppose we grant that I have the following infallible, introspective, justified basic belief:

(a) It appears to me as though there is a cup on the desk.

Suppose my experience is just the way (a) says it is. Still, it should be clear that (d) does not logically follow from (a), since it is logically possible for (a) to be true and for (d) to be false. If, for example, I were deceived

by Descartes's evil demon about the presence of a cup on the desk, then
(a) would be true and (d) would be false. Since (d) does not follow logically
from (a), I cannot deduce (d) from (a). I can't, therefore, be justified in
believing (d) by deducing it from (a). More generally, it does not seem that
(d) would follow logically from *any* combination of propositions which
enjoyed basic justification for me. From those propositions I infallibly
believe about my mental states and some simple logical truths, nothing
seems to follow about the truth of (d). If so, then I cannot be justified in
believing (d) by deducing it from propositions that I am basically justified
in believing.

It does appear, then, that according to classical foundationalism and CF,
I am not justified in believing (d). My belief does not meet the requirements
for justification laid out in CF. But, of course, this is not the only thing which
is unjustified for me. For similar reasons, very few, if any, of our beliefs about
the external world and the past will turn out to be justified according to CF
and classical foundationalism. Again, this is a serious problem. Critics claim
that since we *do* have justified beliefs about the external world and the past,
classical foundationalism is mistaken. Of course, even if we reject classical
foundationalism, it does not follow that other forms of foundationalism
are mistaken. Let us turn to another form of foundationalism.

Modest foundationalism

Modest foundationalism, as the name suggests, is also a kind of foundationalism. It accepts the two central claims of foundationalism, holding
that (i) there are justified basic beliefs and (ii) that all nonbasic justified
beliefs depend ultimately for their justification on justified basic beliefs.
In contrast to classical foundationalism, however, modest foundationalism
has a more relaxed view about the nature of basic beliefs and about the
connections between justified basic beliefs and nonbasic justified beliefs.
Modest foundationalism does not insist that justified basic beliefs must
be infallible. Moreover, modest foundationalism does not hold that the
only way for justification to be transmitted to nonbasic beliefs is through
deduction. Modest foundationalism allows, for example, that nonbasic
beliefs can be justified through various kinds of inductive reasoning, such
as enumerative induction and inference to the best explanation. Let's
consider these points more closely.

Modest foundationalism does not require that basic beliefs be infallible, and so, not surprisingly, the scope of our justified basic beliefs is much broader for modest foundationalists than it is for classical foundationalists. Modest foundationalists typically include among our justified basic beliefs various cognitively spontaneous, noninferential perceptual and memory beliefs. Thus, my perceptual belief that there is a cup on the desk and my memory belief that I had eggs for breakfast would typically be taken as justified basic beliefs, as long as there is no defeating evidence for those beliefs. If classical foundationalism accepts as justified basic beliefs the testimony of introspection and rational intuition, modest foundationalism adds to this the undefeated noninferential testimony of perception and memory.

In addition to taking a more liberal view about justified basic beliefs, modest foundationalism also rejects the view that the only way for justification to be transmitted from one belief to another is through deduction. Suppose, for example, I am justified in believing that (i) two hundred marbles have been drawn from an urn, and (ii) they have all been red. Now consider, (iii) the next marble drawn will be red. According to classical foundationalism, I cannot be justified in believing (iii) on the basis of (i) and (ii) since they do not logically imply (iii). Modest foundationalism rejects this view, and allows that one can be inductively justified in believing (iii) on the basis of (i) and (ii). Similarly, suppose that I am justified in believing that (i) Smith's fingerprints were found at the crime scene, (ii) Smith was seen in the area at the time of the crime, and (iii) the stolen object was found in Smith's room. Now consider, (iv) Smith is a thief. According to classical foundationalism, I cannot be justified in believing (iv) on the basis of (i)–(iii), since (i)–(iii) do not logically imply (iv). Again, modest foundationalism denies this and allows that I can be inductively justified in believing (iv) on the basis of (i)–(iii).

Many philosophers regard modest foundationalism as a more reasonable view than classical foundationalism. Classical foundationalism seems unduly restrictive and appears to imply that much of what we ordinarily believe on the basis of perception and memory is not justified. Modest foundationalists avoid this problem by taking one's noninferential and undefeated perceptual and memory beliefs to be immediately justified and by allowing justification to be transmitted to other beliefs through various forms of inductive inference.

What justifies basic beliefs?

One of the most important questions for any theory of justification is "What makes justified beliefs justified?" Certainly this is an important question for any version of foundationalism and indeed we may ask "What justifies *basic* beliefs?" Even if we think that modest foundationalism is a more plausible view than classical foundationalism, we may still wonder what makes basic beliefs justified. In order to properly appreciate these questions, and to begin to answer them, let us note the following points.

First, many philosophers take epistemic justification to be an evaluative or normative concept or property. When we say that a belief is epistemically justified or reasonable, we are making a positive or favorable evaluation of that belief. Similarly, when we say someone's belief is epistemically unjustified or unreasonable, we are making a negative or unfavorable evaluation of that belief. The same might be said of the concept of knowledge. When we say that someone knows something, we are making a positive or favorable evaluation of his belief. Along with knowledge and justification, other evaluative or normative concepts include good, bad, right, wrong, praiseworthy, blameworthy, beautiful, and ugly.

Second, many philosophers hold that evaluative and normative properties *supervene* or depend on descriptive properties. In other words, a thing has its evaluative or normative properties in virtue of its having certain descriptive properties. Suppose, for example, A is a good apple. If A is a good apple, then it is good in virtue of its having various descriptive properties. Such properties might be its being sweet, crisp, juicy, and worm-free. We might think of those properties as being "good-making" properties of apples. Similarly, if B is a beautiful painting, then it is so in virtue of its having certain descriptive features or properties, such as its having a certain composition and arrangement of colors. If we assume that justification is a normative or evaluative property, then we should assume that if someone's belief is justified, then it is justified in virtue of certain descriptive features or properties of the person or his belief. If I am justified in believing, for example, that there is a cup on the desk, then I am justified in that belief because of certain descriptive properties had by me or my belief, e.g. that I am having such and such perceptual experiences or that my belief is caused by my perceptual experiences.

Of course, *which* descriptive properties an evaluative property supervenes upon is sometimes controversial. Take for example moral rightness. Some utilitarian philosophers hold that it is morally right for S to perform act A in virtue of A's maximizing the total balance of pleasure over pain. Some egoists hold it is morally right for S to do A in virtue of A's maximizing the balance of pleasure over pain for S. Some Kantian moral philosophers hold that it is morally right for S to do A in virtue of S's not treating any human being as mere means in performing A. Though it is controversial what the right making properties of acts are, it is reasonable to think that acts are right or wrong in virtue of some descriptive features of those acts. In epistemology, there are also different views about what makes justified beliefs justified. Still, it is reasonable to think that justification, like other evaluative properties, depends on some set of descriptive features or properties of beliefs.

Finally, many philosophers endorse the following view about supervenience and evaluative properties:

E   Necessarily, if two things share all of their descriptive properties, then they share all of their evaluative properties.

To illustrate E, consider two apples that have the same descriptive properties. They are equally sweet, crisp, juicy, and worm-free. Given that they share the same descriptive properties, E implies that it is impossible for one of the apples to be good, but not the other. Given that they share the same descriptive properties, either they are both good or neither is. Again, suppose that two paintings share the same descriptive properties, they have same colors, subject matter, composition, etc. If the paintings are alike in all their descriptive properties, then, according to E, either they are both beautiful or neither is. By the same token, if two things differ in their evaluative properties, then there must be some difference in their descriptive properties. So, if one painting is beautiful and the other is not, then there must be some difference between them in terms of their descriptive properties. Similarly, if we think that A is justified in believing that p and B is not justified in believing that p, then there must be *some* descriptive difference between A and B. Perhaps, for example, A sees or remembers something that B does not. Whatever it is, there must be some descriptive difference between them which makes the one justified and the other not.

Let us return, then, to the question "What makes justified basic beliefs justified?" Let's distinguish between two types of sources of justification, *doxastic* and *nondoxastic*. A doxastic source of justification is another belief or set of beliefs. Beliefs that are justified by other beliefs have a doxastic source of justification. Nonbasically justified beliefs or inferentially justified beliefs have doxastic sources of justification. In contrast, a nondoxastic source of justification is a source of justification that is not a belief or set of beliefs. Since justified basic beliefs have some source of justification other than one's beliefs, justified basic beliefs must have a nondoxastic source of justification. If there are any justified basic beliefs, there must be nondoxastic sources of justification. But what can these nondoxastic sources be?

One candidate for a nondoxastic source of justification is infallibility. We might say that basic beliefs are justified in virtue of their being infallible. Such a view might be attractive to the classical foundationalist. Indeed, some classical foundationalist might hold that infallibility is the *only* source of justification. Perhaps infallibility is a source of justification. Still, if we reject classical foundationalism in favor of modest foundationalism and allow that basic beliefs need not be infallible, we must find some other source of justification for basic beliefs. Since perceptual and memory beliefs are not infallible, infallibility can't be what makes them justified.

A widely held view among many foundationalists, both classical and modest, is that our basic beliefs are justified in virtue of our *nondoxastic experiences*. A nondoxastic experience is an experience or mental state that is not a belief. Nondoxastic experiences include such things as our sensations and perceptual experiences. Sensations and perceptual experiences differ from beliefs. One difference between them is that beliefs have truth values. Beliefs are true or false. In contrast, sensations and perceptual experiences do not have truth values. The belief that I have a sensation of red, for example, is either true or false. In contrast, the sensation of red is not itself true or false. Similarly, the perceptual experience of seeming to hear a bell is neither true nor false. In contrast, the belief that I hear a bell and the belief that I seem to hear a bell have truth values.

According to many classical and modest foundationalists, our nondoxastic experiences are sources of justification for our introspective beliefs. Consider, for example, our introspective beliefs about our own sensations. Suppose I have the introspective belief that I am in pain. What justifies such a belief? According to the present view, it would be the fact that I am in pain. My introspective belief that I am in pain is justified in virtue of my having the sensation of pain. Similarly, my introspective belief that I am having the sensation of red is justified in virtue of my having the sensation of red. What justifies our introspective beliefs that we have these sensations is our having those very sensations.

Our introspective beliefs that we have certain sorts of perceptual experiences are also justified by our nondoxastic experiences. Consider the introspective belief that one is having a certain sort of perceptual experience. Suppose, for example, that I believe that I seem to see a tomato. (We should bear in mind that my belief in this case is a belief about my own experience. It is not a belief that there actually is a tomato before me. We might express this belief by saying, "It looks as though there were a tomato before me.") According to some foundationalists, my belief that I am having this experience is justified in virtue of my having this experience. In other words, what justifies me in believing that I seem to see a tomato is the fact that I seem to see a tomato. Similarly, my belief that I seem to hear a bell ringing is justified in virtue of my seeming to hear a bell ring.

While many classical and modest foundationalists hold that introspective beliefs can be justified by nondoxastic experiences, many modest foundationalists go even further. They take our perceptual and memory beliefs to be justified by nondoxastic perceptual and memory experiences. Many modest foundationalists, for example, maintain that our perceptual beliefs about the external world can be justified by nondoxastic experiences such as our sensations and perceptual experiences. Suppose, for example, that my perceptual experience is such that it appears to me that there is a cup on the desk. Suppose that I seem to see that there is a cup on the desk. They would say the fact that it appears to me that there is a cup on the desk, or that I seem to see a cup on the desk, is evidence for the proposition that there is a cup on the desk, (d). Similarly, according to this view, if I have the perceptual experience of seeming to see something red, then I have evidence for believing that there is something red. The central point is that according to many modest foundationalists our sensations and perceptual experiences do not merely justify introspective beliefs or propositions about our own mental states, they also "point beyond themselves" by providing evidence about the external world. These experiences are sources of justification for our basic perceptual beliefs.

Can we say simply that if it appears to me that there is a cup on the desk, then I am justified in believing that there is a cup on the desk? No, for it is possible that there is defeating evidence. I might, for example, have that perceptual experience yet also know that I am looking at a extremely realistic hologram of a cup. Or again, I might have that perceptual experience and yet also know that I have taken a drug that causes visual hallucinations. Perhaps I know that the drug typically causes hallucinations of cups. In these cases, even though it appeared to me that there were a cup on the desk, the proposition that there is a cup on the desk would not be justified for me. Instead, we might say that my having that perceptual experience *prima facie* justifies me in believing (d). My perceptual experience justifies me in believing (d) provided I have no defeaters for (d).

Some modest foundationalists also appeal to nondoxastic experiences to justify memory beliefs about the past. Here the claim is that memory experiences *prima facie* justify our memory beliefs. Sometimes, they would say, we seem to remember various things. I might, for example, seem to remember that I had eggs for breakfast or that I visited Washington DC as a child. These memory experiences can, like perceptual experiences, serve as evidence or *prima facie* justification for our beliefs about the past. Thus, if I seem to remember having eggs for breakfast, and I have no defeating evidence for the proposition that I did have eggs for breakfast, then I am justified in believing that I had eggs for breakfast.

Objections to foundationalism

There are a variety of objections to foundationalism. It this section we shall consider two sorts of objections. The first objection claims that the view that nondoxastic experiences can justify beliefs faces a fatal dilemma. The second objection holds we need a better explanation of why some experiences justify beliefs and others don't.

One objection to foundationalism maintains that the view that nondoxastic experiences are sources of justification faces a dilemma. Consider the following passage by Laurence BonJour:

> if [our] intuitions or direct awarenesses or immediate apprehensions are construed as cognitive, at least quasi-judgmental ... then they will be both

capable of providing justification for other cognitive states and in need of it themselves; but if they are construed as noncognitive, nonjudgmental, then while they will not themselves need justification they will also be incapable of giving it.[2]

To understand BonJour's objection we need to understand the difference between a cognitive and a noncognitive mental sate. A cognitive state is one that has a truth value and can have the property of being justified. Doxastic states, such as beliefs and judgments, are cognitive states. They have truth values and they are the sorts of things that can have the property of being justified. A noncognitive mental state is one that has no truth value and cannot have the property of being justified. A sensation of pain is not, we shall assume, a cognitive state. A sensation of pain can have no truth value; it is neither true nor false, and it is not the sort of thing that can be epistemically justified. Given the distinction between cognitive and noncognitive states, we can put the objection as follows:

The dilemma of nondoxastic justification

(1) Our nondoxastic experiences are either cognitive or noncognitive states.
(2) If they are cognitive states, then they can justify beliefs, but they themselves must be justified.
(3) If they are noncognitive states, then they do not need to be justified, but they also cannot give justification.
(4) Therefore, our nondoxastic experiences either (a) cannot give justification or (b) they must themselves be justified.

Foundationalists who take nondoxastic experiences as a source of justification for basic beliefs will not welcome this conclusion. If (a) is true, then nondoxastic experiences are simply not sources of justification. They simply cannot justify basic beliefs. If (b) is correct, our nondoxastic experiences are really no different from beliefs − they can justify beliefs but only if something else justifies them. Our nondoxastic experiences are not the ultimate sources for justification that put an end to the regress of justification. If either (a) or (b) is true, then our nondoxastic experiences do not play the epistemic role the foundationalist says they do.

---

[2] Laurence BonJour, *The Structure of Empirical Knowledge* (Cambridge, MA: Harvard University Press, 1985), p. 69.

Many foundationalists respond to the dilemma by rejecting premise 3, so let's consider it more closely. Why should we assume that if nondoxastic states are noncognitive then they cannot justify basic beliefs? If we focus on beliefs, it seems reasonable to think that a belief must itself have justification in order to confer it on another belief. So, perhaps the idea is that if nondoxastic states don't have the property of justification, then they can't give it to anything else. But it is not at all obvious that this principle is true. Consider the case of right and wrong actions and decisions. Right and wrong are characteristics of actions or decisions, and not properties of states of pleasure and pain or happiness or unhappiness. In some cases, however, it seems that what makes an action right is not some further action or decision, but rather the consequences of that action in terms of pain and pleasure or happiness and unhappiness. In some cases, what makes an action right are its consequences and these consequences do not themselves have the property of being right or wrong. Similarly, consider the property of deserving a punishment or reward. Strictly speaking, deserving a punishment or reward is a characteristic of persons or agents, not actions. We do not, strictly speaking, reward or punish an action. We don't imprison actions or give medals to actions. Still, persons can deserve rewards or punishment *in virtue of* or *on the basis of* their actions. Actions can confer desert on a person, even if actions don't have desert. Actions can make persons worthy of punishment or reward and they can be reasons for punishment or reward. Similarly, we might say that nondoxastic states can make certain things worthy of belief and they can be reasons for belief. Reflection on the evaluative properties of right, wrong, and desert illustrates that a thing can have an evaluative property in virtue of things that do not have that evaluative property. But if this is so, then why assume that a belief can have the evaluative property of being justified only in virtue of things that have that property?

Let's consider a second problem for the view that nondoxastic experiences can be sources of justification. Suppose we think that various kinds of experiences are sources of justification. We might think, for example, that the following are true:

(1) If S has the visual experience of a triangle before him, then S is *prima facie* justified in believing that there is a triangle before him.
(2) If S has the visual experience of something red before him, then S is *prima facie* justified in believing that there is something red before him.

We might think that the experience of seeming to see a triangle and seeming to see to something red, in the absence of defeating evidence, justify certain beliefs. But *why* do they do so? What is it about *those* experiences that make them sources of justification? Perhaps we might explain (1) and (2) by appealing to a more general principle such as:

F   If S has the experience of an X before him, then S is *prima facie* justified in believing that there is an X before him.

But, Principle F seems false. Suppose that I am having the visual experience of a chiliagon (a thousand sided figure) before me. That experience would *not* seem to be a reason for me to believe that there is a chiliagon before me. My having that experience does not *prima facie* justify me in believing that there is a chiliagon before me. But why not? What explains the difference? Some critics of foundationalism, at least of those versions that appeal to nondoxastic experiences as evidence or sources of justification, object that foundationalism does not explain why some kinds of experience are sources of evidence and others aren't. Without such an explanation, the critics say, foundationalism simply offers a scattered plurality of principles such as (1) and (2) without any deeper explanation of why these principles are true. This objection is sometimes referred to as "the scatter problem."[3]

In response, some might object that the visual experience of a chiliagon simply *can't* be a source of justification akin to the visual experience of a triangle. But that seems false. It does not seem impossible for it to be a reason. It seems possible for there to be beings with powers of discrimination much greater than ours, who are such that when they have the experience of a chiliagon before them, they have a reason to believe that there is one. Perhaps Superman or extra-terrestrials are such that when they have that experience, they have a reason to believe that there is one before them.

Indeed, it also seems possible for other creatures to have forms of experience that we don't have, kinds of experience which we find it difficult to imagine, but which serve to justify their beliefs. Perhaps some creatures have forms of experience that are as foreign to us as our visual experience

---

[3] This objection is raised by Ernest Sosa in "The Raft and the Pyramid: Coherence versus Foundations in the Theory of Knowledge," *Midwest Studies in Philosophy, Volume* **V** (Minneapolis, MN: The University of Minnesota Press, 1980), pp. 3–26.

is to an earthworm, and yet those experiences play a crucial role in their epistemic life. Perhaps some extra-terrestrial creatures gain knowledge and justified belief by sensing magnetic fields or forms of radiation we cannot. So, another way of thinking of the scatter problem is to ask what would all these different kinds of experience have in common that makes *them* sources of justification? Critics of the view that our nondoxastic experiences are sources of justification maintain that we need a more satisfactory answer.

In this chapter we have introduced foundationalism and the view that basic beliefs are justified in virtue of nondoxastic experiences. In the next chapter we shall consider additional objections to foundationalism and to the view that there are justified basic beliefs. We shall also look more closely at the coherence theory of justification, one of the main alternatives to foundationalist theories.

4   The coherence theory of justification

In this chapter we will examine the coherence theory of justification. The coherence theory of justification is an important alternative to the foundationalist views we considered in the last chapter. In the first section we shall consider what makes a body of beliefs coherent and examine some simple ways to formulate a version of the coherence theory of justification. Though neither of these simple versions is satisfactory, the ways in which they fail point to problems that any satisfactory version must solve. In the last two sections we shall look at some main arguments in the debate between foundationalists and coherentists. In the second section, we shall consider some further objections to foundationalism. In the final section, we shall look at some objections to the coherence theory of justification.

Coherence and two simple coherence theories

Many of our beliefs seem to be reasonable or justified in virtue of the fact that they cohere or fit with our other beliefs. Suppose, for example, a mother brings her young son, Adam, to the doctor. The child complains that he does not feel well. Upon examination the doctor finds that the boy has a fever, red spots on his skin, and feels itchy. Suppose the doctor also recalls that many children at Adam's school have had the measles. The doctor forms the belief that Adam has the measles. His belief that Adam has the measles fits or coheres with the rest of his beliefs. Similarly, suppose a detective forms the belief that Smith stole some missing object on the basis of his beliefs that Smith's fingerprints were found at the scene, that witnesses saw Smith in the area at the time of the crime, and that the stolen object was found in Smith's room. His belief that Smith stole the object fits or coheres with the rest of his beliefs. In these cases, the fact that a belief fits or coheres with the rest of one's beliefs seems to make it reasonable to hold that belief.

In contrast, the fact that a belief conflicts with one's other beliefs seems to make it less reasonable to hold that belief. Suppose, for example, I believe that my batting average is only .100, that I am not good at hitting curve balls, that this pitcher likes to throw curve balls, and that I have not had a hit in my last fifteen attempts. Now suppose that I believe that I will hit a home run in my next at bat. My belief that I will hit a home run does not cohere with my other beliefs. Since it conflicts with the rest of my beliefs, it seems that this belief is not epistemically justified for me.

Many philosophers distinguish between *positive* and *negative* coherence. We may say that a belief enjoys positive coherence when it is supported on balance by one's total body of beliefs. The doctor's belief that Adam has the measles positively coheres with the rest of his beliefs, and the detective's belief that Smith is a thief positively coheres with the rest of his beliefs. A belief suffers from negative coherence when it conflicts on balance with one's total body of beliefs. My belief that I will hit a home run in my next at bat suffers from negative coherence.

The idea that coherence is relevant to the justification of belief seems quite plausible. Indeed, many foundationalists claim that coherence, both positive and negative, are relevant to the degree of justification that a belief enjoys.[1] Many foundationalists hold that the degree of justification a belief enjoys is enhanced by the fact that it positively coheres with one's other beliefs. Thus, a foundationalist might hold that the doctor's belief that Adam has the measles enjoys a greater degree of justification in virtue of its positively cohering with his other beliefs. Similarly, a foundationalist may hold that the fact that a belief negatively coheres with the rest of one's beliefs lowers its degree of justification. Thus, the fact that my belief that I will hit a home run conflicts with the rest of my beliefs makes it less reasonable than it would be if it did not so conflict.

Coherence theories of justification differ from foundationalist theories insofar as they place a much greater emphasis on the role of coherence.

---

[1] See for example Roderick Chisholm's discussions of "concurrence" in *The Foundations of Knowing* (Minneapolis, MN: University of Minnesota Press, 1982), pp. 33–42, and in *Theory of Knowledge*, 3rd edn. (Englewood Cliffs, NJ: Prentice-Hall Publishing, 1989), pp. 69–71.

Coherentists hold that whether a belief is justified depends *entirely* on how well it fits or coheres with one's other beliefs. Coherentists hold that the justification of a belief is entirely a matter of its relations to one's other beliefs, of its belonging to a coherent web of mutually supporting beliefs. For this reason, the coherence theory of justification is sometimes called a "doxastic" theory of justification. Such a theory holds that the only things which can justify beliefs are other beliefs, and the only things that can serve as reasons or grounds for a belief are other beliefs.

Coherence theories thus differ sharply from foundationalists views. As we saw in the last chapter, foundationalists hold that there are justified basic beliefs that have some degree of justification independently of the support they get from other beliefs. Since coherentists hold that all beliefs depend entirely for their justification on other beliefs, they reject the view that there are any justified basic beliefs. Moreover, many foundationalists hold that nondoxastic experiences can justify beliefs, that such experiences can be reasons or grounds for beliefs. Since coherentists hold that the only things that can justify beliefs are other beliefs, coherentists reject the view that nondoxastic experiences can justify beliefs. We shall examine some of the differences between foundationalism and coherentism more closely in the next sections.

For the moment, let's consider the concept of coherence more closely. Most philosophers distinguish between coherence and logical consistency. A set of beliefs is logically consistent if and only if it is logically possible for every member to be true. Suppose someone believes both p and *not-p*. Since it is not possible for both of these beliefs to be true, his beliefs are inconsistent. Similarly, if someone believes several propositions p, q, r, and s and it is not logically possible for them all to be true, then his beliefs are inconsistent.

It seems clear that two sets of belief can each be consistent and yet differ greatly in their coherence. Consider, for example, the doctor's beliefs that (a) Adam has red spots on his skin, (b) Adam has a fever, (c) Adam feels itchy, and (d) Adam has the measles. Now consider the following set of unrelated beliefs: (a′) Madonna is a singer, (b′) Paris is in France, (c′) Seven is a prime number, and (d′) Snow is white. Both sets of beliefs are consistent, but intuitively the former exhibits much greater coherence than the latter. Indeed, it seems that the latter enjoys no coherence whatever. In any case, since each set is consistent and yet they differ in their coherence, coherence and consistency are not the same things.

Again, consider my belief that I will hit a home run in my next at bat. This belief does not cohere with my other beliefs, that my batting average is .100, that this pitcher loves to throw curve balls and I am not very good at hitting curve balls, etc. But even though my belief that I will hit a home run conflicts with my other beliefs and does not cohere with them, it *is* logically consistent with them. It is logically possible that my other beliefs are true *and* that I will hit a home run my next time at bat. So again, we need to distinguish between the consistency of a set of beliefs and its coherence.

What makes a body of beliefs coherent? What makes one body of beliefs more coherent than another? No single answer enjoys widespread support. Perhaps it is best to hold that there are different factors that contribute to, or detract from, the coherence of a body of beliefs. Just as there are several factors which contribute to or detract from the goodness of an essay, e.g. cogent arguments or poor grammar, so we may think that the coherence depends on a variety of factors. But which factors are these? At least three factors are often cited: (i) logical inconsistency, (ii) explanatory connections, and (iii) inconsistency with norms about belief formation. Let us consider briefly each of these.

One factor that detracts from the coherence of a set of beliefs is inconsistency. If my beliefs are inconsistent, then this detracts from the degree of coherence my beliefs enjoy. If I believe that both *p* and *not-p*, then this detracts from the coherence of my beliefs. Similarly, if I believe several propositions, *p*, *q*, *r*, and *s*, and they cannot all be true, then this also detracts from the coherence of my beliefs. Sometimes a person can believe several propositions without realizing that they are inconsistent. Even if he is unaware of the inconsistency, the fact that his beliefs are inconsistent lowers the degree of coherence his beliefs enjoy.

Some philosophers hold that explanatory connections contribute to the coherence of beliefs. Consider the doctor's beliefs about Adam. His beliefs exhibit several explanatory connections. Adam's having the measles explains his having red spots, a fever, and his feeling itchy. Similarly, Smith's stealing the missing object explains why Smith's fingerprints were found at the crime scene and the presence of the object in Smith's room. The explanatory connections between these beliefs increases the coherence of the detective's beliefs. In general, then, when one's beliefs exhibit explanatory relationships, the coherence of one's beliefs is increased.

Indeed, we may contrast these beliefs with the set of unrelated beliefs noted above, (a')–(d') (Madonna is a singer, Paris is in France, etc.). The presence of explanatory connections between the doctor's and the detective's beliefs explains why they enjoy more coherence than the random (a')–(d').

Sometimes we form beliefs that conflict with our own principles about how we ought to form beliefs. Suppose, for example, I believe that (i) beliefs based on wishful thinking are not likely be true and should be avoided. Now suppose I form some belief, B, on the basis of wishful thinking. Perhaps I believe on the basis of wishful thinking that the sun will shine tomorrow. Suppose that I become aware on further reflection that (ii) B *is* formed on the basis of wishful thinking. B conflicts with my other beliefs in (i) and (ii). B conflicts with my beliefs about how I should form beliefs. Some philosophers hold that this sort of conflict lowers the coherence of one's beliefs.

It is plausible to think that these three factors are relevant to the coherence of a body of beliefs. Perhaps there are others. It is hard to say what makes a body of beliefs coherent. Still, it is important to note that this is not a problem for the coherentist alone. Foundationalists who take coherence to be relevant to the justification of belief will also want a clearer account of what makes beliefs coherent.

Let's assume, however, that we understand in a rough way what makes a body of beliefs coherent. How might we formulate a version of coherentism? One attempt would be the following:

C1   S's belief that p is justified if and only if S's total body of beliefs is coherent and includes the belief that p.

The basic idea behind C1 is that if one's total body of beliefs is coherent, then any belief belonging to it is justified. Unfortunately C1 won't do. Suppose that S's total body of beliefs is coherent and S's belief that p is included in his total body of beliefs. According to C1, S's belief that p is justified. But of course, *all* of S's beliefs are included in his total body of beliefs. Consequently, C1 implies that if S's belief that p is justified, then *all* of S's beliefs turn out to be justified. But that seems an undesirable consequence of C1. C1 implies that if I have some justified beliefs, then *all* of my beliefs are justified. But that is surely false. It seems likely that some of our beliefs are justified and others aren't. Surely some are unjustified because they are based on wishful thinking, prejudice, or insufficient evidence, while others are well justified and instances of knowledge. C1 implies that it is "all or nothing" and, thus, it is not sufficiently discriminating.

In his discussion of coherentism, Richard Feldman suggests the following simple version of a coherence theory of justification:

C2   S is justified in believing that p if and only if the coherence value of S's system of beliefs would be greater if it included a belief in p than it would be if it did not include that belief.[2]

The basic idea between C2 is simple and straightforward. Suppose S believes p. We can compare the coherence value of S's total body of beliefs with the coherence value his total body of beliefs would have if we removed his belief that p. If removing the belief that p lowers the coherence value of his system of beliefs, then S is justified in believing that p. If S does not already believe that p, then we can compare the coherence value of his actual system of beliefs with the coherence value of the system that includes the belief that p. If the system with the added belief has a higher coherence value, then the belief that p is justified.

Let's consider the doctor's belief that Adam has the measles in light of C2. In this case, it seems that C2 yields the right verdict. The doctor believes that Adam has the measles. If that belief were removed from his total body of beliefs, then it seems this would detract from the overall coherence of his beliefs. He would have no explanation for Adam's red spots, fever, and itchiness. The coherence of the doctor's belief is enhanced by his belief that Adam has the measles and so, according to C2, this belief is justified. Consider also the detective's belief that Smith stole the missing object. If we remove this belief from the detective's body of beliefs, then the coherence value of his system of beliefs suffers. That Smith stole the object is part of what explains the presence of his fingerprints at the crime scene, the witnesses' testimony that he was at the crime scene, and the presence of the object in his room. Smith's system of beliefs is more coherent when we include that belief. Consequently, C2 correctly implies that the detective's belief is justified.

---

[2] Richard Feldman, *Epistemology* (Upper Saddle River, NJ: Prentice-Hall, 2003), p. 65. Feldman does not endorse this view. His discussion of coherentism is excellent.

Still, as Feldman notes, there are problems with C2. One problem can be illustrated by the following example. Suppose that the night has turned quite cold and I believe on the basis of wishful thinking that my son took his coat when he left. Let's assume that this belief is unjustified for me. If I have this belief, I might well have other beliefs that are closely connected with it. I might believe, for example, that his coat is not hanging in the closet and that he now has his coat. But now imagine that we remove from my body of beliefs the belief that he took his coat when he left. The problem is that the resulting set of beliefs would seem to be *less* coherent. My belief that he took his coat with him explains my other beliefs that his coat is not hanging in the closet and that he has his coat. If I simply remove my belief that he took his coat when he left, then I have no explanation for these other things I believe. Consequently, this would make my beliefs *less* coherent, and, according to C2, this implies that my belief that he took his coat with him is justified after all. The problem seems clear. Sometimes removing one unjustified belief from a system of beliefs can lower the coherence of the system. C2 gives us the wrong result in such a case. As Feldman notes, "The fact that any belief, even one that is not justified, can still have logical connections to many other beliefs poses a hard problem for coherentists. It is not clear how to revise coherentism to avoid this problem."[3]

A second problem for C2 arises in the following way. Suppose I form on the basis of wishful thinking the belief that (i) my son took his coat. Suppose I reflect on this belief and come to believe that (ii) my belief that my son took his coat is based on wishful thinking. Suppose further I believe that (iii) beliefs based on wishful thinking are not likely to be true and should be avoided. Here it seems that my beliefs in (i), (ii), and (iii) conflict with one another. Setting aside the objection raised above, it seems that if my belief in (i) is eliminated, then the conflict among my beliefs is removed and the coherence value of my beliefs goes up. According to C2, this implies that my belief in (i) is unjustified. But note that the conflict can also be eliminated by eliminating my belief in either (ii) or (iii). Suppose, for example, my belief in (ii) is eliminated. If my belief in (ii) is eliminated, then again I eliminate the conflict and the coherence value of my beliefs goes up. But, according to C2, this implies that my belief in (ii) is also unjustified.

---

[3] *Ibid.*, p. 66.

C2 implies that my belief in (i) is unjustified and that my belief in (ii) is unjustified. But this seems mistaken. It seems false that both of these beliefs are unjustified, and, in particular, it seems false that my belief in (ii) is unjustified. Perhaps C2 can be modified to avoid this problem, but it is not clear how it should be amended.

In sum, it is difficult to say exactly what contributes to the coherence of a body of beliefs or to formulate a clear and simple version of the coherence theory. Still, as we have noted, many foundationalists also believe that coherence is relevant to the justification of belief. Consequently, the problem of explaining what makes a body of beliefs coherent is not a problem for the coherentist alone. Moreover, the failure to find a simple, clear version of the theory hardly shows that the theory is false. Still, the sort of problems noted for C2 are problems that any satisfactory version of the coherence theory must solve.

Coherence vs. foundations: objections to foundationalism

The debate between foundationalists and coherentists often focuses on the existence of justified basic beliefs and the epistemic role of nondoxastic experience. Coherentists deny that there are any justified basic beliefs and deny that nondoxastic experiences can be sources of epistemic justification. In the last chapter, we considered one argument against the view that nondoxastic experiences can be sources of justification. In this section, we shall consider one argument for the view that only beliefs are sources of justification and one argument against the existence of justified basic beliefs. If either of these arguments is sound, then foundationalism is false.

Sometimes the view that only beliefs can be sources of justification is supported in the following way. One begins by noting that in justifying a belief one must appeal to one's other beliefs. To justify a belief is to cite some other belief or set of beliefs in support of it. Often such support takes the form of presenting an argument in which one draws a conclusion from various believed premises.[4] But, the argument continues, if beliefs are the only things one can appeal to in justifying a belief, then beliefs are

---

[4] Compare the following remarks by the political philosopher John Rawls: "... justification is argument addressed to those who disagree with us, or to ourselves when we are of two minds. It presumes a clash of views between persons or within one person,

the only sources of justification. One might then add that to have a justification for a belief is simply to have the beliefs that one would cite in
justifying it.

Perhaps we might formulate the preceding line of thought as follows:

(1) Beliefs are the only things we can appeal to in order to justify our beliefs.
(2) If beliefs are the only things we can appeal to in order to justify our
     beliefs, then beliefs are the only sources of justification.
(3) Therefore, beliefs are the only sources of justification.

Foundationalists are unmoved by this argument. They argue that it overlooks
the distinction between *justifying a belief* and a belief's *being epistemically
justified*. As we noted in the first chapter, justifying a belief is an activity in
which one engages. In contrast, being epistemically justified is a property of
a belief. It is a certain kind of evaluative or normative property. A belief may
have the property of being justified even if one has never attempted to justify
it. Many foundationalists will hold that premise 2 is false. Even if the only
way to justify a belief is to appeal to other beliefs, it does not follow that
beliefs are the only source of justification or the only things that make beliefs
justified. What one appeals to in justifying a belief need not be what makes
that belief epistemically justified or gives it its positive epistemic status.

Consider the apparently analogous case of moral justification. Suppose,
for example, that I am trying to justify some action of mine. I might justify
my action by appealing to certain beliefs I have about it. I might appeal

and seeks to convince others, or ourselves, of the reasonableness of the principles upon
which our claims and judgments are founded. Being designed to reconcile by reason,
justification proceeds from what all parties to the discussion have in common."
A Theory of Justice (Cambridge, MA: Harvard University Press, 1971), p. 580. According to
this view, justification is argument that proceeds from what is believed or, when the
argument is directed at other people, from what is mutually believed. Compare also,
"[Nothing] . . . counts as justification unless by reference to what we already accept, and
there is no way to get outside our beliefs and our language so as to find some test other
than coherence." Richard Rorty, *Philosophy and the Mirror of Nature* (Princeton, NJ:
Princeton University Press, 1979), p. 178. "[N]othing can count as a reason for holding
a belief except another belief . . . [And it] . . . will promote matters at this point to review
very hastily some of the reasons for abandoning the search for a basis of knowledge
outside the scope of our beliefs. By 'basis' I mean here specifically an epistemological
basis, a source of justification." Donald Davidson, "A Coherence Theory of Truth
and Knowledge," in *Kant oder Hegel*, ed. Dieter Henrich (Stuttgart: Klein-Cotta, 1983),
pp. 423–38; p. 426.

to my belief that the action was generous or kind. But even if I appeal to my beliefs about an action in justifying it, it does not follow that the action is morally justified in virtue of my *beliefs* about it or in virtue of any beliefs at all. The action might be morally justified because it is kind or generous or because it has certain consequences. Thus, it might be morally justified in virtue of something that is not a belief.

Let us turn to our second argument, an argument against the existence of justified basic beliefs. This argument is developed by Laurence BonJour. In the last chapter, we considered BonJour's argument that nondoxastic experiences cannot be sources of justification because they are not cognitive states, because they have no truth value and lack epistemic justification. Such an argument, were it successful, would be a serious objection to versions of foundationalism that take such experiences as sources of justification for basic beliefs. BonJour, however, has another objection to empirically justified basic beliefs.[5] The basic idea behind this objection goes as follows. In order for an empirical belief, B, to be justified, one must have some reason to believe that B is likely to be true. According to BonJour, the only way to have such a reason is to believe with justification certain things *about* B. One must be justified in believing both that (i) B has some feature, φ, and (ii) beliefs having φ are likely to be true. In short, in order for one's belief B to be justified one must have certain justified "meta-beliefs" about B. But, according to BonJour, if B is justified only if one has these justified meta-beliefs, then it turns out B is not basically justified after all. BonJour writes:

> If we let φ represent the feature or characteristic, whatever it may be, which distinguishes basic empirical beliefs from other empirical beliefs, then ... belief B could qualify as basic only if the premises of the following justificatory argument were adequately justified:
>
> (1) B has feature φ,
> (2) Beliefs having φ are highly likely to be true.

---

[5] Philosophers often draw a distinction between beliefs which are justified empirically and those that are justified *a priori*. The distinction is roughly that empirically justified beliefs depend on experience for their justification whereas beliefs justified *a priori* do not. One's belief that snow is white depends for its justification on sense experience, e.g. one seeing that snow is white. One's belief that snow is snow does not depend on sense experience. We shall say more about the distinction between empirical and *a priori* justification in chapter 9.

Therefore, B is highly likely to be true.

... The other issue to be considered is whether, in order for B to be justified for a particular person A (at a particular time), it is necessary, not merely that a justification along the above lines exist in the abstract, but also that A himself be in cognitive possession of that justification, that is, that he believe the appropriate premises of forms (1) and (2) and that these beliefs be justified *for him*. In chapter 1, I argued tentatively that such cognitive possession by the person is indeed necessary, on the grounds that *he* cannot be epistemically responsible in accepting the belief unless *he himself* has access to the justification; for otherwise, *he* has no reason for thinking that the belief is at all likely to be true.

But if all this is correct, we get the disturbing result that B is not basic after all, since its justification depends on that of at least one other empirical belief.[6]

Let's consider what this view implies about one's introspective belief that one is in pain. Let's call the belief that one is in pain "B." According to the present view, B is justified only if one has certain justified beliefs about it, certain justified meta-beliefs. What might these be? In this case, let's assume they are something like: (i) belief B is a cognitively spontaneous introspective belief, and (ii) cognitively spontaneous introspective beliefs are very likely to be true. Consider also one's cognitively spontaneous perceptual belief that there is a cup on the desk, B'. Given the present view, B' is justified only if one has certain justified meta-beliefs, e.g. that (i) belief B' is a cognitively spontaneous perceptual belief, and (ii) cognitively spontaneous perceptual beliefs are very likely to be true. BonJour argues that since B and B' are justified only if one has the relevant justified meta-beliefs, B and B' cannot be justified basic beliefs.

Foundationalists have made a variety of responses to BonJour's argument. Suppose we take BonJour to hold that *every* empirical belief must be supported by justified meta-beliefs. Many foundationalists object that the requirement that every empirical belief must be supported by justified meta-beliefs leads to an infinite regress and to skepticism about empirical knowledge and justification. To see why this is so, suppose that I form

---

[6] Laurence BonJour, *The Structure of Empirical Knowledge* (Cambridge, MA: Harvard University Press, 1985), p. 31.

a perceptual belief, B. According to BonJour, in order for B to be justified for me I must be justified in two other beliefs, such as:

(1) B is a cognitively spontaneous perceptual belief, and
(2) Cognitively spontaneous perceptual beliefs are highly likely to be true.

If every empirical belief must be supported by justified meta-beliefs, then in order to for me to be justified in believing (1) and (2), I would need to have other justified beliefs about them. With respect to (1), perhaps the meta-beliefs would take the following form:

(3) My belief that B is a cognitively spontaneous perceptual belief is a cognitively spontaneous introspective belief.
(4) Cognitively spontaneous introspective beliefs are highly likely to be true.

Of course, since (3) and (4) are both empirical beliefs, I would need further justified empirical beliefs about each of them. In the case of (3), I might need to believe both (4) and

(5) My belief that my belief that B is a cognitively spontaneous perceptual belief is a cognitively spontaneous introspective belief is a cognitively spontaneous introspective belief.

Of course, (5) is an empirical belief and so it would need to be supported with yet further justified empirical beliefs, and so on and so on. It seems clear that I do not have the necessary justified meta-beliefs. The requirement that *every* justified empirical belief be supported by justified meta-beliefs requires that we have an infinite number of increasingly complex meta-beliefs and this is a requirement that cannot be met. If that assumption were true, then we would not have any justified empirical beliefs, and that seems false.[7] Many foundationalists, then, reject the requirement that

---

[7] In his "Reply to Steup," *Philosophical Studies*, 55, 58, BonJour denies that *every* empirical belief must be supported by justified meta-beliefs along the lines presented above. He suggests that the requirements of meta-justification only apply to "putatively foundational" beliefs. "It needs to be stressed, however, that the schema was formulated with putatively foundational beliefs, those for which no ordinary inferential justification is offered, in mind and was not necessarily intended to generalize to all cases in which one belief provides a reason for thinking another to be true." It is unclear that this response is satisfactory. Note that the meta-beliefs that justify my

every empirical belief be supported by meta-beliefs because it leads to skepticism.

Foundationalists deny that justified empirical beliefs require these meta-beliefs for other reasons as well. Consider again one's belief that one is pain. Many foundationalists will say that what justifies that belief is one's nondoxastic experience of being in pain. One does not need, in addition to the experience of pain, justified beliefs *about* one's belief that one is in pain and about the reliability of introspective experience. Such meta-beliefs, they would say, are unnecessary. To support this claim foundationalists might make the following three points.

First, it seems clear that when one believes with justification that one is pain, one hardly ever forms the meta-belief that one's belief that one is in pain is an introspective belief. If, for example, I believe that I am in pain because I have burned my hand or struck my thumb with a hammer, I typically don't also form the meta-belief that my belief that I am in pain is an introspective belief. If justified belief that one is pain required that one have that meta-belief, then our beliefs that we are in pain would hardly ever be justified. But that seems mistaken. It is doubtful, then, that such a meta-belief is necessary. In the previous chapter, we considered a similar criticism of classical foundationalism and the view that our knowledge of the external world is based on or inferred from our beliefs about our sensations and the ways we are appeared to. The problem was that we do not generally form the sorts of beliefs this view requires. When, for example, I form the belief that there is a cup on the desk, I typically do not also form some belief about my own experiences. BonJour's requirement of meta-beliefs seems open to a similar objection.

"But," one might object, "even if I don't actually form the meta-belief that my belief that I am in pain is an introspective belief, it is true that I would form such a belief if I were to consider it." Perhaps one might form such a belief on reflection. Perhaps one has the disposition to form the meta-belief. Still, there is a difference between having the belief that p and having

belief B include many introspective beliefs that are putatively foundational beliefs. Would these introspective beliefs (of increasing complexity) not need to be supported by justified meta-beliefs? And if an introspective and putatively foundational belief is involved at each level of meta-support, how is a regress avoided? Quite apart from the problem of a regress, how plausible is it really to think that a simple perceptual belief is ever supported by a meta-belief as complicated as (3) or, worse yet, (5)?

a disposition to form the belief that p. Even if I have the disposition to form the right sort of meta-belief, it does not follow that I actually have the sort of meta-belief BonJour's view requires.

Second, consider the case of brute animals and young children. Children and animals have much in the way of knowledge and justified belief. They know much and have many justified beliefs on the basis of perception and memory. But it is doubtful that animals and children have the intellectual sophistication to form justified meta-beliefs about the relia-bility of perception and memory or that they are able to attribute their perceptual and memory beliefs to those sources. Though animals and children know and are justified in believing much on the basis of perception and memory, they don't know much, if anything, about perception and memory. If justified perceptual and memory beliefs required the sort of justified meta-beliefs that BonJour suggests, then children and animals would not have the knowledge and justified beliefs we take them to have. So, again, the foundationalist would claim, we should reject the view that such meta-beliefs are necessary.

Third, the foundationalist might note that BonJour does *not* require such justified meta-beliefs for some justified *a priori* beliefs. Consider the beliefs that all round things are round, or that if something is red, then it is colored. It seems reasonable to think that these beliefs are justified basic beliefs and that one's justification for believing them does not depend on one's having justified meta-beliefs about them. Should we say, for example, that one's justification for believing that all round things are round depends on one's justified beliefs that (i) this is belief is a cogni-tively spontaneous rational intuition, and (ii) cognitively spontaneous rational intuitions are highly likely to be true? BonJour himself rejects this view. But if the justification of these basic *a priori* beliefs does not require justified meta-beliefs, then what reason is there to require such meta-beliefs for basically justified empirical beliefs? Many foundationalists would say that there is no good reason to treat these two sorts of beliefs differently.

We should bear in mind that a foundationalist can consistently hold that some belief is both (i) a justified basic belief, and (ii) supported by justified meta-beliefs. A justified basic belief is one that has some degree of justification that is independent of the justification it might receive from other beliefs. The fact that it has support from other justified beliefs does not imply that it is not basic. Indeed, while the foundationalist might reject the need for justified meta-beliefs, he need not deny that such beliefs can supply additional support or evidence for our justified basic beliefs. Thus, even if my belief that I am pain does not depend upon my justified beliefs that (i) it is an introspective belief, and (ii) introspective beliefs are highly likely to be true, such beliefs can provide additional support.

Coherence vs. foundations: objections to coherentism

Foundationalists raise several objections to coherentism. One common criticism of coherence theories is that they "cut justification off from the world." This criticism is often taken to mean that coherence theories overlook the relevance of experience to justification. Often this criticism takes the form of the "isolation argument." In order to appreciate this objection, let's imagine two men, A and B. Let's suppose that A has a coherent body of beliefs and that among A's beliefs are the following: I have a splitting headache, I want aspirin, I am in pain. Let us suppose that B's body of beliefs is identical to A's. Let's imagine that B's body of beliefs is an exact duplicate of A's and that among B's beliefs are the following: I have a splitting headache, I want aspirin, I am in pain. Since we are supposing that A and B have the same beliefs, it seems that their beliefs will be equally coherent. According to the coherence theory, since justification is entirely a matter of the coherence of one's beliefs and since A and B have the same beliefs, it seems that their beliefs are equally justified.

But now suppose that A actually has a splitting headache whereas B has none. A really has the painful nondoxastic experience associated with a headache, but B does not. According to proponents of the isolation argument, A's belief that he has a headache is more justified than B's belief that he has a headache. But since the coherence theory implies that their beliefs are equally justified, the coherence theory must be false. Perhaps we can put the objection as follows:

The isolation argument

(1) If the coherence theory of justification is true, then B's belief that he has a headache is as justified as A's belief that he has a headache.

(2) But B's belief that he has a headache is *not* as justified as A's belief that he has a headache.

(3) Therefore, the coherence theory of justification is false.[8]

According to proponents of the isolation argument, A's belief about his headache is more justified than B's belief about his headache. Why is it more justified? Proponents of the isolation argument might answer that A's belief is supported by his nondoxastic experiences in way that B's belief is not.

Let's consider a second version of the isolation argument. Suppose that, as before, A and B have identical bodies of beliefs, but now let's imagine that each man believes: I have no headache, I feel fine, it is a great day to be alive. Again, since their beliefs are identical, the coherence theory implies that their beliefs enjoy equal justification. Suppose that A actually has no headache. He is actually feeling pretty good. But now suppose that B has a terrible headache. Unlike A, B is in considerable pain. Now consider the following argument:

The isolation argument (second version)

(1) If the coherence theory of justification is true, then B's belief that he does not have a headache is as justified as A's belief that he does not have a headache.

(2) But B's belief that he does not have a headache is *not* as justified as A's belief that he does not have a headache.

(3) Therefore, the coherence theory of justification is false.

Proponents of this argument might say that what explains the difference in justification between A and B is the character of their nondoxastic experiences. The fact that A feels pretty good while B actually has a throbbing headache makes A's belief more justified than B's.

Coherentists make a variety of responses to these arguments. First, the coherentist might simply deny that there is any difference in justification

---

[8] For a discussion of this argument and of some of the main issues in the debate between foundationalism and coherence see Ernest Sosa, "The Raft and the Pyramid: Coherence versus Foundations in the Theory of Knowledge," *Midwest Studies in Philosophy*, 5, ed. Peter A. French, Theodore E. Uehling, Jr., and Howard K. Wettstein (Minneapolis: University of Minnesota Press, 1980), pp. 3–25.

between A and B. He might hold that as long as their beliefs are identical, they are equally justified. The difference in their experiences does not affect the justification of the beliefs. But is this response plausible? Let's consider an extreme case. Suppose that at t_1, C has a coherent body of beliefs. He believes that he is working in his office at his computer. Let's suppose that such beliefs are justified. But now suppose C's body of beliefs becomes frozen. Perhaps he suffers some rare brain disorder or is struck by a freakish bolt of cosmic radiation. Imagine, however, that many of his sensations change. Imagine that they change because his colleagues have noticed his bizarre state and he is being rushed to the hospital. At t_2, while he is in the ambulance being rushed to the hospital, his sensations are radically different from those he had in his office; still C continues to believe that he is in his office and working at his computer. Since his beliefs at t_2 are as coherent as his beliefs at t_1, the coherence theory appears committed to the view that his belief that he is in his office working at his computer is as justified or reasonable at t_2 as it is at t_1. To many, this consequence seems mistaken.

Second, the coherentists might challenge the plausibility of the examples used in these objections. These objections ask us to assume that one can have various sorts of sensory experiences without believing that he has them. We are supposed to assume, for example, that someone could have a painful headache and believe that he does not, and to assume that one can believe that one has painful headache when one does not. Indeed, this does seem far fetched. Suppose, then, that it is impossible to believe that one has a headache when one does not and that it is impossible to believe that one does not have a headache when one does. Suppose that one cannot be mistaken about whether one has a headache. If this is so, then we are *infallible* about our headaches. Such a concession would certainly be welcomed by the classical foundationalist. Indeed, now the critic of the coherentist might ask why isn't this sort of infallibility itself a source of justification? Why wouldn't the fact that I cannot be mistaken in my beliefs about my headaches confer some degree of justification quite apart from the justification such beliefs might get from their cohering with others?

Finally, let us consider the following objection. Suppose that Marcia is searching for her lost dog one afternoon. She loves the dog greatly and is worried sick about her. In the distance, she sees a dog. Let's suppose that the dog is too far away for her to identify her dog on the basis of her perceptual experience; nonetheless, on the basis of wishful thinking, Marcia thinks, "There's my dog!" Let's suppose that her belief coheres well with her other beliefs. Let's suppose she believes both that she sees her dog and that she knows what her dog looks like. Yet despite the fact that her belief coheres with her other beliefs, critics of coherentism will hold that Marcia's belief is unjustified insofar as it is based on wishful thinking and insufficient evidence. Perhaps we might put the objection as follows:

(1) If the coherence theory of justification is true, then Marcia's belief that there's my dog is justified.
(2) But Marcia's belief is not justified
(3) Therefore the coherence theory justification is not true.

In response to this argument, one might argue that Marcia's belief is not really coherent with her other beliefs, and therefore premise 1 is false. For example, one might suggest that Marcia's belief is not justified because it conflicts with other beliefs that she has, such as her beliefs that (i) beliefs formed on the basis of wishful thinking are not likely to be true, and (b) my belief that there is my dog is formed on the basis of wishful thinking. It is not clear, however, that this is a satisfactory response. Even if we suppose that Marcia has the first of these beliefs, we can suppose that in our example Marcia doesn't have the second. We can suppose that she does not believe that her belief *is* formed on the basis of wishful thinking. Maybe she will reflect on her belief and come to believe that it is just wishful thinking, but let's imagine that when she forms the belief "There's my dog!" she does not believe that this is mere wishful thinking. Perhaps, however, a defender will find some other reason for thinking that Marcia's belief fails to cohere with her other beliefs. It is not clear, though, what that reason might be.

Alternatively, in response to the objection, one might hold that premise 2 is false. One might insist that Marcia's belief is justified simply because it does cohere with her other beliefs. But given that the dog is too far away for Marcia to identify on the basis of her perceptual experience and that her belief is based on wishful thinking, many will find such a stance mistaken. To many, it seems that what Marcia's belief needs for justification is a certain kind of perceptual experience, one which she would have if her dog were much closer, but one which, under the circumstances, she lacks. Indeed, even if one held simply that Marcia's belief would be *more* justified in virtue of having that sort of experience, then one should reject the coherence theory of justification. For that would be to hold that something other than the coherence of one's beliefs is a source of, or is relevant to, the degree of justification of her belief.

We have considered a variety of objections and arguments in the debate between foundationalism and coherentism. We have also considered different versions of each theory. We should note that there is the possibility of "mixed" theories that combine elements of both foundationalism and coherentism. One might hold, for example, (i) that there are no justified basic beliefs, and (ii) that the degree of justification of any belief can be enhanced by one's nondoxastic experience. With respect to (i), one might maintain that no belief is justified independently of the support it receives from other beliefs. One might thus hold that coherence is essential for any degree of justification, and, thus, there are no basic beliefs. With respect to (ii), one might claim that one's nondoxastic experiences, while not sufficient by themselves to justify belief, can enhance the level of justification a belief enjoys. Insofar as one accepts (i), one rejects foundationalism. Insofar as one accepts (ii), one rejects coherentism, at least a "pure" coherentism that maintains that the only thing relevant to justification is the coherence of one's beliefs. If one accepts (ii), one cannot consistently accept a doxastic theory of justification.

Such mixed theories increase our epistemological options. Still, they too face objections. Pure coherentists will resist the notion that nondoxastic experiences can enhance justification. Foundationalists will ask why it is that nondoxastic experience can enhance justification without being sufficient for it.

Indeed, foundationalists might ask if my beliefs that I think or that I am in pain really need the support of other beliefs in order to have some degree of justification. It might be that proponents of a mixed position can develop responses to these objections. In any event, these mixed theories see some combination of coherence and nondoxastic experience as being the source of epistemic justification. In the next chapter, we shall consider some alternative theories that look for the source of epistemic justification elsewhere.

5   Reliabilism and virtue epistemology

In this chapter, we shall look at a fairly simply form of reliabilism and a form of "virtue epistemology." Reliabilism holds, roughly, that whether a belief is epistemically justified is a function of its being the product of a reliable cognitive process. Virtue epistemologists hold, roughly, that a belief enjoys the positive epistemic status of being "apt" if it is the product of a truth conducive intellectual virtue. Both reliabilism and virtue epistemology maintain that beliefs enjoy some positive epistemic status, "justification" or "aptness," in virtue of being the product of some truth conducive source, either a reliable process or an intellectual virtue.

Reliabilism

In his 1979 essay "What is Justified Belief?" Alvin Goldman provides us with an early and important version of reliabilism. He contrasts "faulty" belief producing processes, processes that typically produce unjustified beliefs, with those that typically produce justified belief. According to Goldman, faulty belief producing processes include such things as confused reasoning, wishful thinking, reliance on emotional attachment, mere hunch, guesswork, and hasty generalization. In contrast, justification conferring processes include standard perceptual processes, remembering, good reasoning, and introspection. Goldman notes that the faulty processes have something in common: "They share the feature of unreliability. They tend to produce *error* a large proportion of the time."[1] On the other hand, the justification conferring processes appear to share the feature of *reliability*. The beliefs that they produce are generally true. Reflecting on

---

[1] Alvin I. Goldman, "What is Justified Belief?" *Justification and Knowledge*, ed. George Pappas (Dordrecht, Netherlands: D. Reidel, 1979), p. 9.

this difference, Goldman suggests that "the justificational status of a belief is a function of the reliability of the process or processes that cause it, where (as a first approximation) reliability consists in the tendency of a process to produce beliefs that are true rather than false."[2]

This view is attractive for several reasons. First, it is plausible to think that perception, memory, introspection, and good reasoning are sources of epistemic justification whereas wishful thinking and hunches are not. But suppose we ask *why* is this so? What makes these diverse ways of forming beliefs sources of justification? Reliabilism offers an appealing and straightforward answer: they are sources of justification in virtue of their reliability. Reliabilism offers a unified explanation for why these different kinds of belief forming processes are sources of justification. It takes the plurality of sources and explains why they are sources of justification in terms of the feature of reliability. Second, to many it seems that there is *some* connection between a belief's being true and its being justified. But what exactly is the connection? Reliabilism offers a fairly direct account of the connection. It tells us that justified beliefs are those produced and sustained by reliable processes, processes that generally produce true beliefs. Indeed, Goldman suggests that whether one belief is more justified than another depends on the comparative reliability of the processes which produced them. In other words, if A is a more reliable cognitive process than B, then the beliefs produced by A are (other things being equal) more justified than those produced by B. Let us consider this view more closely.

According to reliabilism, whether a belief is justified is a function of the reliability of the process that produces or sustains it. It is important to note that in order for one's belief, B, to be justified it is *not* necessary that one know or believe that B is reliably produced. It is enough that it *be* reliably produced. The subject need not have any meta-beliefs about the reliability of his cognitive processes in order for those processes to yield justified belief. Goldman rejects the view that justification requires such meta-beliefs, since, in his view it would preclude children and animals from having justified beliefs and knowledge. It would preclude them from having justified beliefs or knowledge because they typically do not have beliefs about the genesis or reliability of their ways of forming

---

[2] *Ibid.*, p. 10.

beliefs, and they typically lack the relevant concepts to have such meta-beliefs.

The reliability of cognitive processes varies. How reliable must a process be in order to produce justified belief? Goldman says that our concept of justification is vague in this respect, and that there is no precise answer to the question. Still, he denies that perfectly reliable or infallible processes are necessary for justified belief. A process that is less than perfectly reliable can still be a source of justification. The false beliefs produced by such processes could still be justified, but that seems to accord with our ordinary and considered views about justification.

In developing his view, Goldman distinguishes between "process *tokens*" and "process *types*."[3] A process type is a *kind* of process and there can be many tokens or instances of that type. If we think of perception as a type of cognitive process, then there will be a great many tokens of that process. Every individual act of perception is a token of that process. A process token is a particular process that occurs only once. Each individual act of perception, for example, is a token that occurs exactly one time. When reliabilism says that the justification of a belief depends on the reliability of the process that produces it, is it referring to process tokens or process types? Goldman notes that it is only process types that have statistical properties such as being right 80 percent of the time. Process tokens cannot be reliable 80 percent of the time since each process token occurs exactly one time. Goldman suggests, then, that when we think about the reliability of cognitive processes we should think about the reliability of process types.

Goldman also distinguishes between *belief-dependent* and *belief-independent* processes. A belief-dependent process is one that starts with some beliefs and yields other beliefs. Its "inputs" include beliefs and its "outputs" are other beliefs. Reasoning is an example of a belief-dependent process. Reasoning takes us from beliefs in various premises to belief in a conclusion. Memory also provides an example of a belief-dependent process. When I recall a previously formed belief, the process is a belief-dependent process.

---

[3] We may illustrate the general distinction between tokens and types by considering the following three items: a **a** A. Each of these is a token of a *type* or *kind* of letter, the letter A. We have here three tokens of one type, the letter A. Of course, a particular can be a token of several different types. Our three letters, for example, are *also* tokens of other types, such as printed letters, vowels, etc.

In contrast, belief-independent processes have no inputs that are beliefs. Belief-independent processes might include certain basic perceptual and introspective processes. My belief that I am in pain or that something is moving might be examples of beliefs formed on the basis of such processes. Beliefs produced by reliable belief-independent processes are justified *basic* beliefs, since they have some degree of justification independent of the support they receive from other beliefs.

Reliabilism thus offers us another way in which to answer the question "What justifies basic beliefs"? In chapter 3 we considered foundationalist views that held that basic beliefs were justified by our nondoxastic experiences. Such views typically maintain, for example, that my belief that I am having an experience of red is justified in virtue of the fact that I am having an experience of red. Foundationalist views of this sort are sometimes called "foundationalism of the given" or "givenist foundationalism" since they claim that basic beliefs can be justified by what is "given" or "presented" in nondoxastic experience. In contrast, reliabilists maintain that what justifies a basic belief is its being produced by a reliable cognitive process. On their view, what justifies my belief about my experience is not, strictly speaking, my nondoxastic experience, but its being produced by a reliable process, such as introspection.

Goldman also introduces the notion of a *conditionally reliable* process. A conditionally reliable process is one that usually yields true beliefs if the beliefs it starts with are true. Goldman suggests that we think of memory and good reasoning (reasoning in accord with the canons of deductive and inductive logic) as conditionally reliable. Good reasoning is a conditionally reliable process insofar as it usually yields true beliefs when the premises we start from are true. Similarly, memory is a conditionally reliable process insofar as the testimony of memory is usually true when the beliefs which function as "inputs" are true. Still, if the beliefs these processes start with are largely false, then the beliefs yielded by these processes will be largely false. If, for example, most of the beliefs we form and commit to memory are largely false, perhaps due to deception by a Cartesian demon, then most of what memory tells us will be false. If most of the premises from which we reason are false, then it might be that good reasoning hardly ever produces true beliefs.

Let's consider the following simple version of a reliability theory of justification.

R1   S's belief that p is justified if and only if S's belief that p
            is produced by a reliable cognitive process.

Goldman points out that this simple version of reliabilism is unsatisfactory.
Suppose, for example, that Jones believes on the basis of memory that he
owned a pony when he was very young. Let's suppose that his memory is
reliable. But now imagine that Jones is told by otherwise trustworthy
authorities that most of his memory beliefs before the age of seven are
false. His parents and doctors tell him that he suffered from a certain brain
disorder that caused him to have amnesia as a child and later to develop
various pseudo-memories concerning his early childhood. Suppose,
however, that Jones ignores the testimony of his parents and doctors and
persists in believing that he owned a pony. In this case, Jones ignores
evidence or reasons for thinking that his belief was *not* reliably formed.
Even though his belief that he owned a pony is produced by a reliable
cognitive process, it seems that his belief is not justified. If this is so, then R1
must be false.

  Goldman recognizes that R1 is unsatisfactory. The problem, he says, is
that Jones failed to take into account strong evidence against his belief.
If Jones had used the evidence available to him, he would stop believing
that he had owned a pony. According to Goldman, the proper use of
evidence is a conditionally reliable process. In this case, Jones "*fails* to use a
certain conditionally reliable process that he could and should have used."[4]
The lesson we should take from this case, Goldman suggests, is that the
"justificational status of a belief is not only a function of the cognitive
processes *actually* employed in producing it; it is also a function of the
process that could and should be employed."[5] We might now formulate
reliabilism as:

R2   S's belief that p is justified if and only if (i) S's belief that p
            is produced by a reliable cognitive process, and (ii) there is no
            reliable or conditionally reliable process available to S which,
            had it been used by S in addition to the process actually used,
            would have resulted in S's not believing p.[6]

---

[4] Alvin Goldman, "What is Justified Belief?", p. 20.
[5] *Ibid.*, p. 20.
[6] Cf. *ibid.*, p. 20.

Jones's belief that he had a pony does not satisfy condition (ii), since there *is* a conditionally reliable process, "making proper use of evidence," which is such that, had Jones used it, he would not have believed that he had a pony. Unlike like R1, R2 seems to give us the right result in this case.

Still, Goldman admits that there are some problems with R2. For example, what does it mean to say that a process is "available"? Let's consider the following example. Suppose that I believe that Brown's address is 123 Broad Street because I just looked up his address in the local phone book. In this case, it seems plausible that my belief that Brown lives on Broad Street is justified. But suppose that there is some other reliable procedure which is such that had I also followed it, I would *not* have that belief. Suppose, for example, that another source, say the campus directory, lists Brown's address as 123 Baker Street. Let's suppose that the trustworthy campus directory just happens to be mistaken about Brown's address. Now, my having also checked the campus directory would have resulted in my *not* believing that Brown lives on Broad Street. If checking the campus directory is a reliable process that is "available" to me, then according to R2 my belief about Brown's address is *not* justified. Yet that seems to be a mistake. Even if I fail to make use of this additional and available process, it seems that I am justified in believing that Brown lives on Broad street. Does this show that R2 is mistaken? Not necessarily, for it is unclear what counts as an "available" process. Perhaps making use of the campus directory was not an available process. In any event, this case points to the importance of making clear what it is for a process to be available to a subject. As Goldman himself notes, failing to make use of a process that one *could* and *should* have used is relevant to justification. In some cases, we think that not using some reliable process is relevant to justification and in other cases it does not seem relevant. Unfortunately, as it stands R2 does not really tell us when it matters. Perhaps this problem with R2 can be solved.

Three objections to reliabilism

Many philosophers have held that there are more serious problems for a reliabilist account of justification. Three sorts of problems have been widely discussed. These are: (1) the new evil demon problem, (2) the problem of unknown reliability, and (3) the generality problem. Let us consider each of these.

The New Evil Demon Problem. Imagine a possible world in which someone is deceived by a Cartesian demon. The demon causes him to have perceptual experiences very much like ours. Indeed, let's suppose that his perceptual experience is phenomenologically indistinguishable from ours. On the basis of his perceptual experiences he forms lots of beliefs about his surroundings. Unfortunately, almost all of these beliefs are false. In the demon world, our victim's perceptual processes are highly unreliable since they almost always lead him to form false beliefs about his environment. Although his perceptual processes are extremely unreliable and his beliefs about his surroundings massively mistaken, many people would say that his beliefs are, nevertheless, epistemically justified. But if his perceptual beliefs *are* epistemically justified, then, contrary to reliabilism, being produced or sustained by a reliable process is *not* a necessary condition for epistemically justified belief.[7]

The view that our victim of massive deception has justified perceptual beliefs seems quite plausible. To support this view, let's consider the following case of high-tech deception. Imagine two beings, A and B. A is a perfectly normal human being in normal conditions. B, on the other hand, is a brain in a vat connected to a very powerful computer. The computer monitors B's neural states, its inputs and outputs, and stimulates B in such a way as to cause it to have perceptual experiences. Now suppose that A and B have the same perceptual experiences and the same beliefs. For example, both A and B have the perceptual experience of having a body with arms and legs, being in a class with other people, and listening to a lecture. Both believe themselves to be in class, awake, and sitting among friends. However, B's beliefs about his environment are almost all completely false. He has no arms or legs. He is not seated among friends. He is all alone in his vat. Many people would say that if B's beliefs and perceptual experiences are just like A's, and A's beliefs are justified, then B's are too. In other words, if there is no difference in their beliefs and perceptual experiences, and A is justified in believing, for example, that he is in a room with other people, then B is also justified in believing that he is in a room with other people. Again, however, reliabilism implies that since B's perceptual beliefs are not

---

[7] This objection is raised by Stewart Cohen in "Justification and Truth," *Philosophical Studies*, 46, 279–95. Cf. also Richard Foley, "What's Wrong with Reliabilism," *The Monist*, 68 (1985), 188–202.

reliably produced, his perceptual beliefs are not justified. According to many critics of reliabilism, this is false, and reliabilism, therefore, is mistaken.

The Problem of Unknown Reliability. Suppose that one's belief, B, is reliably produced, but one is unaware of that fact. Would the fact that B is reliably produced be sufficient for justification? Consider the following example suggested by Laurence BonJour:

> Norman, under certain conditions which usually obtain, is a completely reliable clairvoyant with respect to certain kinds of subject matter. He possesses no evidence or reasons of any kind for or against the general possibility of such a cognitive power or for or against the thesis that he possesses it. One day Norman comes to believe that the President is in New York City, though he has no evidence either for or against this belief. In fact the belief is true and results from his clairvoyant power under circumstances in which it is completely reliable.[8]

BonJour holds that in this case Norman's belief is not justified even though it is reliably produced. According to BonJour, if Norman has no evidence for or against this belief, and no reason for believing that his belief about the President's whereabouts is reliably produced, then it is not epistemically responsible for him to hold that belief and that belief is not epistemically justified. So, BonJour concludes that being reliably produced is not sufficient for a belief's being justified.

The Generality Problem. Suppose that I am looking out my window one night and see the full moon shining. I form the belief "There's the moon." It seems reasonable to think that my belief is justified. Now, the particular process that produced my belief is a process token. But that process token exemplifies several different process types. It is an instance of (a) perception, (b) visual perception, (c) visual perception at night, and (d) visual perception of a brightly illuminated object at night. It seems reasonable to think that these process vary in their reliability. It seems reasonable to believe, for example, that (d) is more reliable than (c). But which of these processes is relevant to the justification of my belief? If (d) is the relevant process, then we might think that my belief that there's the moon is well justified.

---

[8] Laurence BonJour, *The Structure of Empirical Knowledge* (Cambridge, MA: Harvard University Press, 1985), p. 41.

If (c) is the relevant process, however, then we might think that my belief is not well justified or not justified at all. One problem for reliabilism is to tell us which process types are relevant to justification. Goldman himself is aware of this difficulty. He notes that the theory must tell us which process types are relevant to justification, but it is unclear what degree of generality the relevant type should have.

In trying to determine what process types are relevant to justification one faces the following dilemma. On the one hand, process types can be described so narrowly that *any* true belief will be the product of a type that is highly reliable. Suppose, for example, that Jones simply guesses that *p* at 11:15 on July 7, 2006 while standing in his office. Suppose that *p* is true. Now, consider the following process type: *guessing that* p *at 11:15 am on July 7, 2006 while standing in Jones's office.* That very narrow process type has only *one* token and it produced a true belief. The reliability of this very narrow process type is 100 percent. But surely Jones's guess that *p* is not epistemically justified. So we need some restriction to rule out excessively narrow process types. On the other hand, there is a problem with allowing the relevant process types to be too general. Suppose, for example, that one decides that the relevant process type is some general type, *T*. The difficulty in this case is that there might be two beliefs each produced by tokens of *T* such that one of them is justified and the other is not, or one of them is more justified than the other. In that case, it is not clear that reliabilism can explain why beliefs produced by the same type of process should differ in their justification. Consider the general process type, visual perception. Surely, some beliefs formed on the basis of visual perception are more justified than others and some are even unjustified. For example, consider the visual beliefs that (i) this is a ship, (ii) this is a sailing ship, and (iii) this is a ketch. For a nautical novice, the perceptual beliefs in (i) and (ii) might be highly justified, but his belief in (iii) might not very justified at all and perhaps even unjustified. The same problem arises with more specific or determinate process types. Consider the more determinate process, visual perception of a brightly illuminated object at night. Suppose that one night at sea one sees lights in the distance. One forms the following beliefs: (a) there are two lights, (b) that light is closer than the other one, (c) this light is brighter than that one. Again, it is not hard to imagine that one's belief in (a) is much better justified than one's belief in either (b) or (c). The dilemma is that if one allows very narrow types as relevant to justification, then virtually any true belief turns out to be justified. If, on the other hand, one allows very general types, then one faces the prospect that one's account implausibly implies that all beliefs of that type are justified.

These three problems are important challenges for any form of reliabilism. Reliabilists have offered a variety of responses. It would be fair to say, though, that no responses are widely accepted even among those sympathetic to reliabilism. Still, let us consider briefly a few prominent responses.

Let's begin by considering the problem of unknown reliability. Responses to BonJour's objection and Norman's case vary. Some philosophers hold that, contrary to BonJour's verdict, Norman *is* justified in his belief about the President's whereabouts. They try to support this judgment about Norman's case in a variety of ways. Frederick Schmitt, for example, asks us to imagine an alien race, the Andromedans, who have remarkable clairvoyant powers.[9] Instead of perception, they use their clairvoyant powers to acquire beliefs about their surroundings. Suppose that one of the Andromedans, Abnorman, acquires reliable powers of perception. On the basis of his perceptual powers Abnorman comes to believe various things about his environment. Schmitt argues that if Norman is unjustified in his clairvoyant beliefs, then Abnorman is unjustified in his perceptual beliefs. But, Schmitt claims, Abnorman is *not* unjustified in his perceptual beliefs. Abnorman's perceptual beliefs about his surroundings are justified. But, Schmitt argues, since it is reasonable to believe that Abnorman's perceptual beliefs are justified, it is reasonable to believe that Norman is not unjustified in his clairvoyant beliefs. If this is so, then BonJour's verdict in Norman's case is mistaken.

Schmitt defends reliabilism by defending the view that Norman's clairvoyant beliefs are in fact justified. But it is not clear that the reliabilist must take that approach. Let's recall the previous case in which Jones believes on the basis of his reliable memory that he owned a pony when he was young. In that case, Jones's belief *is* reliably produced, but he ignores the testimony of his parents and doctors that his memory beliefs from that time were almost all false. Jones's belief is reliably produced, but he ignores defeating evidence. Goldman, as we have seen, holds that in this case Jones's

---

[9] Frederick Schmitt, *Knowledge and Belief* (London: Routledge, 1990), pp. 179–80.

belief is not justified. Goldman says that the belief is not justified because there was a process available to Jones, namely, making proper use of evidence, which, had it been used, would have resulted in his not forming that belief. So, Goldman argues that Jones's belief is not justified according to R2.

Perhaps Goldman could take a similar stance concerning Norman's case. Suppose we think of Norman's case in the following way. Suppose that the belief that the President is in New York just pops into Norman's head. Suppose further that Norman is justified in believing both (i) this belief just popped into my head, and (ii) I have no evidence or reasons whatever for believing that this is true. One might hold that, since he is justified in believing both (i) and (ii), Norman has defeating evidence for his belief. In this respect, one might hold that Norman's case is not fundamentally different from Jones's. We might hold that there was an additional reliable process available to Norman, namely, making proper use of evidence, which, had it been used, would have resulted in his not forming that belief. So, perhaps Goldman could argue that Norman's belief is not justified according to R2.

Let us turn to the New Evil Demon Problem. One approach to the new evil demon problem is "normal world chauvinism."[10] This approach holds, roughly, that a belief is justified just in case it is produced by a process that is reliable in a *normal* world. According to this suggestion, whether a belief is justified does *not* depend upon whether it is reliably produced in the world in which it is formed. Instead, it depends on whether the belief is formed by a process that is reliable *in a normal world*. But what is a normal world? Suppose we say that a world, *W*, is normal just in case our general beliefs about the actual world are true in *W*. Now, since one of our general beliefs about the actual world is that perception is a reliable process, a normal world will be one in which it is true that perception is a reliable process. A world in which perception is not reliable, such as a demon-world, will not be a normal world.

How would this suggestion help with the new evil demon problem? It helps in the following way. Since we are now assuming that (i) a belief is justified just in case it is produced by a process that is reliable in a normal

---

[10] For a version of this view see Alvin Goldman, *Epistemology and Cognition* (Cambridge, MA: Harvard University Press, 1986), p. 107.

world, and since (ii) perception is a reliable process in a normal world, it follows that (iii) the perceptual beliefs of the demon's victim *are* justified. To put the point in a slightly different way, consider two worlds, a normal world, W, and a demon world, W'. Perception is a reliable process in W, but not in W'. But since perception is a reliable process in normal world W, perceptual beliefs formed in demon world W' are also justified.

Unfortunately, this response does not seem satisfactory. Consider clairvoyance. One of our beliefs about the actual world is that clairvoyance is not reliable. Thus, in no normal world is clairvoyance a reliable process. But now consider a world, W', that contains Schmitt's Andromedans who have reliable powers of clairvoyance. Since clairvoyance is not a reliable process in a normal world, it follows from normal world chauvinism that clairvoyance is not a source of justification in W'. In *no* world could a belief be justified on the basis of clairvoyance. But that seems mistaken. Consider again Schmitt's Adromedans. It surely seems possible that in their world, W', they might be able to form justified beliefs on the basis of clairvoyance. According to normal world chauvinism the only sources of justification are processes that are reliable in normal worlds. But there is no good reason to think that is true.

An alternative approach to the new evil demon problem is presented in Goldman's 1988 paper, "Strong and Weak Justification."[11] In that essay, he proposes a distinction between two ways in which a belief can be justified. A belief is "strongly justified" if and only if it is the product of a process that is reliable or truth-conducive in the world in which it is produced. In contrast, a belief is "weakly justified" if and only if it is blameless and the product of a process that is unreliable in the world in which it is produced. A weakly justified belief is one that is ill formed but blameless or nonculpable. Since a strongly justified belief is the product of a reliable process and a weakly justified belief is the product of an unreliable process, no particular instance of belief can be both strongly and weakly justified.

To illustrate the concept of a weakly justified belief, consider a society in which predictions based on astrology are widely accepted. These astrological predictions are not reliably formed. Beliefs based on them are not strongly justified. But suppose some ordinary member of the society believes predictions based on what the astrological experts tell him. He is aware

---

[11] Alvin Goldman, "Strong and Weak Justification," *Philosophical Perspectives*, 2, 51–69.

that some predictions have turned out accurately. However, when the predictions are in error, "the community's astrology experts explain that the predictions had been based on misapplications of the method. The experts have techniques for 'protecting' their theory from easy falsification, and only sophisticated methodologies or astronomical theories would demonstrate the indefensibility of such tactics; but these are not available."[12] Under such circumstances we might think that the ordinary members of the society could not be blamed for relying on astrological predictions and we might believe that their beliefs were blameless though not reliably formed. So, their beliefs are weakly justified.

Now consider the victim of demonic deception. Goldman suggests that the victim's beliefs are not strongly justified, since in the victim's environment perception is not a reliable way of forming beliefs. Still, since the victim of demonic deception does not believe that perception is unreliable and since there is not available to him any reliable way of telling that perception is unreliable, Goldman suggests that the victim's belief is blameless. Goldman holds, therefore, that the victim's beliefs are weakly justified since his beliefs, though ill formed, are blameless. In this way, Goldman wants to accommodate the plausible intuition that the demon's victim is justified, without abandoning the core position of reliabilism.

Many critics of reliabilism, however, do not find the distinction between strong and weak justification a satisfactory response. One reason, according to some critics, is that there is nothing "weak" about the justification enjoyed by the demon's victim. They insist the victim's perceptual beliefs are every bit as reasonable and every bit as justified as our ordinary perceptual beliefs. Given that his perceptual experiences are phenomenologically indistinguishable from ours and his beliefs enjoy as much coherence as our beliefs, many critics see no reason to hold that his beliefs are any less justified than ours. They think that weak justification is simply *too* weak a form of epistemic appraisal to capture the status of the victim's beliefs. Perhaps we can see why some think it too weak by considering beliefs that one simply cannot avoid having, or that one simply cannot give up. We might hold that one is blameless or nonculpable in holding a belief that one cannot avoid having or that one cannot give up. Perhaps, though, one might have some really crazy beliefs that one cannot avoid having.

[12] *Ibid.*, p. 57.

One might have paranoid beliefs or delusions that cannot be given up. Indeed, one might even recognize that one's delusional beliefs are crazy and in deep conflict with one's evidence, and be unable to give them up. Such beliefs might be "ill formed" yet blameless and nonculpable, and thus "weakly justified" in Goldman's sense. Still, one might think blameless beliefs of this kind fall short of the positive epistemic status enjoyed by the beliefs of the demon's victims. At least, the beliefs of the demon's victims enjoy a kind of coherence and experiential support that a blameless or nonculpable belief need not have.

Virtue epistemology

It is fair to say that the reliabilists' responses we have considered so far remain controversial. At this point, however, let us turn to consider one form of "virtue epistemology." Virtue epistemology emphasizes the role of intellectual virtues in knowledge and justification. There are different forms of virtue epistemology, but we shall focus on the form developed by Ernest Sosa. Sosa introduced the concept of an intellectual virtue into contemporary epistemology in a series of challenging, yet subtle essays. While reliabilism holds that beliefs enjoy a positive epistemic status in virtue of being the product of a reliable cognitive process, Sosa's virtue approach maintains that beliefs enjoy a positive epistemic status in virtue of being the product of a truth conducive intellectual virtue.

There are at least two reasons to consider Sosa's version of virtue epistemology. First, Sosa distinguishes between two kinds of positive epistemic states, the *aptness* of a belief and its *justification*. A belief is apt in virtue of its being the product of a truth conducive intellectual virtue. A belief is justified in virtue of its coherence. In accepting both forms of epistemic merit, Sosa's view attempts to reconcile elements of reliabilism and coherentism while doing justice to the guiding intuitions behind both views. Second, Sosa's view offers alternative responses to the objections that have been raised against reliabilism. His responses are worth considering carefully.

Let us begin by considering briefly Sosa's account of intellectual virtue. In general, a virtue is an excellence of some kind, an excellence that is either innate or acquired. It is a disposition, skill, or competence that makes one good at achieving some goal. Consider the difference between a lucky shot in archery and a skillful shot. Both hit the target, but a skillful shot is successful due to some virtue in the archer. The shot of the skillful archer is a manifestation of his virtue or excellence as an archer, a virtue that makes him successful in attaining his goal of hitting the target. Because of his virtue he would mostly succeed in hitting it. The skillful archer has some "inner nature" which enables him to succeed, a nature which, in this case, is typically acquired by long hours of practice. Suppose we call that nature I. Of course, his having I does not make him likely to succeed in every environment and in every set of conditions. For example, even given I he would not be likely to hit the target in a hurricane. Similarly, given I, he is unlikely to succeed at hitting a target at every range. Given his nature, he would not be likely to hit the target if it were, say, a mile away. So the skillful archer's nature, I, enables him to succeed only relative to a certain set of conditions and to targets in a certain range.

What then is an intellectual virtue? An intellectual virtue is a competence by which one would mostly attain the intellectual end of believing the truth and avoiding error. More precisely Sosa says, "Let us define an intellectual virtue or faculty as a competence in virtue of which one would mostly attain truth and avoid error in a certain field of propositions F, when in conditions C."[13] To have an intellectual virtue is to have an inner nature, I, in virtue of which one would mostly attain true belief and avoid error in a certain range of propositions in a certain set of conditions. So, consider one's visual endowment, an endowment which includes among other things one's eyes, brain, and nervous system. To have that visual system is to have a certain inner nature. Again, let's call that inner nature, I. Because of I one would most likely attain the truth and avoid error in a certain field of propositions under certain conditions. So, for example, in virtue of having I one would mostly be right about a certain field of propositions concerning the shape and color of an object viewed at arm's length in broad daylight. Such a field might include, for example, propositions about whether the object was red, green, or blue, or round, triangular, or square. One's visual endowment, I, makes one virtuous relative to that field of propositions and those conditions (being viewed at arm's length, in broad daylight, etc.).

---

[13] Ernest Sosa, "Reliabilism and Intellectual Virtue," in *Knowledge in Perspective* (Cambridge: Cambridge University Press, 1991), p. 138.

Of course, having *I* need not make one virtuous with respect to other fields and conditions. So, for example, consider propositions about whether a perceived object is a dodecagon or a chiliagon. For most us, these propositions would be outside the field of our competence. We would not be able to judge rightly whether the object were a dodecagon or a chiliagon. Still, it seems quite possible that someone, Superman or Martians, have such a virtue or competence with respect to such propositions. Superman, for example, might be able to simply see that something is a chiliagon. Again, one's ability to judge correctly with respect to a field of propositions is relative to certain conditions. Even concerning red or blue, round or square, one cannot judge correctly in some conditions. Relative to the pitch blackness of a coal mine or a world of demonic deception *I* provides us with no intellectual virtue. Though, again, Superman might have a different nature which grounds his superior abilities. He would be able to see such things even in a coal mine.

Believing something on the basis of a virtue is a reliable process for getting at the truth. But not every reliable belief forming process is a matter of believing something on the basis of a virtue. Sosa offers the example of someone who, whenever he hears the cannonade in Tchaikovsky's 1812 Overture, forms the belief that there is a large gray object nearby. Now, suppose that one day he hears the cannonade and forms the belief that a large gray object is nearby. His belief is true because nearby there is an elephant with a radio hanging from his neck and the radio is tuned to the classical station and the Overture's cannonade happens to be playing. Relative to those highly specific circumstances, his doxastic process is highly reliable. But is his believing in this way virtuous? Is it the mani-festation of an intellectual virtue? "Has it thereby earned much credit, however, as a faculty to develop and admire? Of course not, since the circumstances in question are unlikely to be repeated sufficiently often in anyone's life. And if they happen to be repeated often for someone, that is just a fantastic accident that he could not have expected with any reasonable assurance, and that others cannot expect for themselves."[14] Having the disposition to believe that there is something large and gray nearby when one hears the cannonade turned out to be reliable. Still that disposition is not a virtue since the circumstances in which that disposition

[14] Ernest Sosa, "Intellectual Virtue in Perspective," in *Knowledge in Perspective*, p. 277.

led one to judge rightly are unlikely to be repeated sufficiently often in one's life.

Sosa introduces a distinction between *aptness* and *justification*. He writes:

> The "justification" of a belief B requires that B have a basis in its inference or coherence relations to other beliefs in the believer's mind – as in the "justification" of a belief derived from deeper principles, and thus "justified," or the "justification" of a belief adopted through cognizance of its according with the subject's principles, including principles as to what beliefs are permissible in the circumstances as viewed by that subject.

> The "aptness" of a belief B relative to an environment E requires that B derive from what relative to E is an intellectual virtue, i.e. a way of arriving at belief that yields an appropriate preponderance of truth over error (in the field of propositions in question, in the sort of context involved).[15]

According to Sosa, the justification of a belief is a matter of its coherence with other beliefs, including coherence with one's principles about what it is reasonable or permissible to believe. In contrast, the aptness of a belief is a matter of the intellectual virtue that yields it. Apt beliefs are reliably formed beliefs. To illustrate this distinction consider my perceptual belief that there is a coffee cup on the desk. My belief that there is a coffee cup on the desk is an apt belief. It is formed on the basis of perception which, relative to this environment (good lighting, the surface of the earth, etc.), is an intellectual virtue. My belief that there is a coffee cup on the desk is also a justified belief since it fits coherently with my other beliefs. It coheres with my beliefs that there was a cup here a moment ago, that I frequently have a cup of coffee at this time of day. Moreover, my belief that there is a coffee cup on the desk fits with my own views about what it is reasonable to believe. I believe, for example, that it is a perceptual belief made in favorable conditions and that perceptual beliefs made in such conditions are likely to be true.

A belief could have much in the way of justification and yet fail to be apt. Consider the victim of the Cartesian demon and his beliefs about his surroundings. His beliefs enjoy a great deal of coherence and thus they have a great deal of justification. But his beliefs fail to be apt relative to his demonic environment. By the same token, a belief could be apt without

---

[15] Ernest Sosa, "Reliabilism and Intellectual Virtue," in *Knowledge in Perspective*, p. 144.

having much justification. The perceptual or memory beliefs of a child or animal might be apt, without having much justification, since they lack the relevant sort of meta-beliefs about their faculties and their beliefs. They lack the appropriate intellectual perspective.

In addition to the distinction between aptness and justification, Sosa introduces a distinction between *animal knowledge* and *reflective knowledge*. He says, "For animal knowledge one needs only belief that is apt and derives from an intellectual virtue or faculty. By contrast, reflective knowledge always requires belief that is not only apt but also has a kind of justification, since it must be belief that fits coherently within the epistemic perspective of the believer."[16] To have animal knowledge all one needs is true belief that is apt, that derives from an intellectual virtue. Suppose, for example, that a child forms the true belief that there is a cup on the table. Let's suppose that this belief is formed on the basis of perception and that the belief is apt. In this case the child's belief is an instance of animal knowledge. But now suppose that the child's father also forms the true belief that there is a cup on the table. The father's perceptual belief is also apt, but, in addition, his belief is supported by its coherence with his other beliefs. He believes, at least implicitly, for example, that he sees the cup, that his vision is working normally, that he is a good judge of the presence of cups in conditions like these. He believes that his belief comes from a good source and one employed in a favorable environment. The father has background beliefs that help support his belief about the presence of the cup. He enjoys a coherent perspective about his own cognitive powers and his own intellectual virtue.

Having such a perspective is valuable since it is useful for us to know how we formed our belief and under what conditions beliefs of that sort are likely to be true. Having some idea about our intellectual powers, their reliability, and their limits makes us better able to employ them to meet our goal of attaining truth and avoiding error. Moreover, we find it useful to know on what basis others believe things and this makes us better able to assess what they tell us. For an information sharing species, such as ours, knowing on what basis others form their beliefs is a valuable thing. Suppose, for example, the father says that there is a cup on the desk and we

---

[16] *Ibid.*, p. 145.

ask how he knows this? It would be helpful to us if he can cite his beliefs that he saw the cup and did so in good light with 20/20 vision.

In our discussions of foundationalism, coherentism, and reliabilism, we have focused on the concept of *justified* belief. But Sosa introduces, in addition to the concept of justified belief, the notion of *apt* belief. Why do we need the concept of aptness in addition to the concept of justification? First, according to Sosa, aptness is necessary for knowledge, whether animal or reflective. Consider the victim of the Cartesian demon. Imagine that the victim forms beliefs about the external world on the basis of his sensory experiences and suppose further that his beliefs are coherent with one another and with his beliefs about his own cognitive powers. Suppose the demon's victim forms on the basis of his sensory experience the belief that there is a chair in the room. Further, let us suppose that on this occasion there is by sheer luck a chair in the room. Would such a true belief count as knowledge? Surely not, says Sosa. Even though such a belief is supported by experience and coherent with the rest of his beliefs, it fails to be knowledge. It falls short, according to Sosa, because the victim's belief is not apt relative to his demonic environment. So, Sosa concludes aptness is essential for knowledge.

Second, in chapter 3 we considered a problem for the view that our nondoxastic experiences were sources of justification. The problem is that it seems that some experiences, but not others, provide justification for our perceptual beliefs. For example, one's perceptual experience of a triangle seems to provide *prima facie* justification for one's belief that there is a triangle before one. In contrast, one's perceptual experience of a chiliagon does not provide such *prima facie* justification. Why is there this difference? According to Sosa's view, one's perceptual beliefs about triangles are apt, and one's perceptual beliefs about chiliagons are not. One is virtuous with respect to the one, but not the other. That is why the former have a greater positive epistemic status than the latter. Of course, for someone with greater virtue, such as Superman, both beliefs might be apt.

In sum, Sosa's virtue epistemology differs from the simple forms of reliabilism we considered above. First, knowledge requires not just any reliable mechanism of belief formation, it requires that the belief derive from an intellectual virtue. Second, it distinguishes between aptness and justification. An apt belief is one derived from an intellectual virtue, whereas a justified belief is one that fits coherently within the perspective of the believer. Third, it distinguishes between animal and reflective knowledge. For the former, apt true belief is sufficient. Reflective knowledge requires not only belief that is true and apt, but also belief that is justified, that fits coherently within the subject's epistemic perspective.

Let us return to the three problems for reliabilism considered above. Let us begin by considering again the new evil demon problem. Imagine that S is your cognitive twin. S's beliefs and phenomenological states are just like yours, only S is being deceived by a Cartesian demon. Since S's beliefs are not reliably produced, reliabilism apparently implies that S's beliefs are not justified. To many philosophers this seems to be a mistake, and reliabilism is therefore mistaken.

What does Sosa's virtue epistemology imply about this case? First, if justification is, as Sosa suggests, a matter of internal coherence then S's beliefs are "justified." Indeed, they would seem to be no less justified than our own. Still, relative to his demonic environment, D, S's coherence seeking reasoning is not a virtue, since the more he reasons about his world the more false beliefs he forms. His search for coherence leads him deeper into error. The same is true about his perceptual beliefs. Relative to D, S's perceptual faculties are not virtues, for they lead him deep into error. So, relative to D neither coherence seeking reason nor perception are intellectual virtues.

However, relative to the actual world A, both perception and coherence *are* virtues. Relative to the actual world, A, S's beliefs are virtuous. Indeed, relative to A, S's beliefs are *as* virtuous as our own. We need not say, therefore, that S's beliefs are merely "weakly justified," simply blameless but ill-formed. In this way, Sosa's virtue epistemology tries to make sense of the strong intuition that the S's belief are as good epistemically as ours. They are as good epistemically insofar as they are, relative to the actual world, just as virtuous.

Turning to the problem of unknown or accidental reliability, let us consider again Norman the clairvoyant. Norman's belief that the President is in New York is formed on the basis of a reliable power of clairvoyance. But Norman has no evidence for or against the existence of such a power and no evidence for or against his having such a power. Suppose we assume that from Norman's perspective, his belief simply comes out of the blue. He has no belief about why he believes that the President is in New York. On Sosa's view, we may say that Norman's belief about the President is apt, but not justified. It is not justified, since from his perspective he has no reason to believe that it is true. Perhaps we might concede to Norman a kind of animal knowledge of the President's whereabouts, but Norman lacks reflective knowledge.

Finally, how does Sosa's virtue epistemology deal with the generality problem? Here the answer is less clear and it is also less clear that the response is satisfactory. As we have seen, to have a virtue is to have a competence such that one would most likely attain the truth and avoid error in a certain field, F, of propositions, when in certain conditions, C. Sosa recognizes that his view faces a problem akin to the generality problem of reliabilism. Suppose one forms a true belief that p. Suppose that one's belief that p is a simply a guess made at 11:15 am on July 7 in one's office. Now consider the following very narrow F/C pair, namely, p/being formed at 11:15 am on July 7 in one's office. Given that narrow pair, one would mostly attain the truth with respect to p in *those* circumstances. If we allow ourselves such narrow fields and narrow circumstances, then we will have a competence with respect to virtually *any* truth and virtually any true belief will turn out to be justified. On the other hand, there is a problem if our F/C pairs are too general. Consider one's perception of simple shapes in broad daylight. Most of us are competent judges of simple shapes in broad daylight. So consider the F/C pair: simple shapes/viewed in broad daylight. Shall we say, then, that any perceptual belief about simple shapes viewed in broad daylight is the product of a virtue and therefore justified? No, for clearly some perceptual beliefs about simple shapes made in broad daylight will *not* be aptly formed and not justified. This might be the case if the belief is about an object that is too far away, very small, or if one has had four martinis. If our F/C pairs are too generic, then we face the problem that a subject could have two beliefs from that faculty or virtue where one is justified or apt and the other not.

Clearly, in providing an account of the virtues and competences we need some restrictions on fields and circumstances. Sosa notes that not just any restrictions will do.

> Such restrictions must heed a twofold objective: (a) that F and C, not be made so specific that one is always perfectly reliable and justified whenever one's belief is true; but also (b) that they not be made so generic that one cannot explain how a subject could have two beliefs both derived from a given

faculty (e.g. from his sight, or more generally yet, his sensory perception), though one is justified while the other is not.[17]

But what restrictions are appropriate? Sosa makes a variety of comments that point in the direction of a solution.

> Just how fields are to be defined is determined by the lay of interesting and illuminating generalizations about human cognition, which psychology and cognitive science are supposed in time to uncover . . . Human intellectual virtues are abilities to attain cognitive accomplishments in "natural" fields, which would stand out by their place in useful, illuminating generalizations about human cognition.[18]

> We care about justification because it tends to indicate a state of the subject that is important and of interest to his community, a state of great interest and importance to an information-sharing social species. What sort of state? Presumably, the state of being a dependable source of information over a certain field in certain circumstances. In order for this information to be obtainable and to be of later use, however, the sort of field F and the sort of circumstances C must be projectible, and must have some minimal objective likelihood of being repeated in the careers of normal members of the epistemic community.[19]

Sosa suggests the relevant fields and circumstances must be selected so as (1) to provide *useful* generalizations to the epistemic community and (2) there must be some likelihood that those circumstances will be *repeated* in the lives of normal members of the community. In some respects, these comments seem promising. Consider again the very narrow F/C pair that consists simply of *p*/being formed at 11:15 am July 7 in one's office. It seems clear that these circumstances are *not* likely to be repeated in the careers of normal members of the epistemic community and that they do not provide the basis for *useful* generalizations about one's cognitive powers.

It is less clear, however, how Sosa's comments help with the problem of F/C pairs that are too generic. Consider again the F/C pair simple shapes/ viewed in broad daylight. It is implausible to think that *all* beliefs about simple shapes formed in broad daylight are aptly formed or justified.

---

[17] *Ibid.*, p. 284.

[18] Ernest Sosa, "Knowledge and Intellectual Virtue," in *Knowledge in Perspective*, p. 236.

[19] Ernest Sosa, "Intellectual Virtue in Perspective," in *Knowledge in Perspective*, pp. 282–83.

Surely one's ability to discern shapes is affected by such things as the size of the object, its distance, and whether one has had too much alcohol. Perhaps we might opt then for a more determinate, less general F/C pair. Suppose we opt for the narrower: simple shapes/viewed in broad daylight at arm's length when the object is medium sized and one is sober. Still, even here it seems possible that two beliefs formed about a simple shape under these conditions might be such that one was apt or justified and the other not. Consider sober Jones who in daylight looks steadily at a white card with a black triangle held at arm's length. Now consider sober Smith who gets only a fleeting glimpse of a similar card containing a red hexagon on an orange background. It seems plausible to think that Jones's belief is more justified than Smith's. Again, we might think that some further narrowing of the field and conditions would help solve the problem. But can we be sure that a similar problem will not arise again for the more narrow F/C pair? Perhaps this problem can be solved, but it is not clear what the response should be. In any case, it is safe to say that many philosophers regard the generality problem as one that does not yet have a clear and widely accepted solution.

6 Internalism, externalism, and epistemic circularity

In the last chapter, we examined a reliability theory of justification. In this chapter, we will continue to explore issues concerning justification, knowledge, and reliability. In the first section, we will focus on the debate between "internalism" and "externalism," two very general views about the nature of epistemic justification. In the last two sections, we shall consider some issues concerning how we know that any of our ways of forming beliefs, such as perception and memory, are reliable. Suppose, for example, that the only way to support the reliability of memory involves using memory. Would that way of supporting the reliability of memory be epistemically unacceptable? Would it prevent us from knowing that it is reliable? We shall consider some different answers to such questions. We shall focus mainly on the views of William Alston and Ernest Sosa.

Internalism and externalism

In the previous chapters, we considered a variety of theories about epistemic justification, including different forms of foundationalism, coherentism, and reliabilism. In the past twenty years, many philosophers have classified these theories of epistemic justification as either *internalist* or *externalist*. Internalism and externalism are general views about what is relevant to epistemic justification. Assessing the debate between internalists and externalists is difficult because different writers often use the terms "internalism" and "externalism" to mean different things. Still, it is worth considering some of the main issues that arise in the debate.

Let's consider one common way of drawing the distinction between internalism and externalism. According to this approach, the difference between internalism and externalism concerns the sorts of factors that make beliefs epistemically justified. According to internalism, the epistemic justification of a subject's belief is entirely determined by factors "internal" to the subject's perspective. Externalism, in contrast, denies that epistemic justification depends entirely on factors internal to the subject's perspective.

What does it mean to say that some factor is "internal to the subject's perspective"? Laurence BonJour suggests that according to internalism, justification depends "on elements that are internal to the believer's conscious states of mind in a way that makes them accessible to his conscious reflection (at least in principle)."[1] Similarly, Matthias Steup says that according to internalism, the factors that determine the justification of a belief must be "*internal to the subject's mind* or, to put it differently, *accessible on reflection.*"[2] These remarks suggest that we should think of something as internal to the subject's perspective just in case it is accessible to him on reflection.

But what is it for something to be "accessible on reflection"? Perhaps we might illustrate the concept by considering our beliefs and perceptual experiences. Many of my beliefs and perceptual experiences are accessible on reflection in the sense that I can direct my attention to them and tell through introspection whether I do in fact have those beliefs or perceptual experiences. Thus, various beliefs, sensations, and perceptual experiences are accessible on reflection. In contrast, a great many things are not accessible on reflection. Whether I have a brain tumor or whether my cholesterol is too high is not accessible to me on reflection

Let us take internalism, then, to hold that the epistemic justification of a subject's belief depends solely on factors internal to the subject's perspective, factors directly accessible to him through reflection. We may take externalism to be the denial of this view. Coherentism is typically taken to be a form of internalism since it holds that the factors that determine justification are one's beliefs.[3] Presumably one's beliefs are accessible on reflection. Similarly, givenist foundationalism holds that the factors that determine justification are one's beliefs and one's nondoxastic experiences.

---

[1] Laurence BonJour and Ernest Sosa, *Epistemic Justification* (Malden, MA: Blackwell, 2003), p. 7. The view here is BonJour's.

[2] Matthias Steup, *An Introduction to Contemporary Epistemology* (Upper Saddle River, NJ: Prentice-Hall, 1996), p. 84.

[3] Must the fact that one's beliefs cohere *also* be accessible on reflection? That's a good question. I shall simply note that different internalists answer this question differently.

Again, such factors are taken to be accessible on reflection. In contrast, reliabilism is taken to be an externalist view because it holds that the epistemic justification of a belief depends at least in part on its being the product of a reliable cognitive process. However, the reliability of one's cognitive processes need not be accessible through reflection. It need not be accessible through such reflection *which* cognitive process produced one's belief or *whether* that process is reliable. What matters, according to the reliabilist, is whether one's belief is reliably produced, not whether the reliability of the process is available through reflection. Reliablism does not limit the factors relevant to justification to those internal to the subject's perspective.

In the previous chapters we considered various forms of givenist foundationalism, coherentism, and reliabilism as well as several objections to each. In this respect, we have already considered some important representative forms of internalism and externalism. Still, the failure of some particular form of givenist foundationalism does not show that all forms internalism are mistaken and the failure of some particular form of reliabilism does not show that all forms of externalism are mistaken. Let us, however, set aside consideration of particular forms of internalism and externalism and consider the general views themselves.

Internalism is a very plausible view and supported by some powerful intuitions about the nature of epistemic justification. Internalism holds that what justifies a belief depends solely on factors internal to the subject's perspective. Suppose we take the internalist to hold that justification supervenes solely upon those states that are accessible upon reflection, upon those states that are internal to the subject's perspective. We might take the internalist to hold that if whatever is internal to A's perspective is also internal to B's perspective and *vice versa* and A is justified in believing that p, then B is also justified in believing that p. If there is no difference from their perspectives concerning their beliefs, sensations, perceptual states, etc. and A is justified in believing some proposition, then B is also justified in believing that proposition.

Again, this is a very plausible view. But how might it be supported? Sometimes internalism is supported by assumptions about epistemic justification and epistemically responsible belief. Let us examine two of these assumptions. First, some philosophers assume that there is a connection between epistemic justification and epistemic responsibility.

Sometimes it is suggested that to be epistemically justified is just to believe in a way that is epistemically responsible. According to this view, S is epistemically justified in believing that p if and only if S is epistemically responsible in believing that p. Second, it is sometimes assumed that whether one is epistemically responsible in believing that p depends only upon factors to which one has cognitive access, upon factors that are internal to one's perspective. It seems plausible that if some factor lies beyond one's internal perspective, then it cannot matter to one's believing responsibly. According to this view, whether one believes responsibly at some time is a matter of what is accessible upon reflection at that time. Given these assumptions the internalist might argue that (i) S's belief that p is epistemically justified if and only if S is epistemically responsible in believing that p, (ii) epistemic responsibility depends only on what is internal to one's perspective, therefore (iii) epistemic justification depends only on what is internal to one's perspective.

This line of argument and the assumptions which support it are controversial. Consider the first assumption that epistemic justification is a matter of epistemically responsible believing. Some critics reject the connection between epistemic justification and epistemic responsibility. Consider, they would say, what it is to *act* responsibly. They would argue that in order for S to act responsibly, it must be the case that his actions are voluntary, that they are under his control. If someone's actions are not under his control, the objection goes, then he does not act responsibly and he is not responsible for his actions. Some critics would argue that the same is true of our beliefs. If some of our beliefs are not under our control or not voluntary, then we are not epistemically responsible for them. But, the critic argues, it seems plausible that some of our beliefs are *not* voluntary and not under our control. Take, for example, one's beliefs that one thinks, that one exists, that $2 = 2$. Are such beliefs really voluntary? Is it within one's power to withhold belief in such things? To many, it seems that such beliefs are not voluntary, and therefore that one is not responsible for believing them. Yet even if we are not responsible for them, such beliefs are epistemically justified for us. Indeed, these are among our most highly justified beliefs. So, the objection concludes, we should not construe epistemic justification as a matter of epistemically responsible believing.

Let us consider the second assumption, that what lies beyond a subject's internal perspective cannot matter to his believing responsibly. Let's consider the following case. Suppose that Doctor Jones occasionally prescribes a drug, Pseudoxin, for his patients. He has prescribed it for several years and none of his patients have suffered any harmful side effects. On Monday, he receives an official looking letter. Written on the envelope is the following: "Important Information Concerning Potentially Fatal Side Effects of Pseudoxin." Dr. Jones thinks to himself, "This could be important. I should read it." Unfortunately, he puts the letter aside and completely forgets about it. The next day Dr. Jones prescribes pseudoxin to one of his patients. Dr. Jones believes, as he has for years, that the drug is perfectly safe. Now, some critics will argue that Dr. Jones's belief on Tuesday is *not* an epistemically responsible belief. His negligent failure to take account of relevant evidence on Monday makes his belief on Tuesday epistemically irresponsible. But, the critics argue, what makes his belief epistemically irresponsible is *not* something internal to his perspective on Tuesday. What makes his belief epistemically irresponsible is his negligent failure to have read the letter he received, and that failure is not something internal to his perspective on Tuesday. On Tuesday, he has forgotten about the letter. If this is right, then it is false that the only factors relevant to epistemically responsible believing at a time are those internal to the subject's perspective at that time.

With respect to the preceding point, however, some philosophers might suggest that whether a subject's believing that *p* is epistemically responsible at *t* does not depend upon what is internal to S's perspective at *t*. They might hold, instead, that whether S's belief is epistemically responsible at *t* depends on what is accessible to S's perspective at *t* or *before t*. One might argue, for example, that on Monday, the fact that he was ignoring relevant evidence was internal to his perspective, and so his believing in a manner that is epistemically irresponsible was dependent on something internal to his perspective at that earlier time.

This is an interesting response. Still, it is not clear that it is consistent with internalism, since it concedes that what is relevant to a subject's being justified at some time need not be internal to the subject's perspective at that time. It allows that what is relevant to a subject's justification at *t* might be some factor to which the subject has absolutely no cognitive access at *t*. In any event, there still remains the problem of epistemically justified beliefs which do not seem to be voluntary and for which people do not seem responsible. I think it is safe to say that attempts to support internalism by appealing to considerations about epistemic responsibility remain controversial.

It is not clear, however, that the internalist needs to support his position by appealing to considerations about epistemic responsibility. Indeed, an internalist might agree that we should carefully distinguish between epistemically *justified* belief and epistemically *responsible* belief. He might suggest that epistemic justification is *not* to be understood in terms of epistemic responsibility, but rather in terms of what it is *reasonable* to believe given one's evidence. To say that a person is justified in holding a belief at a time is to say that it is reasonable for him to hold that belief given his evidence at that time.[4]

So, consider again Dr. Jones's belief on Tuesday that it is safe to prescribe Pseudoxin. The internalist might suggest that even if the doctor has been negligent in the past with respect to considering evidence, the question of justification concerns what it reasonable for him to believe now. Given the evidence he has on Tuesday, what is the justified or reasonable attitude for him to take concerning the safety of Pseudoxin? It seems that there are only three attitudes he can take toward the proposition that the drug is safe. He can believe it, disbelieve it, or withhold belief in it. Now, Dr. Jones seems to remember having safely prescribed the drug for years, seems to remember having read that it is approved by the government, and has completely forgotten about yesterday's letter. The internalist might say that given what is accessible from his perspective the epistemically justified or reasonable attitude is to believe that the drug is safe. Such a view seems quite plausible.

The general view that justification depends solely on what is accessible on reflection has a strong intuitive pull.

Externalists, however, deny that justification depends solely upon what is internal to the subject's perspective. Externalists hold that whether a belief is justified might also depend on whether it came about in the right way, through good intellectual procedure or on the basis of an intellectual virtue. These are factors that need not be accessible to the subject on reflection. Consider the following example from Ernest Sosa.

> Mary and Jane both arrive at a conclusion C, Mary through a brilliant proof, Jane through a tissue of fallacies. Each has now forgotten her reasoning,

---

[4] Cf. Richard Feldman, *Epistemology* (Upper Saddle River, NJ: Prentice-Hall, 2003), pp. 47–48.

however, and each takes herself to have established her conclusion validly. What is more, each of their performances is uncharacteristic, Jane being normally the better logician, Mary a normally competent but undistinguished thinker, as they both well know. As of the present moment, therefore, Jane might seem as well justified as Mary in believing C. We know the respective aetiologies, however; what do *we* say? Would we not judge Jane's belief unjustified since based essentially on fallacies? If so, then a belief's aetiology can make a difference to its justification.[5]

Jane and Mary each believe C, and each believes that she has validly established C, though neither recalls the reasoning. Given their internal perspectives, internalism would imply that Jane and Mary are each justified. But Sosa suggests that Jane's belief is *not* as justified as Mary's since Jane's belief is based on fallacies. He suggests that the aetiology or ancestry of the belief can make a difference to its justification. But since the aetiology of the belief can lie outside the subject's perspective, as it does for both Jane and Mary, internalism is false. Indeed, a similar verdict might be offered concerning Dr. Jones. Even though the doctor's belief is supported by what is internal to his perspective at the time, it seems to be the product of bad intellectual procedure, the negligent failure to consider relevant evidence. It seems plausible to think that bad intellectual procedures such as fallacious reasoning and the negligent failure to consider relevant evidence are relevant to the justification of belief even when the subject is unaware of them.

Let us consider a second example.

Tom and Bob are each asked to look at some shapes and to report the number of sides they see. They are not to count the number of sides and the images pass too quickly to allow for counting. Suppose that they are each presented with the same image of an irregular octagon. Each of them responds confidently that it has eight sides. But suppose that, unbeknown to him, Bob is extremely gifted when it comes to recognizing the number of sides. With respect to figures of great complexity, he almost always gets the number of sides right. Indeed, Bob is as good with respect to octagons as Tom is concerning triangles. Tom on the other hand is no better than average, and is right by sheer luck.

---

[5] Laurence BonJour and Ernest Sosa, *Epistemic Justification*, p. 151. This is Sosa's example. For a resposne to the example by BonJour see pp. 179–81.

Given their internal perspectives, their beliefs and their nondoxastic experiences, internalism would seem to imply that each is justified in his belief. But, the externalist might argue, Bob's superior ability makes his belief more justified. Bob's belief is produced by a reliable cognitive process or an intellectual virtue and this is relevant to the justification of his belief. However, that he has that intellectual virtue or that his belief is produced by a reliable cognitive process is not something accessible to him on reflection.

Reflection on examples such as these lead some philosophers to reject internalism. It leads some philosophers to hold that whether a belief is justified depends, at least in part, on whether it is the product of good intellectual procedure or a truth conducive intellectual virtue, upon factors that might not be accessible upon reflection. Still, intuitions about such cases vary and philosophers differ about their importance.

While examples such as these play a role in assessing the merits of internalism and externalism, they are not, of course, the only relevant considerations. In evaluating internalism and externalism, one might also consider the extent to which particular forms of each come close to providing satisfactory theories of justification. If, for example, one finds that some form of coherentism provides the most satisfactory theory of justification, then one will have some reason to believe that internalism is true. If, on the contrary, one finds that some form of reliabilism provides the most satisfactory theory of justification, then one will have some reason to believe that externalism is true. Thus, one might try to assess the merits of internalism and externalism, by seeing how well particular versions of each succeed in explaining what makes beliefs justified. If this is right, then our critical examination of the various forms of givenist foundationalism, coherentisim, reliabilism, and virtue approaches in previous chapters has put us in a better position to understand not only the strengths and weakness of those particular views, but also internalist and externalist accounts of justification. Of course, since these particular views themselves remain controversial, so too do the more general views. The debate between internalism and externalism remains unresolved.

Sometimes, however, philosophers suggest that there is another way of looking at the debate between internalism and externalism. According to this view, there are different *kinds* of epistemic evaluation or different kinds of epistemic merit. Some forms of epistemic evaluation are to be understood along internalist lines, others externalistically. As we have seen, some internalists suggest that we should distinguish epistemic justification from other kinds of epistemic appraisal such as epistemic responsibility. They would say that these are two distinct forms of epistemic appraisal. Furthermore, an internalist might concede that while epistemic justification is an internal matter, epistemic responsibility is not. Similarly, as we saw in the last chapter, Sosa distinguishes between "justification" and "aptness." Both are positive epistemic evaluations, but Sosa treats the former as a matter of internal coherence and the latter as a manifestation of intellectual virtue. He suggests that justification should be understood internalistically, and aptness externalistically. The main point is that even if one concedes that there is some concept of justification which is internalist, one might think that there are other forms of positive epistemic status which are to be understood externalistically and that these forms of epistemic evaluation are important.

Perhaps the importance of externalist concepts such as reliability or aptness can be illustrated by considering the concept of *knowledge*. Consider Jane's belief in her conclusion, C. Even if her belief that C is true and justified from her perspective, it still seems to fall short of knowledge. The same would seem true of Tom's belief that the figure before him has eight sides. Even if his belief is justified from his perspective, it falls short of knowledge. But in what way do they fall short? One might hold that knowledge requires that these beliefs need to be not only justified, but also apt or reliably produced. Thus, even if one concedes that there is an important notion of justification which is internalist, an adequate understanding of knowledge requires that we consider other kinds of positive epistemic status which are externalist, such as those exemplified by Mary and Bob.

Similarly, consider someone generally deceived by a Cartersian demon. Suppose he has the (generally unreliable) perceptual experience of there being a chair in the room and he believes, coherently with his other beliefs, that there is a chair in the room. Yet in this case, suppose that his belief is true. His true belief is justified from his internal perspective, but it falls short of knowledge. His belief seems to fall short of knowledge given the general unreliability of his faculties. Here perceptual knowledge appears to require that one's perceptual faculties must be reliable or apt. Again, the externalist would hold that in order to be a case of knowledge his belief must enjoy something like reliability or aptness, some form of epistemic merit beyond that of internalist justification.

The problem of epistemic circularity

Whatever one's position on internalism and externalism, it is an important question whether our faculties and ways of forming beliefs are reliable. Even if one's belief that p need not be reliably formed in order to be epistemically justified, it seems plausible to think that knowing that p requires that one's belief that p be reliably formed. It seems plausible, for example, that one has perceptual knowledge that p only if one's perceptual belief that p is reliably formed and one has mnemonic knowledge that p only if one's mnemonic belief that p is reliably formed.

But how is one to know whether one's faculties are reliable? Consider one's own faculties of perception and memory. How does one know, for example, that they are reliable? Consider how one might try to support one's belief that one's memory is reliable. One might reason in roughly the following inductive way, (i) my memory was reliable on Monday, (ii) my memory was reliable on Tuesday, (iii) my memory was reliable on Wednesday, therefore, (iv) my memory is reliable. Of course, in reasoning in this way, one's belief in the premises is based on memory. One is using memory to support the reliability of memory. Now consider how one might try to support the reliability of perception. Suppose one looks at an eye chart and writes down what one sees. One then walks up closer to the chart and compares what one sees with what was written. One notes that one accurately identified the larger letters on the chart and concludes that one's perception is reliable. But of course, in this simple procedure one is still relying upon sense perception to read the chart and to read what one has written down. In this case, one is using sense perception to support the reliability of sense perception. These simple procedures seem somewhat silly. Surely none of us bases his belief in the reliability of memory or perception on such simple procedures. But these simple procedures raise some important issues. Can one use memory to support the reliability of memory? Can one use sense perception to support the reliability of sense perception?

Many philosophers would say "no." Many would hold that one cannot use beliefs from a source, A, to support the reliability of A. They would tell us that such a procedure is epistemically unsatisfactory. Concerning this issue, the Scottish philosopher Thomas Reid objected that if a man's honesty were called into question it would be ridiculous to trust his own testimony concerning his honesty.[6] More recently, Richard Fumerton writes, "You cannot *use* perception to justify the reliability of perception! You cannot *use* memory to justify the reliability of memory! You cannot *use* induction to justify the reliability of induction! Such attempts to respond to the skeptic's concerns involve blatant, indeed pathetic, circularity."[7] But if we cannot use memory to justify the reliability of memory or sense perception to justify the reliability of sense perception, then how can we be justified in believing that they are reliable?

Let us say that a way of supporting the reliability of a source of belief, A, is *epistemically circular* if it makes use of beliefs that have A as their source. One's justification for believing that a source of belief is epistemically circular if it relies upon beliefs based on that source. So, any argument for the reliability of memory that makes use of what we remember would be epistemically circular. Similarly, any reasoning for the reliability of sense perception that makes use of premises accepted on the basis of sense perception would be epistemically circular. So, we might ask whether a way of supporting the reliability of some source of belief is epistemically unsatisfactory if it is epistemically circular. Alternatively, we might ask does epistemic circularity prevent us from knowing that our ways for forming beliefs are reliable?

William Alston has examined the problem of epistemic circularity with care and subtlety. Let us begin by considering Alston's discussion of the following "track record" argument for the reliability of perception:

(1) At t_1, I formed the perceptual belief that p, and p.
(2) At t_2, I formed the perceptual belief that q, and q.
(3) At t_3, I formed the perceptual belief that r, and r.

(And so on)

Conclusion: My perception is a reliable source of belief.

---

[6] Thomas Reid, *Essays on the Intellectual Powers of Man* (Cambridge, MA: The MIT Press, 1969), essay VI, chapter 5, p. 630. Reid's views are, however, complicated. I discuss them at some length in *Common Sense: A Contemporary Defense* (Cambridge: Cambridge University Press, 2004), pp. 67–84

[7] Richard Fumerton, *Metaepistemology and Skepticism* (Lanham, MD: Rowman and Littlefield, 1995), p. 177.

In a track record argument for the reliability of perception, we reason inductively from a wide sampling of perceptual beliefs, noting that the vast majority of them have been true, and conclude that perception is reliable. Thus, I might reason that at t_1 I formed the perceptual belief that it was raining, and it was raining; at t_2, I formed the perceptual belief that there was a dog in the yard, and there was a dog in the yard. After noting a wide variety of such judgments, I conclude, then, that my perception is reliable.

Let us say that an argument is *logically circular* just in case the conclusion is identical to one of the premises. An argument of the form p, q, r, therefore p is logically circular. Logically circular arguments seem to be epistemically unsatisfactory ways of *conferring* justification on the conclusion. If one is not justified in believing premise p, then the reasoning does not confer justification on the conclusion. If, on the other hand, one is justified in believing premise p, then it seems the conclusion already enjoys justification, and it is not the reasoning or argument that confers justification on the conclusion. Whatever the defects of logically circular arguments, Alston points out that the track record argument is *not* logically circular since the conclusion is not identical with one of the premises.

Still, Alston concedes that the track record argument *is* epistemically circular. According to Alston, epistemic circularity "consists in assuming the reliability of a source of belief in arguing for the reliability of that source. That assumption does not appear as a premise in the argument, but it is only by making that assumption that we consider ourselves entitled to use some or all of the premises."[8] How in this track record argument are we assuming the reliability of perception? Consider the second conjunct of each premise. How do I know that it is true? On the basis of sense perception itself. It is only by *using* sense perception or *relying* on it that I can know the truth of the premises.

Alston, however, does not think that epistemic circularity renders an argument epistemically useless. He writes, "Contrary to what one might suppose, epistemic circularity does not render an argument useless for justifying or establishing its conclusion. Provided that I can *be* justified in certain perceptual beliefs without already being *justified* in supposing perception to be reliable, I can legitimately use perceptual beliefs in an

---

[8] William Alston, "A 'Doxastic Practice' Approach to Epistemology," *Empirical Knowledge*, 2nd edn., ed. Paul K. Moser (Lanham, MD: Rowman and Littlefield, 1996), p. 271.

argument for the reliability of sense perception."[9] How can one be justified in particular perceptual beliefs without already being justified in supposing the conclusion that perception is reliable? Well, Alston suggests, suppose that our perceptual beliefs are *basically* justified. Perhaps they are justified in virtue of our sensory experience, as some foundationalists suggest, or suppose that they are justified in virtue of their origin in a reliable faculty of perception. If our perceptual beliefs are basically justified, then the second conjunct of each premise of the track record argument is basically justified. But if it is basically justified, then it has some degree of justification that is independent of the conclusion. In that case, our justification for believing the premises would not be based on our being justified in believing the conclusion.

"But," one might object, "you cannot have perceptual knowledge that *p* unless you know that perception is reliable and you cannot have mnemonic knowledge unless you know that memory is reliable. One's knowledge of the premises in a track record argument for memory or perception *must* be based on knowledge of the conclusion. This makes the argument as bad as a logically circular argument." This objection implies that there are no instances of *basic* perceptual and mnemonic knowledge. I shall simply note two difficulties with the view that particular instances perceptual and mnemonic knowledge must be based on knowledge of the reliability of those sources. First, such a view would seem to preclude brute animals and young children from having perceptual and mnemonic knowledge. Brute animals and young children seem to lack the requisite concept of reliability and perhaps lack the necessary self-awareness to form such a belief, but it seems reasonable to think that they have much in the way of perceptual and mnemonic knowledge. They have a lot of perceptual and mnemonic knowledge without knowing anything about perception and memory. Second, such a requirement does not seem plausible with respect to other sorts of belief. Consider one's belief that $2 = 2$. It seems plausible that this is an instance of basic knowledge. Consequently, it would be a mistake to hold that one's knowledge that $2 = 2$ must be based on one's knowledge that reason is reliable. Again, it seems that one knows in the basic way that one thinks. If so, then it is a mistake to hold that one's knowledge that one thinks must be based on one's knowledge that introspection is reliable.

---

[9] *Ibid.*, p. 271.

But if these instances of introspective and rational knowledge do not depend on knowledge of the reliability of their sources, why insist on it for perceptual and mnemonic knowledge?

In any event, Alston holds that epistemically circular arguments are not useless for justifying or establishing their conclusions. Still, in spite of this, he thinks that epistemically circular arguments are *not* satisfactory ways of discriminating between reliable and unreliable sources of belief. But why not? What problem does he see with epistemically circular arguments? Alston says that if we allow ourselves to use beliefs from a source to show that it is reliable, then any source can be validated. Consider crystal ball gazing. The seer gazes into his crystal ball and makes a series of pronouncements: p, q, r, s ... Alston writes, "Is this a reliable mode of belief formation? Yes. That can be shown as follows. The gazer forms the belief that p, and using the same procedure, ascertains that p. By running through a series of beliefs in this way we discover that the accuracy of this mode of belief formation is 100 percent!"[10] Alston concludes:

> If we allow the use of mode of belief-formation M to determine whether the beliefs formed by M are true, M is sure to get a clean bill of health. But a line of argument that will validate any mode of belief formation, no matter how irresponsible, is not what we are looking for. We want, and need, something much more discriminating. Hence the fact that the reliability of sense perception can be established by relying on sense perception does not solve our problem.[11]

According to Alston, track record arguments are not sufficiently discriminating. Some epistemically crazy methods can be supported in that way. Presumably, any epistemically circular way of supporting the reliability of some source would, in Alton's view, face the same problem.

In order to get around this problem, Alston favors a different approach. He favors an appeal to "practical rationality." He argues that it is practically rational for us to rely on our ways of forming beliefs, or "doxastic practices." How does this argument go? In brief, Alston points out that many of our ways of forming beliefs are firmly established. It does not seem to be in our power (easily) to avoid forming beliefs on the basis of those practices. It would not be easy for us to avoid forming beliefs, for example,

[10] *Ibid.*, p. 271.
[11] *Ibid.*, p. 272.

on the basis of doxastic practices such as perception and memory. Though there are alternative practices we might try to take up, it would be difficult for us to do so. Moreover, what reason would we have to think that these alternative practices would be more reliable? The very same problems of epistemic circularity that beset our attempts to support the reliability of our current practices would confront these alternatives. So, given these facts, Alston concludes that it is practically rational for us to continue engaging in our own firmly established practices.

Suppose we take Alston's reasoning to be something like the following:

(1) We have various ways of forming beliefs – sense perception, memory, reason, introspection – that are firmly established. So firmly established that we cannot help forming beliefs in these ways.

(2) It would be enormously difficult for us to abandon these ways of forming beliefs and to take up others.

(3) One cannot support the reliability of these alternative ways of forming beliefs without facing the same problems of epistemic circularity that beset attempts to support the reliability of sense perception, memory, reason, and introspection.

(4) Therefore, it is reasonable for us to continue forming beliefs the way we standardly do on the basis of sense perception, memory, reason, and introspection.

Alston's argument faces a number of objections. First, some critics object that his argument does not avoid epistemic circularity any more than the track record argument. Suppose we ask, for example, how do we know that sense perception and memory are firmly established practices? Wouldn't our answer be that we know that on the basis of sense perception and memory? It seems that we would be using sense perception and memory to support the conclusion that it is reasonable to form beliefs in those ways. If epistemic circularity is a vice that makes track record arguments unsatisfactory, then is it any less of a vice here?

Second, some critics note that Alston rejects track record arguments because they are not sufficiently discriminating. The crystal ball gazer can appeal to gazing to argue for the reliability of those sources. But isn't there an analogous problem for the sort of argument that Alston advances? Couldn't the gazer appeal to gazing to argue that gazing is a firmly established way of forming beliefs? He looks into his crystal ball and "sees" that it is. He then argues that since gazing is firmly established, and that any other way of forming beliefs will face the problems of epistemic circularity, it is, therefore, practically rational for him to continue to form beliefs on the basis of gazing. Given that the gazer can reason in an analogous way for the practical rationality of his way of forming beliefs, how would Alston's appeal to firm establishment provide a more discriminating approach? If we are to reject track record arguments because gazers can use that form of argument to support the reliability of their practices, then shouldn't we also reject Alston's appeal to being firmly established insofar as the gazer can appeal to gazing to argue that it is firmly established, and thus reasonably engaged in?[12]

One might argue that the difference between the gazer's reasoning and Alston's is that perception and memory, for example, *really are* firmly established. But if it is *actually* being firmly established as opposed to being merely thought to be so that makes the one line of reasoning better, then why not simply say that it is *actually* being reliable as opposed to being merely believed to be reliable that makes the difference between perceivers and gazers? Why not simply point out that what makes the difference between a track record argument for perception and a track record argument for gazing is that perception *really is* reliable? Defenders of reliabilism and virtue theories might argue that the views of the perceivers are epistemically superior to those of the gazers because perceiving is, unlike gazing, reliable or apt. On this view, what would make the position of the perceivers epistemically superior to that of the gazers would not be the logical structure of their arguments; these, after all, are parallel. Neither would the difference between them be a matter of coherence, for we might suppose the beliefs of the gazers could be as coherent. What would make the position of the perceivers epistemically superior is that their beliefs in the reliability of their way of forming beliefs are actually rooted in reliable faculties or intellectual virtues.

Indeed, a similar approach seems open to the givenist foundationalist. He might hold that what makes the position of the perceivers epistemically superior to that the gazers are the nondoxastic perceptual experiences

---

[12] This objection is made my Ernest Sosa in "Philosophical Scepticism and Epistemic Circularity," *Empirical Knowledge*, 2nd edn., ed. Paul K. Moser (Lanham, MD: Rowman and Littlefield, 1996), pp. 317–18.

of the perceivers. Such experiences he might hold make the perceivers' beliefs justified, but do not justify the beliefs of the gazers. So, even if the gazers can offer an argument for the reliability of their ways of forming beliefs which parallels the structure of the perceivers' arguments, the perceiver need not treat the arguments as being on a par epistemically.

Let us consider another response to the problem of epistemic circularity. Ernest Sosa concedes that any reasoning for the reliability of our faculties will be, if pushed far enough, epistemically circular. This is so if only because any reasoning for the reliability of our faculties must rely on or use reason. To see this, suppose that I give an argument for the reliability of some source of beliefs, A. In giving this argument I rely upon reason. I use reason to form the argument and infer the conclusion that A is reliable from the premises. But I can always ask how do I know that my reason is reliable? If I give an argument for the reliability of my reason then I will be using my reason to support its reliability. Such a procedure would be epistemically circular. It seems that we cannot give an argument for the reliability of reason that is free of epistemic circularity.[13] But how else am I to support the reliability of my own reason? Again, it seems that any reasoning for the reliability of our faculties will be, if pushed far enough, epistemically circular. So, Sosa holds that epistemic circularity is inescapable.

But must our inability to give arguments free from epistemic circularity preclude our knowing that our ways of forming beliefs are reliable? Sosa thinks not. Sosa makes the following suggestion. Suppose, he suggests, that W is our total way of forming beliefs. Suppose we use W, and W assures us that it is reliable. Suppose also:

(1) "W *is* reliable (and suppose, even, that, given our overall circumstances and fundamental nature, it is the *most* reliable overall way we could have)."

(2) "We are *right* in our description of W; it is exactly W that we use in forming beliefs; and it is of course (therefore) W that we use in forming the belief that W is our way of forming beliefs."

---

[13] Laurence BonJour makes the same point. He writes, "Obviously, no *argument* can be used to show that reasoning is trustworthy without implicitly begging the questing." *The Structure of Empirical Knowledge* (Cambridge, MA: Harvard University Press, 1985), p. 195.

(3) "We *believe* that W *is reliable* (correctly so, given [1] above), and this belief, too, is formed by means of W."[14]

In this situation, Sosa asks, what more do we need for an epistemically satisfactory understanding of ourselves and our own reliability? Of course, our belief that W is reliable is itself formed by means of W. We have not, therefore, avoided epistemic circularity. But our belief that W is reliable is (1) true, (2) reliably formed by our best intellectual procedures, and (3) fits coherently in our view of ourselves and our intellectual endowments. Though we have not avoided epistemic circularity, asks Sosa, in what way do we fall short? Sosa concludes that the mere presence of epistemic circularity would not preclude our knowing ourselves to be reliable.

Sosa asks what exactly is the problem with epistemically circular arguments? Why should we think that they are epistemically unacceptable ways of supporting the reliability of our faculties? Recall Alston's complaints about track record arguments. Alston objects that someone with decidedly unreliable doxastic practices might be able to support the reliability of his ways of forming beliefs with a coherence equal to our own. The gazer, it is urged, might be able to reach a view of his powers that is as well supported by such an inference as is our view about the reliability of our powers of perception, memory, and the like. However, Sosa argues that though the gazer might be able to achieve a coherent view about the reliability of gazing, we need to distinguish justification from aptness. As we saw in the last chapter, Sosa treats "justification" as a matter of internal coherence and a belief is "apt" if it is the product of a truth conducive intellectual virtue. The gazer, Sosa suggests, might be "justified" in his beliefs about the reliability of gazing. But his gazing based beliefs and his belief about the reliability of gazing fail to be "apt." We need not hold, Sosa claims, that the gazer's beliefs, though supported from his perspective by a track record argument, are epistemically on a par with our own. Though enjoying the internal justification of coherence, the gazer's conclusions fall short insofar as they rest on premises that fail to be apt.

Consider the cartoon character Mr. Magoo, whose perceptual faculties are terribly unreliable. Magoo might reason brilliantly from his flawed

---

[14] Ernest Sosa, "Philosophical Scepticism and Epistemic Circularity," *Empirical Knowledge*, 2nd edn., p. 318.

perceptual beliefs, and his belief might enjoy a level of coherence comparable to our own. But Magoo's view of the world is flawed by epistemic vice, and fails to manifest overall virtue. Sosa holds that coherence is a good thing, but it is not the only epistemic virtue. We should not hold that if two bodies of belief enjoy equal coherence, then they enjoy equal epistemic status. Neither should we conclude that if someone can support the reliability of his flawed ways of forming beliefs through arguments that mirror our own in terms of structure and coherence, then his premises and conclusion are as good epistemically. So, Sosa concludes that Alston's fear that the use of epistemically circular arguments by the gazer will yield a view that is epistemically on a par with our own is unfounded once we take into consideration the aptness of one's ways of forming beliefs.

The problem of Roxanne

Sosa argues that epistemic circularity does not prevent us from knowing that our ways of forming beliefs are reliable. But let us consider the following case suggested by Jonathan Vogel.[15] The main target of Vogel's criticism is a view he calls "Neighborhood Reliabilism" (NR). We may take NR to be:

NR S knows that p if and only if S's belief that p is true and S's belief that p is produced by a reliable cognitive process.

Vogel argues that NR is false. His criticism of it raises some important questions about epistemic circularity and it poses a challenge to what Vogel calls a "bootstrapping" procedure for defending the reliability of one's ways of forming beliefs.

Suppose that Roxanne is driving a car with a highly reliable, well-functioning gas gauge. Roxanne, however, does not know this. She has never checked it out, has never been told anything about its reliability, and has no background information about whether gauges like hers are likely to be working. She has never taken any special steps to see whether the gauge is going up or down as it should. She does, however, look at her gauge often and forms a belief about how much gas is in her tank. She also takes note of

---

[15] Jonathan Vogel, "Reliabilism Leveled," *The Journal of Philosophy*, 97 (Nov. 2000), 602–25.

the state of the gauge itself. So when the gauge reads "F," she believes that the tank is full, F, and she believes that the gauge reads "F." Roxanne combines these beliefs and accepts:

(1) On this occasion, the gauge reads "F" and F.

Now the perceptual process by which Roxanne forms the belief that the gauge reads "F" is a reliable one. Moreover, we are assuming that her belief that the tank is full is also reached by a reliable process. So, given NR, Roxanne knows (1). From (1), Roxanne deduces:

(2) On this occasion, the gauge is reading correctly.

Since deduction is a reliable process, NR implies that Roxanne knows (2) as well. Suppose Roxanne repeats this procedure. She reads that the gauge says "X" and forms the belief that the tank is X. Given NR, she comes to know on each of these occasions that the tank is reading accurately. Putting these bits of information together she concludes by induction that:

(3) The gauge reads accurately all the time.

Since induction is a reliable process, NR implies that Roxanne knows (3) too. From (3), Roxanne infers:

(4) The gauge is reliable.

Vogel argues that, according to NR, Roxanne knows (4). Her belief in (1) is reliably formed and she infers (4) through a series of steps each of which yield knowledge according to NR. But Vogel argues Roxanne does not know (4). Therefore, NR is false. But Vogel also criticizes Roxanne's procedure. He writes, "This extraordinary procedure, which I shall call *bootstrapping*, seems to allow us to promote many, if not all, of one's beliefs that were formed by reliable processes into *knowledge* that those beliefs were formed by a reliable process. I assume that bootstrapping is illegitimate. Roxanne cannot establish that her gauge is reliable by the peculiar reasoning I have just described."[16]

Vogel's judgment that Roxanne does not know (4) seems quite plausible. But Roxanne's procedure clearly resembles the track record argument that we considered above. If Roxanne's procedure is unacceptable, then how

---

[16] *Ibid.*, pp. 614–15.

could a track record argument for perception or memory be any better? If Roxanne's epistemically circular procedure fails to yield knowledge of her conclusion, must other epistemically circular procedures also fail?

As we have seen, Sosa argues that epistemic circularity need not prevent us from knowing that our ways of forming belief are reliable. Since we have been considering Sosa's views on the matter, let us ask how Sosa's virtue epistemology might respond to the problems raised by the case of Roxanne.

First, Sosa would reject NR. In the last chapter we noted that Sosa distinguishes between belief that is produced by an intellectual virtue and belief that is produced by a reliable cognitive process. According to Sosa, knowledge requires more than reliably produced belief; it requires belief produced by an intellectual virtue. So, Sosa would agree with Vogel that NR is false. Sosa would say that the mere fact that Roxanne's belief in her first premise is true and reliably produced does not imply that she knows it.

Second, it is open to Sosa to hold that in order for the use of an instrument, such as a gas gauge, to yield knowledge one needs certain background beliefs about its reliability. To yield knowledge one must know that the gauge is reliable and, moreover, reliable in the environment in which it is used.[17] But what is required for the competent, knowledge-yielding use of instruments, such as gas gauges, need not be required for the use of basic virtues such as perception and memory. Even if the use of instruments requires background beliefs about the reliability of the instruments to yield

---

[17] Sosa draws a distinction between fundamental and derived virtues. "*Derived* virtues are virtues acquired by use of the more fundamental virtues as when one learns how to read and use an instrument through a friend's teaching or through reading a manual or through empirical trial and error methods." Ernest Sosa, "Intellectual Virtue in Perspective," *Knowledge in Perspective* (Cambridge: Cambridge University Press, 1991), p. 278. A derived virtue is acquired and sustained by the use of more fundamental virtues such as perception, memory, and inductive inference and is based on correlations established through the use of more basic virtues. In order for the use of instruments to yield knowledge, one must have certain background beliefs about the reliability of those instruments, including beliefs about the reliability of the environments in which they are employed. So, one's knowledge that *p* formed on the basis of using an instrument, *I*, depends on one's knowing that *I* is indeed reliable. But what is required for the use of derived virtues to yield knowledge need not be required for the knowledge yielding use of the fundamental virtues.

knowledge, the use of basic virtues does not. Roxanne's lack of knowledge about the reliability of gas gauges like hers explains why she does not know her first premise, and why her reasoning is poor. But lack of knowledge concerning the reliability of perception and memory does not preclude one from having perceptual or memory knowledge. It would not prevent one from having what Sosa calls "animal knowledge." It does not prevent one from knowing the premises of a track record argument for perception and memory. So, even if we reject Roxanne's track record argument, we need not reject all track record arguments, and we need not reject all forms of support for the reliability of our ways of forming beliefs that are epistemically circular.

Third, Sosa is not committed to the view that one's knowledge of the reliability of one's ways of forming beliefs actually comes about through the sort of simple track record argument we have been considering. While Roxanne has no background information concerning the reliability of gauges like hers, no normal adult human lacks background information concerning the reliability of perception and memory. It would be very strange for any normal adult to base his belief that perception and memory are reliable on a simple track record argument or for such an argument to yield such knowledge where there was none before. For the vast majority of people, knowledge of the reliability of one's faculties does not arise in this simple self-conscious way. Perhaps Sosa would hold that knowledge of the reliability of one's faculties depends on both the overall coherence and aptness of one's beliefs, upon the coherence of beliefs virtuously acquired. For most of us, the belief in the reliability of perception and memory is already well anchored in a virtuous and vast coherent web before we begin to engage in philosophical reflection about their reliability. Most of us believe things like: (i) many people drive cars safely, (ii) they use perception to navigate the roads, (iii) I find my way home every night, (iv) I use perception and memory to find my way home, (v) many people find their way home using perception and memory. Clearly, this just touches the surface of any normal adult's body of beliefs. But we also believe (vi) perception and memory are reliable. What could make it reasonable for us to accept (vi) is the greater explanatory coherence it brings to our other beliefs, beliefs which are themselves aptly or virtuously formed. Such support is epistemically circular but it does not seem epistemically vicious or unacceptable.

It should be clear that one could agree with Sosa's conclusion that epistemic circularity need not prevent one from knowing that one's ways of forming beliefs are reliable without sharing his virtue epistemology. No doubt many philosophers more sympathetic to other forms of externalism or to varieties of foundationalism or coherentism will support Sosa's general conclusion. Many philosophers will also reject that conclusion. They will hold that any way of supporting the reliability of one's faculties that exhibits epistemic circularity is epistemically unsatisfactory. It is fair to say that the debate is unresolved.

7   Skepticism

Most people take themselves to know various things about the external world, the past, and other minds. We assume, for example, that we know that there are cars and trees, that we were alive yesterday, that others are happy or sad, and that they believe various things. Moreover, we believe that almost everyone knows many of the same kinds of things. We don't assume, for example, that such knowledge is the purview of only a handful of philosophers. Still, many of us are skeptical about some claims to knowledge. Suppose someone claims to know who will win the World Series in ten years or that there is life on some other planet. We are skeptical about such claims to knowledge. We deny that those who make such claims really do know what they claim to know. We might also deny that such claims are justified or reasonable. We might be skeptical about the claim that such beliefs are justified.

While almost all of us are skeptical about some knowledge claims, skeptical arguments in philosophy typically purport to show that we do not know or are not justified in believing many of the things we ordinarily assume we know or reasonably believe. These arguments often conclude that we do not know or are not justified in believing anything about the external world, the past, or other minds. In some cases, these surprising conclusions follow from premises that seem quite plausible. In this chapter we shall look at some skeptical arguments and consider some responses to them.

Skepticism comes in many forms. We may distinguish skepticism about knowledge from skepticism about justification. Skepticism about knowledge denies that people have, or can have, certain kinds of knowledge. Skepticism about justification denies that people are, or can be, justified in believing certain sorts of things. One can be a skeptic about knowledge without being a skeptic about justification. One might hold that people are justified in believing various kinds of things, but maintain that the level of justification people have for believing those things is not high enough for knowledge. One might hold, for example, that people are somewhat justified in believing many things about the external world, but deny that these beliefs ever reach the level of justification needed for knowledge. Similarly, one might be a skeptic about justification without being a skeptic about knowledge. Suppose, for example, one held that knowledge does not require justification, but only reliably produced or aptly formed true belief. One might deny that beliefs of a certain kind were justified, but still amounted to knowledge.

We can also distinguish between *global* and *local* skepticism. Global skepticism about knowledge denies that we do, or can, have any knowledge at all. If global skepticism about knowledge is true, then no one knows anything at all. Of course, if global skepticism about knowledge is true, then no one knows that it is. One could not consistently claim both (i) that global skepticism about knowledge is true, and (ii) that one knows it is. Moreover, if global skepticism were true, then no belief in it could be based on premises which are known. In contrast, local skepticism about knowledge holds that we do not, or cannot, have knowledge about some particular domain, such as knowledge about other minds, the past, or the external world. The local skeptic need not deny that we have *some* kinds of knowledge. He might allow, for example, that we know our own mental states and some simple logical truths. Clearly, one can be a local skeptic without being a global skeptic. Similar remarks would apply to global and local skepticism about justification. So, for example, if global skepticism about justification were true, no one could be justified in believing it. If global skepticism were true, then no one would have any good reasons for accepting it. At least, no one would be justified in believing any premises which support it.

In this chapter we will consider several skeptical arguments and a variety of responses to them. Unfortunately, we will not be able to consider all or even most of the responses to skeptical arguments. We shall only skim the surface of a deep debate. Still, some people think there is no point in examining skeptical arguments. Some will think that considering such arguments is an idle waste of time since no one is really going to give up his beliefs in the external world, other minds, or the past on the basis of skeptical arguments. One can imagine someone saying, "These arguments are just *stupid*. No one is going to quit believing there are other people because of an argument like *that*." Let's suppose that reflecting on skeptical arguments will not lead any one to actually give up beliefs about the external world, the past, or other minds. Does it follow that examining skeptical arguments or responding to them is a waste of time? Not at all. First, reflection on skeptical arguments might lead one to give up the belief that one has *knowledge* or *justified belief* about the external world. Even if one cannot give up the belief that there is an external world, it is not so clear that one cannot give up the belief that one *knows* there is. So, we might want to consider skeptical arguments to see whether they give us good reasons to give up our claims to knowledge and justification. Second, even if we are convinced that we do have the sort of knowledge that the skeptic denies we have, skeptical arguments usually presuppose some views about the nature of knowledge or justification. Often, these views are quite plausible. Reflecting on skeptical arguments can sometimes lead us to reject some plausible assumptions about the nature of knowledge and justification. It can lead us to revise, and perhaps improve, our views about the nature of knowledge and what knowledge requires.

Certainty, infallibility, and error

Reflection on skepticism often begins with a consideration of various skeptical scenarios. In his first Mediation, Descartes introduces one of the most famous. Descartes raises the possibility that he is being deceived by an evil demon who causes his sensory experiences. The demon manipulates Descartes's sensory experience to create the illusion of a body and a physical world and tries to deceive him into believing that he has a body and that he is surrounded by material things. More recent skeptical scenarios are less supernatural. According to one scenario, the subject is nothing but a brain in a vat being monitored by a computer. The computer monitors the brain's inputs and outputs and stimulates the brain's nervous system to create sensory experiences. In this way the computer deceives the subject about his having a body and about the nature of his environment. The computer might even deceive the subject into believing that he has a body and that he is holding a philosophy book. Maybe reading a chapter on skepticism.

When we reflect on such examples, it seems clear that our sensory experience does not guarantee that our beliefs about the external world are true. But why should that support or even suggest that skepticism is true? One reason is that reflection on such scenarios suggests to many philosophers that our beliefs about the external world are less than certain. But now suppose further that one thinks knowledge that p requires that one be certain that p. Given these two assumptions we might formulate the following skeptical argument:

The certainty argument

(1) One cannot be certain about what the external world is like.
(2) One knows that p only if one is certain that p.
(3) Therefore, one cannot know what the external world is like.

According to this argument knowledge requires certainty, and since I cannot be certain that I have a body or that there is a desk before me, I cannot know such things. Note that this argument concerns our knowledge of the external world. It could easily be formulated, however, as a skeptical argument about other domains, such as our knowledge of other minds or the past. To the extent that our beliefs in these other domains are less than certain, then they too would fall short of knowledge.

In evaluating this argument, we might ask what does it mean to say that a proposition is "certain" for a person. It seems clear that the term "certain" can mean different things, but suppose we say that a proposition is certain for someone just in case it is maximally justified for him. In other words, a proposition is certain for a person just in case it enjoys the highest possible degree of justification. Perhaps the propositions that you think or that you exist or that $2 = 2$ or that all squares are squares are propositions that are certain for you.

Suppose we do understand the concept of certainty in this way. In that case, it seems reasonable to believe that the first premise of the argument is true. Even if one's beliefs about the external world are highly justified, it does not seem very many of them, if any, are *maximally* justified. For example, I take myself to be highly justified in believing that there is a desk before me. But it does not seem that my belief that there is a desk before me is as justified as some of my beliefs about my own mental states, e.g. that I think that there is a desk before me or that it appears that there is a desk before me. Moreover, my belief that there is a desk before me does not seem as justified for me as the propositions that I think, that I exist, or that $2 = 2$. But if my belief about the desk is not as justified for me as these propositions, then it is not maximally justified, and, therefore, it is less than certain. It seems reasonable to believe that the same could be said of many, if not all, of our beliefs about the external world.

What about the second premise of the argument? The second premise of the argument seems false. While it is reasonable to think that knowledge requires some degree of justification, even a fairly high degree of justification, it does not seem to require certainty. At least this seems true of our ordinary concept of knowledge. People often take themselves to know things that are less than certain. I take myself to know, for example, that I own a car, that Lincoln was the sixteenth president, that Paris is the capital of France. But none of these things is as justified for me as the proposition that I think or that I exist. So, it seems that our ordinary concept of knowledge does not require certainty. Moreover, the view that knowledge requires certainty implies that all instances of knowledge must enjoy the same maximal degree of justification, that instances of knowledge cannot differ in the degree of justification they enjoy. But that again does not seem to fit our ordinary concept of knowledge. We do sometimes distinguish between knowing something and knowing it with absolute certainty. In drawing such a distinction we presuppose that knowing something does not require certainty.

Of course, someone might use some concept of knowledge which *does* require certainty. One might say, for example, "When I use the term 'knowledge,' I am using it to refer to something that does require certainty." Given *that* concept of knowledge, with its extremely high standard of justification, no one knows much of anything about the external world. But from the fact that there is no knowledge of the external world given *that* concept of knowledge, it hardly follows that there is no knowledge of the external world according to our ordinary concept of knowledge. In other words, even if we concede (a) that there is some concept of knowledge that requires certainty, and (b) no one knows much about the external world in *that* sense of knowledge, nothing follows about whether we have knowledge of the external world in our ordinary sense. To see this, suppose Jones says, "When I use the term 'doctor' I mean someone who can cure any disease in ten minutes." Furthermore, suppose Jones points out that no one in town can cure any disease in ten minutes. Jones then concludes that there are no doctors in town. It should be obvious that even if Jones has shown that there are no doctors, given his extremely demanding concept of "doctor," nothing follows about whether there are doctors in the ordinary sense of the term. It would clearly be a mistake to think that Jones had given us any reason to doubt that there were doctors in town according to our ordinary concept of doctor. By the same token, even if the skeptic shows that our beliefs about the external world do not satisfy an extremely high and demanding concept of knowledge that requires certainty, nothing would follow about our having knowledge in the ordinary sense.

Another argument for skepticism holds that knowledge requires infallibility. Like the previous argument, it assumes a very high standard for knowledge.

The infallibility argument

(1) We are not infallible about the existence and character of the external world.
(2) If S knows that p, then S is infallible about p.
(3) We do not have knowledge about the existence and character of the external world.

Let's assume that one is infallible about p just in case it is impossible for one to be mistaken about p. If so, then it seems that the first premise of the argument is true. The skeptical scenarios illustrate some ways in which it is possible for us to be radically mistaken in our beliefs about the external world. But like the previous argument, the infallibility argument presupposes a mistaken view about what knowledge requires, at least where our ordinary concept of knowledge is concerned. The mere fact that it is *possible* for us to be mistaken about p does not imply that we do not know that p.

Sometimes, however, people get confused about the relationship between knowledge and infallibility. To see how this can happen, let's consider the following claim:

(1) If S knows that p, then S is not mistaken about p.

(1) is true. It tells us that if someone knows a proposition, then he is not mistaken in believing it. Moreover, (1) doesn't just happen to be true. (1) expresses a *necessary* truth about knowledge. So, along with (1), we should also accept:

(2) Necessarily, if S knows that p, then S is not mistaken about p.

But now consider the following claim:

(3) If S knows that p, then necessarily S is not mistaken about p.

(3) is false. (3) tells us that if one knows that p, then it is impossible for him to be mistaken about p. (3) implies that if one knows that p, then one is infallible with respect to p. Problems arise when people confuse (2) and (3) or think that (3) follows from (2). From (2) they mistakenly infer that knowledge requires infallibility.

To see that this is a mistake consider the following claims:

(1′) If John is a brother, then John has a sibling.
(2′) Necessarily, if John is a brother, then John has a sibling.
(3′) If John is a brother, then necessarily John has a sibling.

Both (1′) and (2′) are true. (2′) tells us that (1′) expresses a necessary truth about being a brother and having a sibling. However, (3′) is false. It tells us that if John is a brother, then it is a necessary truth that he has a sibling. (3′) tells us that if John is a brother, it is *impossible* for him not to have a sibling. But that's just false. Even if John is a brother, it is *not* a necessary truth that he has a sibling. Even if he is a brother, he *might* have been an only child. In sum, (3′) does not follow from (1′) or (2′). By the same token, (3) does not follow from (1) or (2). One can't support the view that knowledge requires infallibility by inferring (3) from (1) or (2).

Let's consider a third sort of skeptical argument. Let's consider the following sort of case, suggested by John Tienson. Imagine that a detective is investigating Black and White, who are suspected of embezzling.

> After a lengthy and painstaking investigation, he has exactly the same evidence that Black is not the embezzler and that White is not the embezzler. Suppose that Black is in fact the guilty party, and that White is perfectly innocent. Now, given the assumption that [the detective's] evidence is exactly

the same in both cases ... no matter how good the evidence is, he does not know that White is innocent.[1]

In this example we are to assume that the detective has strong evidence that White is innocent and equally strong evidence that Black is innocent. So, the detective has equally strong evidence for both:

p Black is innocent.

q White is innocent.

The detective does *not* know p (since it's false). From his perspective both p and q appear true. He has strong evidence for each. Tienson suggests that since the detective does not know p, and since his evidence for q is no better than his evidence for p, he does not know q either. Perhaps we might formulate the argument in more general terms as:

The argument from error

(1) If S's total evidence for q is no better than S's total evidence for p, and S's belief that p is not an instance of knowledge, then S does not know that q.
(2) S's total evidence for q is no better than S's total evidence for p.
(3) S's belief that p is not an instance of knowledge.
(4) Therefore, S does not know that q.

This is argument from error insofar as it assumes in premise 3 that S is mistaken about p (or would be mistaken about p in some hypothetical scenario.)

Clearly, this line of reasoning is relevant to our concerns about skepticism. For skeptics often suggest that the evidence we have for our beliefs about the external world is no better than the evidence we would have for those beliefs in some skeptical scenarios. So, given (i) that we do not have knowledge of the external world in the skeptical scenarios, and (ii) that our present evidence for the existence of external things is no better than the evidence we would have in those scenarios, this line of reasoning concludes that we do not have knowledge of the external world.

---

[1] John Tienson, "On Analyzing Knowledge," *Philosophical Studies*, 25, 289f.

Nonskeptics typically reject premise 1. They argue that the first premise is much too strong. Let's consider the following case. Suppose, for example, I am walking down the street and I see two people looking into a store window. I form the belief that it's my friend, Tom, and his wife, Lisa. I have known them both for many years. But suppose I am completely unaware that Lisa has an identical twin, Laurie, who just happens to be visiting from out of town, and that the woman I see with Tom is Laurie. Of course, I do not know that I see Lisa, since the proposition that I see Lisa is false. However, since my evidence that I see Tom is as good as my evidence that I see Lisa, and since I don't know that I see Lisa, it follows from premise 1 that I also do not know that I see Tom. To many people this seems implausible. Indeed, if premise 1 were true, I would not know most of my friends when I saw them since my evidence in all those cases is no stronger than my evidence in this case that I see Lisa.

The chief problem with premise 1 and the argument from error is that it implicitly denies that there can be nonconclusive or fallible evidence that is strong enough for knowledge. Recall that in chapter 1 we said that nonconclusive evidence is evidence that does not guarantee the truth of the proposition for which it is evidence. Whenever we believe something on the basis of nonconclusive evidence, it is always *possible* that we are mistaken. My evidence that I see Lisa is nonconclusive evidence. So too is my evidence that I see Tom. Indeed, in each case it is very strong evidence. Yet, according to premise (1), since there is *one* case where such very strong evidence fails to yield knowledge, there is *no* case where one's evidence is just as strong and an instance of knowledge. This is basically to deny that very strong nonconclusive evidence can ever be strong enough for knowledge. In this respect, the argument from error resembles the certainty argument and the infallibility argument in setting a very high standard for knowledge. The argument from error seems to imply that knowledge requires conclusive or infallible evidence. But there is no more reason to accept such a requirement than there is to accept that knowledge requires infallibility.

The argument from ignorance

The three skeptical arguments we have considered so far presuppose fairly high standards for knowledge. But let us consider another line of argument that many think is more troubling.

Let us begin by considering the following epistemic principle:

The principle of exclusion (PE)

S knows that p only if S can rule out (know to be false) any proposition S knows to be incompatible with p.

According to PE, if you know that p and you also know that p is incompatible with q, then you can know that q is false. So, according to PE, I know, for example, that Smith is the thief that robbed the bank only if I know that it was *not* some other man, Jones, who robbed the bank. If I cannot rule out Jones as the thief, then I do not *know* that Smith is the thief. PE seems like a reasonable principle.

Now consider the proposition,

(h) I have hands.

According to PE, I know (h) only if I can rule out any proposition that I know to be incompatible with (h). Now clearly, there are lots of propositions that I know to be incompatible with (h). These include: I have hooks instead of hands, I have no hands, I have giant lobster claws instead of hands, etc. According to PE, I know (h) only if can know that these propositions are false. But it seems that I can know these propositions are false. I can see that they are false. Again, PE seems quite plausible.

But now consider the following skeptical hypothesis:

(v) I am a handless brain in a vat being caused to have perceptual experiences as if I had hands.

Clearly, (v) is incompatible with (h). After all, if (v) is true, then (h) is false, and vice versa. So, according to PE, I know (h) only if I can rule out (v). In other words, according to PE, I know (h) only if I can know not-(v). But that, says the skeptic, is something we cannot do. We might believe that we are not deceived envatted brains, but according to the skeptic that is not something we can *know*. Given these considerations, the skeptic might now offer:

The argument from ignorance

(1) You know that (h) only if you know that not-(v).
(2) But you do not know that not-(v).
(3) Therefore, you don't know that (h).

To many, this argument seems more plausible than the others we have considered, since it seems plausible to them that one cannot know not-(v), that one cannot rule out the skeptical hypothesis, (v). Of course, we have focused on just one skeptical hypothesis, namely (v). It should be clear, however, that there are other skeptical hypotheses we might have chosen instead, e.g. that one is a disembodied mind being deceived by a Cartesian demon into believing that one has hands. It should also be clear that though we have focused on our knowledge of (h), arguments of the same type could be used to support skepticism about many other sorts of things, including skepticism about the external world in general, the past, and other minds.

When we think about the argument from ignorance, we might wonder why should we think that premise (2) is true. Why accept that we don't know that the various skeptical hypotheses are false? Of course, the skeptic might appeal to one of the arguments we considered above to support (2). He might argue, for example, that (2) is true because our belief that not-(v) is not certain or infallible. But since those arguments do not seem compelling, let's consider another line of reasoning in favor of premise (2).

In order to appreciate this line of reasoning for (2), let's recall a case from chapter 2. In discussing causal theories of knowing, we considered the case of Henry. Henry is driving in an area that is filled with barn facades. The facades are so cleverly constructed that tourists like Henry often mistake them for barns. Suppose that Henry looks out his car window and sees the one real barn in the area. He forms the true belief "There's a barn." Many philosophers hold that in this case, Henry does not know that he's seeing a barn. Even though his belief is true, he seems to be right only by accident.

Some philosophers explain Henry's failure to know by claiming that Henry's belief is not sufficiently "sensitive" to the truth or falsity of what he believes. Though his belief that there's barn is true, if it had been false, he would have still held it. Suppose we define the concept of sensitivity:

D14   S's belief that p is sensitive = Df. If p were false, then S would not believe that p.

While Henry's belief that there's a barn is not sensitive, many of our beliefs are. Consider my perceptual belief that there is a cup on the desk. I am looking right at the cup and believe that it is on the desk. It seems true that if the cup weren't on the desk, then I would not have that belief. In those close possible worlds where it is false that the cup is on the desk, where, for example, it is put away in the cupboard, I would not have that belief. The same seems true for my belief that I have hands. If I didn't have hands, then I wouldn't believe that I did. In those close possible worlds where I did not have hands, where, for example, I'd lost them in an accident, I would not believe that I had hands.

Suppose, then, we accept the following "sensitivity requirement" on knowledge:

The sensitivity requirement on knowledge (SRK)

S knows that p only if S's belief that p is sensitive.

If SRK is true, then it seems that the skeptic is right in claiming that we do *not* know that not-(v). This is because one's belief that not-(v) is not sensitive. If one's belief that not-(v) were false, one would still believe not-(v). In other words, if (v) were true, if one were a handless brain in a vat being caused to have experiences as if one had hands, one would still believe not-(v). The skeptic, then, might appeal to SRK to support the claim that (2) is true.

It is not clear, however, that SRK is true. There are at least three objections to it.[2] First, consider our knowledge of necessary truths, e.g. that $2 = 2$ or that all squares are rectangles. It is not clear that our belief in such propositions is sensitive since it is not possible for those propositions to be false. Since a necessary truth is true in every possible world, there is no possible world in which it is false. It is hard to see how our knowledge of necessary truths could be understood in terms of a sensitivity requirement.

Second, suppose that I drop a bag of trash down the chute in my high rise apartment. I have done this many times. Presumably, I know that the bag will soon be in the basement. But what if the bag were not to arrive there, perhaps because it was snagged on the way down or because of some other incredibly rare occurrence. My belief that the bag will soon be in the basement is not sensitive since if the belief were false (say, because of

---

[2] These three objections can be found in Ernest Sosa's "How to Defeat Opposition to Moore," *Philosophical Perspectives*, 13 (1999), 141–53.

the snagging), I would still hold it. SRK implies that I do not know that the bag will soon be in the basement. But that seems false.

Finally, some philosophers raise the following objection. Consider the following propositions:

p The cup is on the desk.

q My belief that the cup is on the desk is true.

Suppose that I am looking at the cup and I believe both p and q. Let's assume that my belief that p is sensitive and that I know that p. But what about my belief that q? My belief that q does not seem to be sensitive since in those close possible worlds where q is false, I would still believe it. But if my belief that q is not sensitive, then, according to SRK, I cannot know that q. Thus, according to SRK, I can know that p, but I cannot know that q. To many, however, it seems implausible to hold that I can know that p, but cannot know that q. So, they would hold that SRK is false.

In sum, it is not clear that SRK is true. It is not clear that it offers any support to the skeptic's position. Still, even if SRK is not the best way to support premise 2, many people find that premise to be plausible. It seems to them to have a certain intuitive pull. They think about it and wonder how *could* one possibly know that the skeptical scenarios are false? Many people think that whatever our evidence might be in terms of our sense experiences, memories, and our justified beliefs, it is not sufficient to rule out the skeptical hypotheses. Perhaps this is right. In any case, let us consider four responses to the argument from ignorance. These are (a) the Moorean response, (b) the relevant alternatives response, (c) the contextualist response, and (d) the inference to the best explanation response.

The Moorean response

Philosophers have made a variety of responses to the argument from ignorance. One of the most famous comes from G. E. Moore, an important "common sense" philosopher from the first half of the twentieth century. Moore claims that we do in fact know many of the things that we ordinarily think we do. We know that there are other people, that we have hands, that we have lived on the surface of the earth for many years. Moore holds that since we *do* know such things it follows that any skeptical argument that implies we don't know such things must be mistaken. The following is a fairly typical statement of Moore's view concerning skeptical arguments:

> [I]t seems to me a sufficient refutation of such views as these, simply to point to cases in which we do know such things. This, after all, you know, really is a finger; there is no doubt about it: I know it, and you all know it. And I think we may safely challenge any philosopher to bring forward any argument in favour either of the proposition that we do not know it, or the proposition that it is not true, which does not at some point rest upon some premiss which is beyond comparison, less certain, than the proposition which it is designed to attack.[3]

Moore claims that since we *do* know such things as "this is a finger," it follows that skeptical arguments that imply that we don't must be mistaken. Either one or more of the premises in the skeptical argument is false or the conclusion does not follow from the premises. Furthermore, Moore claims that skeptical arguments concerning the existence of the external world, other minds, or the past always rest on some premise or assumption which is *less* reasonable than the claims about knowledge or justification they are designed to refute. Since they are less reasonable to believe, it is not reasonable for us to abandon our knowledge claims.

Let's consider again the argument from ignorance. Recall that (*h*) is the proposition that I have hands and (*v*) is the proposition that I am a handless brain in a vat being caused to have perceptual experiences as if I had hands.

The argument from ignorance

(1) You know that (*h*) only if you know that not-(*v*).
(2) But you do not know that not-(*v*).
(3) Therefore, you don't know that (*h*).

---

[3] G. E. Moore, "Some Judgments of Perception," *Philosophical Studies* (London: Routledge and Kegan Paul, 1960), p. 228.

In his 1941 lecture, "Certainty," Moore suggests a "counterargument" to the argument from ignorance. Adapting his line of reasoning to our present case, the Moorean argument would go:

Moore's counterargument

(1′) You know that (h) only if you know that not-(v).

(2′) You know that (h).

(3′) Therefore, you know that not-(v).

Moore takes as his second premise the negation of the skeptic's conclusion. So, while the skeptic reasons, *A only if B, not-B, therefore not-A*, Moore argues *A only if B, A, therefore B*. Both are logically valid forms of argument. Both the skeptic and Moore accept (1). But Moore holds that since (2′) is true, the argument from ignorance must be mistaken. Moore turns the skeptic's argument "on its head" by taking as one of his premises the negation of the skeptic's conclusion.

Furthermore, Moore claims that skeptical arguments rest on some premise or assumption that is less reasonable to believe than the conclusion it is designed to attack. Our version of the argument from ignorance is designed to attack proposition (2′). So we may take Moore to claim that the skeptic's argument rests at some point on some premise that is less reasonable to believe than (2′). So, perhaps we may take Moore to claim that

(2′) You know that you have hands

is more reasonable to believe than at least one of the following:

(1) You know that you have hands only if you know that you are not a handless brain in a vat being caused to have perceptual experiences as if I had hands, or

(2) You do not know that you are not a handless brain in a vat being caused to have perceptual experiences as if I had hands, or

one of the assumptions that might support (1) or (2), such as PE, SRK, or one of the views about knowledge we considered above, e.g. that knowledge requires certainty or infallibility. Moore would claim that since (2′) is more reasonable to believe than at least one of these other propositions, it would be unreasonable to accept the argument from ignorance.

Some critics might object that (2′) is false since Moore has not *proved* that (h) is true. He has not, for example, deduced (h) from other premises that are known. According to these critics, knowledge requires proof, and Moore offers no proof for (h). However, Moore points out that one can know things without proof.[4] Immediate or basic knowledge does not require proof. Indeed, in some places Moore suggests that our knowledge of some external objects such as hands, pencils, and fingers is basic or immediate knowledge.[5] Moreover, Moore might also note that perhaps his critics have confused "proof" with "evidence." While it is plausible to think that knowledge requires evidence, we should not confuse this with a requirement for proof. One might have evidence for a proposition on the basis of sense experience, memory, or induction. Such evidence might be strong enough for knowledge even if it is not proof. In any event, Moore insists that the fact he has not or cannot give a proof of (h) is no reason for thinking that (2′) is false.

Still, we might ask how *do* we know that (h) is true? How do we know that it more reasonable for us to accept (2′) than (2)? Surely these are important questions. Moore, however, writes, "We are all, I think, in this strange position that we do *know* many things, with regard to which we *know* further that we must have had some evidence for them and yet we do not know *how* we know them, i.e. we do not know what the evidence was."[6] Moore suggests that in order to know that one proposition is more reasonable to believe than another, one need not know what makes it so. One might know, for example, that it is more reasonable to accept (2′) over (2) without knowing why this is so.

While Moore's claims seem plausible to many, his position might leave us unsatisfied. As philosophers, we might want to know not only that it is more reasonable to believe one thing rather than another, but *why* this is so. We might want to know why it is more reasonable to believe (h) than (v) and why is it more reasonable to believe (2′) over (2). Though he himself does not do so, Moore, or one of his followers, might go on and try to explain why it is more reasonable to believe (2′) than (2). In fact, he might appeal to one of the theories about the nature of justification we have considered in the previous chapters. He might note, for example, that his belief in (2′) coheres with the

---

[4] G. E. Moore, "Proof of an External World," *Philosophical Papers* (New York: Macmillan, 1959), p. 150. Moore writes, "I can know things which I cannot prove."

[5] G. E. Moore, "Hume's Philosophy Examined," *Some Main Problems of Philosophy* (New York: Macmillan, 1953), p. 142.

[6] G. E. Moore, "A Defence of Common Sense," *Philosophical Papers*, p. 44.

rest of his beliefs much better than (2). He might defend (2') by pointing out that his belief in (h) is formed on the basis of perception and perception is an intellectual virtue. He might point out that, given his total evidence which includes his experiences and his justified beliefs, it is more reasonable for him to believe (2') than (2). He might, perhaps, point out that he has a great deal of evidence for (h), that he seems to see his hands, that he seems to feel his hands, that he seems to remember having had hands for many years, that in general people are highly reliable about whether they have hands. He might also point out that he has evidence against (v). He has evidence that technology has not yet reached the point where brains can be kept alive in vats, much less stimulated in such a way as to cause such perfect deceptions. He has evidence to believe that no one has ever been such a deceived envatted brain. So, Moore might concede that his evidence does not prove that (h) is true or that (v) is false, or prove that (2') is more reasonable than (2). Still, he might hold that his evidence makes it highly reasonable for him to believe (h) and to believe that (v) is false, and more reasonable to believe (2') than (2).

The relevant alternatives response

Some philosophers agree with Moore that we do know much about the external world. But, unlike Moore, they agree with the skeptic that we cannot rule out various skeptical hypotheses. But unlike both Moore and the skeptics, these philosophers reject the Principle of Exclusion (PE) and premise 1 of the Argument from Ignorance. According to this response, knowledge that p does *not* require that one be able to rule out every proposition one knows to be incompatible with p. Instead, we are only required to rule out *relevant* alternatives. Ordinarily, they say, we expect someone who knows something to be able to rule out *some* alternatives, but we do not expect that he will be able to rule out *every* incompatible alternative, especially "far-fetched" alternatives involving envatted brains or malicious Cartesian demons.[7]

---

[7] The classic presentation of the relevant alternatives approach can be found in Fred Dretske's "Epistemic Operators," *Journal of Philosophy*, 67, no. 24 (December 24, 1970), 1007–23; see also Gail Stine, "Dretske on Knowing the Logical Consequences," *Journal of Philosophy*, 68, no. 9 (May 6, 1971), 296–99.

This approach is sometimes called "the relevant alternatives approach." Those who favor this approach would reject PE in favor of:

PE'

S knows that *p* only if S can rule out (know to be false) any *relevant* alternative S knows to be incompatible with *p*.

A proponent of this view, a "relevantist," claims that in order for me to know that I have hands, (*h*), I have to be able to rule out some alternatives, e.g. that I have no hands or that I have hooks instead of hands. These we might deem relevant alternatives to (*h*). But, according to this view, the skeptical hypothesis, (*v*), is *not* a relevant alternative. So, according to PE', knowing that one has hands does not require that one be able to exclude (*v*).

How does this help us respond to the skeptic? Recall premise (1) of the Argument from Ignorance:

(1) You know that (*h*) only if you know that not-(*v*).

According to the relevantist, (*v*) is not a relevant alternative to (*h*). So, premise (1) of the argument from ignorance is false. It is false that you know (*h*) only if you can rule out (*v*). According to the relevant alternative approach, the skeptic mistakenly assumes that PE and (1) are true. Of course, since Moore also assumes that PE and (1) are true, he and his followers make the same mistake.

There are, however, two difficulties with the relevant alternatives approach. First, what exactly counts as a "relevant" alternative? Why should "I do not have hands" or "I have hooks instead of hands" count as relevant alternatives, but not (*v*)? Perhaps we might say that any alternative that seems far-fetched is not a relevant alternative. But what counts as a far-fetched alternative? And why should that matter? That I have lobster claws instead of hands is pretty far-fetched, but presumably in order to know that I have hands I should be able to rule out that alternative. It is not clear that there is any principled way of determining what counts as a relevant alternative. But perhaps the relevantist can find one.

Second, the relevant alternatives approach seems to have what many regard as intuitively implausible consequences. It seems to permit an "abominable" conjunction — namely, that I know that I have hands *and* I do not know that I am not a handless brain in a vat being caused to have experiences as if I had hands. In other words, it seems to permit both that I know (*h*) and I do not know that not-(*v*). How is it that I can know the one and not the other? Moreover, the relevantist's view implies that I can know (*h*) and further know that (*h*) implies not-(*v*) and yet not know not-(*v*). Again, many philosophers think that these implications are mistaken and, therefore, we should reject the relevant alternatives approach.

The contextualist response

Let us consider briefly a third response to the argument from ignorance. According to contextualism, the standards for applying the word "knows" vary from one context to another. In some contexts, the standards for "knows" are fairly low and easily met. In those cases, what we express by saying "S knows that *p*" is likely to be true. In other contexts, the standards for "knows" are very high. In those cases, they are very hard if not impossible to meet and what we express by "S knows that *p*" is not likely to be true. So, in some contexts, where standards for knowledge are low and easily met, attributions of knowledge will often be true, and in other contexts where standards for knowledge are high, attributions of knowledge will be typically, if not always, false.

In order to understand this view better, let's consider how the word "tall" seems to function. Suppose that I am walking down the street and I see a man who is a little over six feet in height. I might say to my wife, "Look at that tall man over there. He plays professional basketball. In fact, he'll be playing in the game we are going to see." Now suppose that later that evening my wife and I go to the game. The man we saw earlier in the day is now on the court huddled with his teammates. I turn to my wife and say, "Look at that short man. The one who is not tall. He's the one we saw this afternoon." Suppose my wife, being in a playful mood, says, "Earlier today you said he was tall. Now you are saying he's short. Quit contradicting yourself. Make up your mind." Now, ordinarily I might just laugh off her comment in a good-natured way. But suppose tonight I actually try to defend myself. I might say that when we call someone "tall" we have a class of comparison in mind. Often that class of comparison is not explicitly stated, but it is usually understood in the context. So, when I called him "tall" this afternoon, I was comparing him to most people. Given that the standard of comparison is most people, then my claim that he is tall is true. But just now when I said he was not tall I was using a different standard. I was comparing him to the other basketball players on his team. Relative to that group, my statement that he is not tall is true. So, I was not contradicting myself. It is simply that the standard for being tall changed in the two contexts.

Contextualists think that "knows" functions in a similar way. In some contexts, our standards of knowledge are low and fairly easy to satisfy. In other contexts, the standards for knowledge are higher and harder to satisfy. Some contextualists think of lower and higher standards in terms of ruling out alternatives. Where the standards are low, we don't have to rule out as much in the way of alternatives as we do when standards are high. So, for example, suppose someone asks me if I know whether Chris is in the room. I might say, "Sure, I know he's here. I can see him." Given our ordinary low standards of knowledge, I need only rule out some fairly simple alternatives. I just need to rule out, for example, that the person I am seeing is Tom or Harry. Since I can rule out such alternatives, I know that Chris is here. But now suppose someone raises the possibility that I am being deceived by a Cartesian demon. According to the contextualist, when someone introduces such skeptical scenarios, the standards for knowledge are raised. In these contexts, where skeptical scenarios are in play, the standards are higher. In these contexts, I need to be able to rule out these skeptical scenarios. According to these higher standards, I need to be able to rule out such demonic deception. But that's not something I can do. I can't know that I am not demonically deceived. So, according to these higher standards, I do *not* know that Chris is in the room.

Contextualists claim that their theory actually explains our reactions to various claims about knowledge. In ordinary contexts we are quite willing to say that we and others know a lot about the external world. However, many people become very reluctant to claim that they or others have such knowledge once skeptical scenarios are introduced. This often happens in epistemology classes when skeptical hypotheses are first encountered. According to contextualists, these different attitudes are explained by the fact that in ordinary cases, standards are low and easily met. When skeptical scenarios are introduced, standards are raised and not met.

How, then, does the contextualist respond to skepticism? According to the contextualist, the skeptic is mistaken in claiming no one ever knows anything about the external world. In ordinary contexts, we have lots of knowledge about the external world. In ordinary contexts, where standards are low and we do not need to rule out much in the way of alternatives, I can know, for example, that I have hands. But in other contexts, where we are considering skeptical claims and the standards for knowledge are raised, it is false that I know I have hands. In those contexts, I must rule out skeptical scenarios such as (*v*), and since I cannot do that, I do not have knowledge.

According to the contextualist, Moore's counter-argument fails because in the context where one would assert the premises of that argument, skeptical scenarios are in play and we are using higher standards of knowledge. Given those higher standards, (2′) turns out to be false. So, Moore's counter-argument is unsound. Does this mean that skepticism is true? Again, according to the contextualist, the answer is "no." In ordinary contexts, where skeptical scenarios are not being entertained, we do know we have hands.

The contextualist's position also differs from that of the relevantists. One difference between them concerns what we know when skeptical hypotheses are being entertained. According to the relevantist, we can know that (*h*) even when we are confronted with skeptical scenarios like (*v*). According to the relevantists, knowing that (*h*) does *not* require that we be able to rule out (*v*). According to the relevantists, knowledge only requires that we rule out relevant alternatives and (*v*) is not a relevant alternative. In contrast, the contextualist denies this and holds that when skeptical scenarios are being entertained we *do* have to rule them out. According to the contextualist, when skeptical scenarios are raised, skeptical hypotheses become relevant. Since we cannot rule them out, the contextualist would say that in those contexts we do not know (*h*). Another way of capturing this difference concerns premise (1) in the argument from ignorance. As we have seen, the relevantist denies premise (1). But according to the contextualist, premise (1) is true. When skeptical hypotheses are being considered, they become relevant. So, on their view, one knows that (*h*) only if one knows that not-(*v*).

In spite of its appeal, contextualism faces a variety of objections. Many philosophers, including Mooreans and relevantists, believe that they *do* know various things about the external world *even* when skeptical scenarios are introduced. These philosophers would hold that contexualists concede too much to the skeptic in holding that we do not have knowledge about the external world in those contexts. Moreover, many philosophers think that there are problems with skeptical arguments. They believe that there are plausible responses to these arguments. Both Mooreans and relevantists, for example, believe that they have plausible responses to the argument from ignorance. But, if contextualism is correct, then the argument from ignorance actually succeeds. Contextualism does not offer a way of refuting the argument from ignorance. On the contrary it endorses it. Again, to many philosophers this seems to concede too much to the skeptic.

Furthermore, contextualists claim that "knows" functions like "tall." But this is not so clear. Consider again our judgments about whether someone is tall. When I see the player on the street, I say that he is tall. When I see him huddled with his teammates, I say he is not tall. There does not seem to be any contradiction between these two claims. I might say that in the first case I am saying he is tall compared to most people. In the second case, I am saying he is not tall compared to his teammates. Both statements can be true. Moreover, recognizing the truth of the second statement does not lead me to question or reject the truth of the first. But in this respect, "tall" seems importantly different from "knows." Suppose, for example, that one becomes convinced by skeptical arguments that we do not have knowledge about the external world. Suppose one finds that such arguments lead him to believe claims to know are false. But if one finds that claims to knowledge are false when one examines skeptical arguments, wouldn't this lead one to question or reject ordinary claims to know? If so, then it is not so clear that we are using one set of standards for "knows" in the skeptical context and another set of standards in the ordinary context.[8]

The "inference to the best explanation" response

Suppose you are sitting in your room late one night. Suddenly, you hear at your door "Knock, knock, knock." Feeling philosophically perverse, it occurs to you that there are several hypotheses to explain the knocking:

(A) Someone came to your door and knocked three times.
(B) Three people came to your door and each knocked once.

---

[8] For contextualist views, see Stewart Cohen, "Contextualism, Skepticism, and the Structure of Reasons," *Philosophical Perspectives*, 13 (1999), pp. 57–89; also Keith DeRose, "Solving the Skeptical Problem," in *Skepticism: A Contemporary Reader*, ed. Keith DeRose and Ted A. Warfield (New York: Oxford University Press, 1999), pp. 183–219. For responses to these views, see Richard Feldman, "Skeptical Problems, Contextualist Solutions," *Philosophical Studies*, 103 (2001), 61–85; and Ernest Sosa, "How to Defeat Opposition to Moore."

(C) Two people came to your door and one knocked twice and the other only once.

It seems possible that the sound at your door was produced in any of these three ways. Still, it seems that the best explanation for the knocking is (A). (A) seems to be the "simplest" or most "economical" answer. It explains the knocking with just one knocker. The other answers seem needlessly complicated, involving several knockers who knock within seconds of one another. Moreover, (A) fits better with your "background information." In your experience, the sound you heard is usually caused by one person and people do not typically knock within seconds of one another. So, you infer that (A) is true. This sort of inference is called "inference to the best explanation" or "abductive inference."

Here's another case. Walking on the beach, you find the remains of a fire, empty beer and soda cans, empty bags of potato chips, and many foot prints. You realize that there are several hypotheses to explain what you observe. Here are two:

(A) There was a party here.
(B) A gang of smugglers came ashore and built a fire to stay warm. The police came and chased them off and ate the potato chips. College students, attracted by the commotion, drank the beer and soda.

Again, it seems more reasonable to believe (A) because (A) is the best explanation for what you observe. (A) seems to be a simpler and more economical explanation for what you observe than (B). (B) seems to involve needless complexity. Again, (A) fits better with your background information. It is very rare for smugglers to come ashore in your area. None have ever been foolish enough to light fires to keep themselves warm. Beach parties are not a rare thing.

It is not easy to say what makes one explanation better than another. There seem to be a variety of factors that contribute to the "goodness" of an explanation. Many philosophers cite such factors as "simplicity," "economy," "comprehensiveness," and "fit" with background information. Explanations might vary in the degree to which they exhibit one of more of these features. It is not clear that there is any systematic way to balance these factors against one another in determining which explanatory hypothesis is the best. Despite the difficulty in explaining what makes one explanation better than another, we do sometimes have a clear sense that one explanation is better than another, as the examples above illustrate.

The inference to the best explanation response to skepticism holds that the hypothesis that there is a material world of roughly the sort we believe there to be is the best explanation for our sense experience. Bertrand Russell, a contemporary of Moore's, was an early proponent of this view:

> There is no logical impossibility in the supposition that the whole of life is a dream, in which we ourselves create all the objects that come before us. But although this is not logically impossible, there is no reason whatever to suppose that it is true; and it is, in fact, a less simple hypothesis, viewed as a means of accounting for the facts of our own life, than the common-sense hypothesis that there are really objects independent of us, whose action on us causes our sensations.[9]

More recently Peter Lipton writes:

> [As] part of an answer to the Cartesian skeptic who asks how we know that the world is not just a dream or that we are not just brains in vats, the realist may argue that we are entitled to believe in the external world since hypotheses that presuppose it provide the best explanation of our experiences. It is possible that it is all a dream, or that we are brains in vats, but these are less good explanations of the course of our experiences than the ones we all believe, so we are rationally entitled to our belief in the external world.[10]

So, consider my sense experience of my hand. One explanation for my having this experience is that there is a hand before me and I see it. Of course, there are other possible explanations for why I have that sense experience. It could be the product of a Cartesian demon, a computer stimulating my envatted brain, or the product of an extremely orderly and realistic dream. But, according to the proponent of this approach, these explanations are much more complicated. Since these are less good explanations of my experience than the explanation that there really is a hand before me, I am justified in believing that there is a hand before me.

---

[9] Bertrand Russell, *The Problems of Philosophy* (Oxford: Oxford University Press, 1912), pp. 22–23.

[10] Peter Lipton, *Inference to the Best Explanation* (London: Routledge, 1993), p. 72.

Let us return to the argument from ignorance. A proponent of the inference to the best explanation approach, an "abductivist," might hold that my sense experience of a hand is so well explained by the hypothesis that there is a hand before me that I know it to be true. In other words, he might hold that it is such a good explanation, that (2') is true and (2) is false. Like Moore, the abductivist holds that we know that (h), but he holds that such knowledge can be supported by inference to the best explanation. More generally, he might argue that the existence an external world of roughly the sort we take there to be is such a good explanation that we know that such an external world exists.

There are, however, a variety of objections to this view. Some philosophers wonder whether the hypothesis that there is a hand before me is the best explanation for my experience. Consider, for example, Bishop Berkeley's view that our sense experience is caused, not by a plurality of material objects, but by God. On Berkeley's view, there is just one divine cause for *all* sense experiences. In some respects, this is an extremely simple and economical hypothesis. In other respects, it might be a less satisfactory explanation. We might wonder, for example, how does an immaterial being such as God cause other immaterial beings to have sensations? Whether the hypothesis that there is an external world is a better explanation for our experiences than all competitors is certainly debatable.

Another objection questions whether the degree of justification that we get from inference to the best explanation would be sufficient for knowledge. Sometimes an explanatory hypothesis is better than alternatives and reasonable to believe without its being justified to the extent required for knowledge. So, for example, suppose that the police know that the art museum was robbed, that Jones was seen near the art museum the night of the crime, and that Jones has been arrested for burglary in the past. The hypothesis that Jones robbed the museum might be a better explanation than any alternative, but it might not be sufficiently justified to count as knowledge. So, consider again the passage by Lipton. Lipton claims that we are rationally entitled to believe in the external world because that hypothesis is the best explanation of our experience. A critic might wonder, however, just how high is that degree of justification? Even if the hypothesis that there is an external world is a good explanation, and better than all competitors, a critic might object that the degree of justification it enjoys is not high enough for knowledge.

Finally, let us consider the following objection. Suppose that a certain hypothesis, p, is the best explanation for S's data. Does this make S justified in believing that p? Or does S have to be justified in believing that p is the best explanation? Let us consider the first alternative. Suppose that S is having a certain sense experience. Let's suppose that it is the sense experience of a regular dodecagon, a twelve sided figure. Suppose further that S has not counted the sides and is not very good at visually identifying shapes with more than five sides. Now, it seems that in one sense the best explanation for his having that sense experience is that there is a dodecagon before him and he sees it. So, let's assume that the hypothesis that there is a dodecagon before him and he sees it is the best explanation for S's experience. But does this fact make S justified in believing that there is a dodecagon before him? It seems that the answer is "no." If S were to happen to believe that there is a dodecagon before him, it does not seem that this belief is justified and it does not seem that his belief would be an instance of knowledge. So, it does not seem that the fact that p is the best explanation for S's sense experience makes S justified in believing that p. If this is right, then the fact that the hypothesis that there is an external world is the best explanation for our experiences would not by itself make us justified in believing that it is true.

Let us consider the second alternative. Suppose that S *is* justified in believing that p is the best explanation for his experience. In this case, it seems plausible to think that S is justified in believing that p. In particular, it seems plausible to think that if one is justified in believing that the best explanation for one's sense experiences is that there is an external world of roughly the sort we think there is, then one is justified in believing that hypothesis.

Some critics argue, however, that very few people have in fact considered or weighed the merits of the various alternative explanations, so very few people actually *are* justified in believing that the external world hypothesis is the best explanation for their sense experiences. Thus, they claim that the inference to the best explanation account fails as an explanation for ordinary people's knowledge of the external world, not to mention the knowledge enjoyed by children and animals. If our knowledge of the external world depended on such an inference, then very few people would have such knowledge. But since it is false that very few have such knowledge, they conclude that our knowledge of the external world does not depend on such an inference. This objection does not claim that inference to the best explanation is not a source of knowledge of the external world. It claims, rather, that such an inference is not required for such knowledge.

Suppose we agree, however, that we *do* know a great deal about the external world even without being justified in believing that the external world hypothesis is the best explanation for our sense experiences. In that case, we might wonder why we can't respond to the skeptical arguments in some other way, say, for example, in Moorean fashion. Why would we *need* the abductivist's inference in order to respond to the argument from ignorance? Perhaps it would be good to have such an inference available. But it is not clear that one must take this approach in order to respond to the argument from ignorance or, more generally, to skepticism.

We have considered several skeptical arguments and a variety of responses to them. Some of these responses will seem better than others. There are also responses we have not considered, and to many these responses will seem superior to those we have briefly discussed here. As we noted at the beginning of this chapter, we have only skimmed the surface of a deep debate.

8 The problem of the criterion

In examining theories about what makes beliefs justified or instances of knowledge and in considering various responses to skepticism, we have assumed that we can pick out instances of justified belief and knowledge. We have rejected various philosophical claims about knowledge and justification because they were incompatible with what we take ourselves to know or be justified in believing. For example, when we considered in the last chapter the view that knowledge required certainty, we argued that since we *do* know things that aren't certain, knowledge does not require certainty. We rejected a view about what knowledge required because it conflicted with what we took ourselves to know. Similarly, we have assumed in various chapters that children and animals have knowledge, and therefore certain theories of knowledge are mistaken. To some it may seem that this is the wrong way to approach the problems of epistemology. To others this seems like a reasonable approach. In this chapter we shall consider one way of defending this approach to the problems of epistemology and we shall consider a variety of objections to it.

Chisholm and the problem of the criterion

In *The Problem of the Criterion*, Roderick Chisholm identifies two main questions in the theory of knowledge:

A *What* do we know? What is the *extent* of our knowledge?
B How are we to decide *whether* we know? What are the *criteria* of knowledge?

Chisholm distinguishes between three general approaches to these questions: skepticism, methodism, and particularism. Let us consider briefly what he says about each. He tells us that we can formulate the skeptical view as: "You cannot answer question A until you have answered question B. And you cannot answer question B until you have answered question A. Therefore, you cannot answer either question. You cannot know what, if anything, you know, and there is no possible way for you to decide in any particular case."[1] Chisholm's remark suggests that he is concerned with a "second level" skepticism. This sort of skepticism does not deny that we know things. It holds, rather, that if we do know anything, we cannot know that we know it.

Unlike the skeptic, the methodist assumes that he has an answer to question B, and he then tries to work out an answer to question A. In other words, he begins with a criterion of knowledge and then uses it to determine the extent of his knowledge. Chisholm takes the empiricism of John Locke and David Hume to be a species of methodism. According to Chisholm, Locke held that in order for a belief to be an instance of knowledge it had to be related in certain ways to our sensations. Hume followed Locke in adopting the empiricist criterion, and found that when it is applied consistently we have no knowledge of the physical world or other minds. Indeed, it seems that a consistent application of the empiricist criterion implies that we cannot have knowledge of the past either. All we can know is that there are certain sensations here and now.

The particularist thinks he has an answer to A, and then he tries to work out an answer to B. Chisholm takes G. E. Moore and the eighteenth-century Scottish philosopher Thomas Reid to be particularists. Reid believed that Hume's criterion implied that we do not know there are physical objects and other people, and since, Reid held, we *do* know such things, we know *ipso facto* that Hume's criterion is false. Moore held that he knew a great many things about the world — for example, that there are other people, that they have bodies and think and feel, that he was smaller when he was born, and so forth. And Moore held that he *knew* that he knew these things and that others know similar things. Given the options of skepticism, methodism, and particularism, Chisholm says, "I suggest the third possibility is the most reasonable."[2]

---

[1] Roderick M. Chisholm, *The Problem of the Criterion* (Milwaukee: Marquette University Press, 1973), p. 14.

[2] *Ibid.*, p. 21.

Let us consider more closely what is involved in methodism and particularism. There are two general points worth making. First, there are different ways of understanding methodism and particularism. One way is to view them as making claims about which justifies which of two sorts of *epistemic* knowledge.[3] Methodism claims that our knowledge of particular epistemic propositions is based on our knowledge of general epistemic principles, while particularism says that it is the other way around. Particularism claims that our knowledge of general epistemic principles is based on our knowledge of particular epistemic propositions. Second, Chisholm's two questions concern the extent and criteria of *knowledge*. But clearly we could ask similar questions about other important epistemic concepts, such as justification. We might ask, for example, what is the extent of our justified belief, and what are the criteria of justification? I shall construe particularism and methodism to be making claims not only about knowledge, but about justification as well.

In order to clarify these views, let's consider the following three propositions:

(a) I have hands.

(b) I know I have hands.

(c) I am justified in believing that I have hands.

Propositions (b) and (c), unlike (a), are *epistemic* propositions. Both (b) and (c) make epistemic claims about what I know or am justified in believing. Furthermore, (b) and (c) are *particular* epistemic propositions rather than general epistemic principles or criteria that tell us under what conditions a belief is justified or an instance of knowledge. Methodism tells us that our knowing particular epistemic propositions such as (b) and (c) depends on our knowing some general epistemic principle or criterion. Particularism says that it doesn't. On the contrary, particularism holds that our knowing general epistemic principles depends on our knowing particular epistemic propositions. In holding that our knowledge of particular epistemic propositions does not depend on our knowing general epistemic criteria of the sort the methodist thinks we need, we should not assume that the

---

[3] This is the view that Ernest Sosa takes. See his "The Foundations of Foundationalism," *Nous*, 14 (November 1980).

particularist is claiming that knowledge of particular epistemic propositions is basic knowledge. The particularist's claim is actually a fairly modest
one. He is simply claiming that one sort of knowledge or justified belief is
not based on another sort of knowledge or justified belief, and to say
that knowledge of A is not based on knowledge of B is not to imply that
knowledge of A is basic.

In describing particularism and methodism, Chisholm refers to "criteria
of knowledge." What sort of criteria does he have in mind? Chisholm
himself does not say, but presumably these would be principles that tell
us under what conditions a belief has some epistemic feature, such as being
an instance of knowledge or justified. Such principles would have the
following form, "If belief B has F, then B is an instance of knowledge
(justified)" or "Belief B is an instance of knowledge (justified) if and only if B
has F." Since the methodist holds that knowledge of particular epistemic
facts depends on our knowing general epistemic principles, I assume that
the relevant criteria and principles would enable us to pick out particular
epistemic facts by picking out nonepistemic facts and properties. Also,
I assume that while F might be a very complex property, it won't itself
contain any epistemic properties. If F did contain some epistemic property,
then presumably the methodist would hold that we would need some *further*
criterion in order to know that a belief had F.

The sort of principle I take the methodist to require has its analogue in
ethics. Consider, for example, moral principles of the form, "If act A has F,
then act A is right." Simple hedonistic utilitarianism holds, roughly, that
if an act A produces as much utility as any alternative act, then A is right.
This simple form of hedonism attempts to tell us what nonethical feature of
acts − e.g. producing a certain balance of pleasure over pain − makes acts
right. Immanuel Kant offers a similar sort of formula in suggesting that
one's performing some act is right if and only if in performing that act one
treats no one as a mere means. Such criteria in ethics would, if they were
true, enable us to pick out right actions by picking out the nonethical
features of actions.

But what about principles of the following form: If belief B has F, then B is
prima facie an instance of knowledge (justified)? Could methodism be committed only to the more modest view that knowledge of some particular
epistemic propositions depends on our knowing such *prima facie* principles?
I assume, perhaps controversially, that the answer is "no." I take the

methodist to hold that we need a criterion or epistemic principle that will tell us when a belief is justified or an instance of knowledge. But principles of *prima facie* justification can only tell us when a belief is *prima facie* justified or *prima facie* an instance of knowledge. Even if we know a principle of the form, "If belief B has F, then B is *prima facie* justified," and we know that B has F, nothing follows about whether B *is* justified. *Prima facie* principles don't provide the sort of criterion that the methodist thinks we need.

As we have seen, Chisholm endorses particularism. But the kind of particularism that Chisholm favors and the kind he finds in Reid and Moore is a "common sense" particularism that holds that we and others know various facts about the world around us. These include such obvious truisms as, there are other people, they have bodies, they think and feel, and so on. They also include various epistemic propositions – for example, that most people know their own names, they know they have bodies, they know that there are other people. Common sense particularists deny that our knowledge of such particular epistemic facts depends on our knowledge of general epistemic principles of the sort the methodist requires.

The common sense particularism that Chisholm endorses is only one form of particularism. There can certainly be different kinds of particularists. One might be, for example, a "Cartesian" particularist and hold that one's knowledge is confined to one's own existence and mental states, to some simple necessary truths, and to the epistemic propositions that we know such things. He would hold that he is thinking and that he knows that he is thinking. The class of epistemic facts the Cartesian particularist claims to know is only a small subset of what the common sense particularist claims to know, but, like the latter, the Cartesian particularist holds that his knowledge of those particular epistemic propositions does not depend on his knowing some general epistemic principle. On the other hand, one might be a particularist and claim to know much more than the common sense or the Cartesian particularist. Someone might claim that among the things he knows is that there has been no evolution, that his people have always inhabited the land they now occupy, and that he is God's appointed messenger. Yet he still might be a particularist insofar as he held that his knowledge of such epistemic facts did not depend on his knowing any general epistemic principle.

What's wrong with methodism?

Chisholm offers a variety of criticisms of methodism. Some of these, however, do not seem compelling. For example, according to Chisholm, the methodist holds that we must begin with a general criterion of knowledge. Chisholm objects, "How can one *begin* with a broad generalization?...[The methodist] leaves us completely in the dark so far as concerns what *reasons* he may have for adopting this particular criterion rather than some other."[4] But as Robert Amico points out, there are several problems with this objection.[5] First, if Chisholm is objecting to the broadness of the criterion, it is not clear why being broad is a problem. Isn't broadness a desirable feature of a criterion? As Amico suggests, being broad would seem to be a desirable feature of a criterion because it suggests that the criterion would be applicable to many cases. Furthermore, Chisholm objects that the methodist offers no reasons for his criterion. Perhaps he means to object that the methodist gives no argument why one should adopt this criterion rather than some other. But it is not clear why this is a fatal objection to methodism. Suppose the methodist held that knowledge of the criterion was basic or direct knowledge, that it was not based on inference. Perhaps he would hold that knowledge of his criterion was a matter of direct *a priori* insight.

If methodism is not to be rejected because it begins with a broad criterion, or because no reasons or arguments are given for the criterion, then what's wrong with methodism? What is to be said in favor of Chisholm's common sense particularism?

In thinking about methodism, we might begin with the following observations from St. Augustine:

> [H]e who says "I know I am alive" says that he knows one single thing. Further, if he says, "I know that I know I am alive," now there are two; but that he knows these two is a third thing to know.[6]

---

[4] Roderick M. Chisholm, *The Foundations of Knowing* (Minneapolis: The University of Minnesota Press, 1982), p. 67.

[5] Robert P. Amico, *The Problem of the Criterion* (Lanham, MD: Rowman and Littlefield, 1993), pp. 78–79.

[6] St. Augustine, *On the Trinity* in *The Essential Augustine*, ed. Vernon J. Bourke (Indianapolis: Hackett, 1974), p. 35.

By "alive," I take Augustine to mean conscious or thinking. More importantly, I take him to hold that we can know that we are conscious or thinking, and that we can know *that* we know this. But our epistemic knowledge in this case is not epistemically dependent on our knowing some general criterion of knowledge. It is not deduced from such a principle. It is not as though St. Augustine says that when he knows that he knows he is thinking, he knows *three* things: (i) that he is thinking, (ii) that he knows he is thinking, and some criterion of knowledge from which knowledge of (ii) is deduced.

Along these same lines, we might consider the following passage from Descartes's third *Meditation*:

> I am certain that I am a thinking thing. Do I not therefore know what is required for my being certain about anything? In this first item of knowledge there is simply a clear and distinct perception of what I am asserting; this would not be enough to make me certain of the truth of the matter if it could ever turn out that something I perceived with such clarity and distinctness is false. So now I seem to be able to lay it down as a general rule that whatever I perceive very clearly and distinctly is true.[7]

In this passage, Descartes begins with a particular epistemic fact – his being certain that he is a thinking being. He then asks, "Do I not therefore also know what is required for my being certain of anything?" The general rule that "whatever I perceive very clearly and distinctly is true" seems to be supported by his recognition of his certainty that he exists. The recognition of that particular epistemic fact does not seem to be based on his apprehension of the general principle.

St. Augustine and Descartes both suggest that we know that we think and, moreover, we know that we know this. Neither holds that this epistemic knowledge is based on our knowing some general criterion. If they are right, then it seems that methodism is false. More generally, we may say each of us knows a lot about his own mental states. We know, for example, that we are happy or sad or thinking about Boston. Not only do we know such things, we know that we know them. But most of us would be hard pressed to cite any general criterion of knowledge on which it is based.

---

[7] Descartes, René, *Meditations* in *The Philosophical Works of Descartes*, vol. II, ed. J. Cottingham, R. Stoothoff, and D. Murdoch (Cambridge: Cambridge University Press, 1991), p. 24.

Indeed, it is not clear that reflective epistemologists would all point to the same epistemic principles in order to explain how they know such a thing. So, it seems that our knowing that we know things about our own mental states does not depend on our knowing some general criterion of knowledge. If this is right, then methodism is false.

Now, the sort of epistemic knowledge that Chisholm and the common sense particularists take themselves to have is not confined to knowledge of one's existence and one's own mental states. Their particularism ranges more broadly and includes more. Consider, for example, the following epistemic propositions:

(i) It is beyond reasonable doubt that I was alive five minutes ago.
(ii) I know that I was alive five minutes ago.

Now, suppose Chisholm argues this away:

Argument A

(1) If methodism is true, then I know (i) and (ii) only if I know the relevant criterion of knowledge.
(2) I don't know the relevant criterion of knowledge.
(3) But I do know (i) and (ii).
(4) Therefore, methodism is false.

It seems that many people know propositions like (i) and (ii) without knowing the relevant criteria. Indeed, many philosophers know things like (i) and (ii) without knowing the relevant criteria. Many philosophers disagree about what the relevant criteria are. Just as one might reject methodism because it would rule out our having the sort of knowledge that St. Augustine and Descartes point to, so we might reject methodism because it would rule out our knowing (i) and (ii). As Chisholm says, one of the merits of his brand of particularism is that it is compatible with the fact that "there are many things that, quite obviously, we do know to be true."[8] What Chisholm is telling us is that if methodism and skepticism were true, we would not know particular epistemic propositions like (i) and (ii). But since we do know them and since we don't know the relevant principles, methodism and skepticism are false.

---

[8] Roderick Chisholm, *The Foundations of Knowing*, p. 69.

Chisholm claims that one advantage of his common sense particularism is that it corresponds with what we do in fact know. But one might object that this advantage is not unique to particularism. Couldn't there be a "common sense" methodism that corresponds with what we ordinarily think we know? Amico writes, "Chisholm's position does have the merit of corresponding to what we ordinarily take ourselves to know . . . [But there] is nothing about methodism that precludes the possibility of its coinciding with our common sense beliefs."[9]

Perhaps someone could know much of what common sense particularists claim to know on the basis of a "common sense" criterion of knowledge. But Chisholm might hold that this misses the point. The problem with methodism is not that it implies that it is impossible to know particular epistemic propositions such as (i) and (ii). The problem is rather that from methodism *and* our ignorance of the relevant general principles, it follows that we don't in fact know (i) and (ii). Given that we don't know the relevant principles, methodism implies that we don't know the sorts of things we do know. So, Chisholm might say, *that's* what's wrong with methodism.

The objection from supervenience

There are a variety of objections to particularism and to Chisholm's brand of common sense particularism. One line of objection arises in connection with the evaluative nature of epistemic concepts, like knowledge and justification. As we noted in Chapter 3, many philosophers hold that normative and evaluative properties supervene on nonnormative and nonevaluative properties. So, just as the goodness of an apple depends on its having certain good-making properties and the rightness of an action depends on its having certain right-making properties, so too one's belief is justified in virtue of its having certain justification-making properties. How might this be thought to support methodism? Consider the following passage from R. M. Hare's *The Language of Morals*:

> [I]f we knew all of the descriptive properties which a particular strawberry had . . . and if we knew also the meaning of the word 'good', then what else should we require to know, in order to be able to tell whether a strawberry was a good one? Once the question is put this way, the answer should

---

[9] Amico, pp. 84–88.

be apparent. We should require to know, what are the criteria in virtue of which a strawberry is to be called a good one, or what is the standard of goodness for strawberries. We should require to be given the major premiss.[10]

In Hare's view knowledge of the descriptive or nonevaluative properties of a strawberry is not sufficient for one to know it to be good. Knowing that a particular strawberry is good requires or depends on knowing a standard or criterion for the goodness of strawberries. Though Hare refers to our knowledge of the goodness of strawberries, we may take him as making a general claim about our knowing the goodness of other sorts of particulars. A similar view about our knowledge of right and wrong is suggested by John Stuart Mill. Mill writes, "A test of right and wrong must be the means, one would think, of ascertaining what is right or wrong, and not a consequence of having already attained it."[11]

Some philosophers have taken a similar view in epistemology. For example, William Alston writes:

> In taking a belief to be justified, we are evaluating it in a certain way. And, like any evaluative property, epistemic justification is a supervenient property, the application of which is based on more fundamental properties . . . Hence, in order for me to be justified in believing that S's belief that p is justified, I must be justified in certain other beliefs, viz., that S's belief that p possesses a certain property Q, and that Q renders its possessor justified. (Another way of formulating this last belief is: a belief that there is a valid epistemic principle to the effect that any belief that has Q is justified.)[12]

Alston suggests that in order to be justified in believing that some particular belief is justified one must be justified in believing some general epistemic principle. He supports this view by appealing to the supervenient character of epistemic properties.

Reflection on the passages by Hare and Alston suggests the following principle:

E: One is justified in believing that x has F (where F is an evaluative property) only if one is justified in believing both (a) that x has some

---

[10] R. M. Hare, *The Language of Morals* (Oxford: Oxford University Press, 1952), p. 111.

[11] John Stuart Mill, *Utilitarianism* (Indianapolis: Hackett, 1979).

[12] William Alston, "Two Types of Foundationalism," *The Journal of Philosophy*, 73 (April 1976), 170; cf. "Some Remarks on Chisholm's Epistemology," *Nous*, 14 (November 1980), 579.

nonevaluative property Q, and (b) a general principle to the effect that whatever has Q has F.

According to E, one is justified in a particular attribution of an evaluative property only if one is justified in believing some general evaluative principle. E seems to be a rationale for accepting methodism. But is E true? Does it provide us with a good reason for accepting methodism?

Many critics would say "no." First, we should be careful not to confuse claims about exemplification with claims about application. In assuming that evaluative properties are supervenient, we assume that they are *exemplified* in virtue of the exemplification of nonevaluative properties. But from this it does not follow that the *application* or attribution of evaluative properties must be based on justified belief that a thing has those properties or in a general evaluative principle. So, E does not follow from the mere fact that evaluative properties are supervenient. Accepting the supervenient character of epistemic properties does not commit one to accepting E.

Second, it seems plausible that there are justified attributions of supervenient properties that do not depend on justified belief in general principles. Many philosophers hold, for example, that mental properties supervene on physical properties. The mental properties of being in pain or being conscious supervene on various physical properties, e.g. physical properties of one's brain. But does our knowledge that we are in pain depend on our knowing some other propositions such as (a) I have F, and (b) whatever has F is in pain? Surely, I can know that I am in pain or conscious without knowing what physical properties pain or consciousness supervene on or even knowing that I have those properties. My knowledge that I am in pain does not depend on my knowing some general principle about the connection between being in a certain physical state and being in pain.

Third, it seems plausible that there are justified attributions of evaluative properties that are not based on justified belief in general evaluative principles. Consider, for example, someone driving in the mountains and suddenly coming on a spectacular mountain vista. He thinks, "That's beautiful!" It is plausible to think such a belief can be justified without one's being justified in believing some general principle about beautiful-making properties. We often form justified beliefs about the beauty of things when we are *struck* by their beauty. In such cases, our beliefs seem based on our experience of the thing and not based on beliefs that it has some property F and that whatever has F is beautiful.

Accepting the evaluative and supervenient character of epistemic properties does not, then, commit one to accepting Principle E or methodism. More importantly, it does not commit one to rejecting particularism.

Does particularism stifle epistemic inquiry?

Laurence BonJour criticizes the common sense particularism of Chisholm and Moore. Concerning particularism, BonJour writes:

> to accept commonsense convictions as Moore and other particularists do, does appear to rule out illegitimately even the possibility that skepticism might in fact be true, that common sense might be mistaken. And, equally importantly, if this solution is taken at face value, it would have the effect of stifling or short-circuiting epistemological inquiry at least as effectively as would simply acquiescing in skepticism.[13]

BonJour makes a variety of objections here. Let us begin with the objection that particularism "stifles" epistemological inquiry. Is this true? It does not seem that particularism stifles the inquiry into criteria of knowledge and justification. On the contrary, Chisholm took the search for such criteria to be one of the principle aims of epistemological inquiry. Even if we assume that we do know various things about the world around us, we might still wonder how we know them. We might still seek philosophical answers to that question. Chisholm might suggest that our situation in epistemology is no different from that which one might find in moral philosophy. We might be convinced, for example, that certain actions are morally wrong, and yet seek to explain why they are wrong. I am convinced, for example, that it would be morally wrong for me now to torture my secretary to death. But is it wrong because it fails to maximize utility, because it fails to treat her as an end in herself, or for some other reason? Even if we assume that such an action is wrong, why would that stifle our attempts to discover criteria of right and wrong? Moreover, even if we assume that we do know the sorts of things that the skeptic denies we do, we need not treat skeptical arguments as "idle" and hold that they ought to be ignored. One might adopt a particularist approach and continue to take skeptical arguments seriously, attempting to identify what plausible, yet mistaken, assumptions

---

[13] Laurence BonJour, *Epistemology* (Lanham, MD: Rowman and Littlefield, 2002), p. 265.

yield skeptical conclusions. We might think that the serious consideration of skeptical arguments reveals a lot about the nature of knowledge and justification. It does not seem, therefore, that particularism stifles epistemological inquiry.

BonJour also objects that particularism appears to rule out illegitimately the possibility that skepticism is true. But here we must be careful. Does particularism rule out the possibility that skepticism is true? Not if the relevant sense of "possibility" is that of "logical possibility." Both Chisholm and Moore admit that it is logically possible that skepticism is true. They grant that it is logically possible that we know nothing or next to nothing about the external world. They grant the possibility of deception by evil demons or dream experiences. Of course, both Chisholm and Moore would deny that skepticism is "epistemically possible" in the sense that, given what we know, it is reasonable to believe that skepticism is true. Both would hold that since we do know that we know much about the external world it is not reasonable to accept skepticism about the external world. But why should this be to rule out the possibility of skepticism *illegitimately*?

Moser's objections to common sense particularism

Paul Moser raises a variety of objections to Chisholm's common sense particularism. First, he points out that common sense judgments are sometimes false. Second, he raises questions about the epistemic status of the particular epistemic judgments that the common sense philosopher takes as data. Finally, Moser expresses doubts about "question-begging" philosophical strategies. Let's consider Moser's criticisms more closely.

Moser takes the common sense tradition to hold "that we have pretheoretical access, *via* 'intuition' or 'common sense,' to certain considerations about justification, and these considerations can support one epistemological view over others." Yet, Moser writes,

> Intuitive judgments and common sense judgments can, and sometimes do, result from special, even biased, linguistic training. Why then should we regard such judgments as *automatically* epistemically privileged? Intuitive judgments and common-sense judgments certainly can be false, as a little reflection illustrates. Such judgments, furthermore, seem not always to be supported by the best available evidence. Consider, for instance, how various

judgments of "common sense" are at odds with our best available evidence from the sciences or even from ordinary perception. It is unclear, then, why we should regard our intuitive or common sense judgments as the basis for our standards for justification.[14]

Moser points out that some "common sense" judgements are false and at odds with the evidence we have from science and even ordinary perception. Given this fact, why should we take common sense judgments as data for epistemological inquiry?

In reply to Moser, the common sense particularist might make the following points. First, he might agree that there are some things that might be called "common sense" that are false and contrary to the evidence we have from the senses and science. Moore, for example, in his essay "A Defence of Common Sense" wrote:

> The phrases 'Common Sense view of the world' or 'Common Sense beliefs'
> (as used by philosophers) are, of course, extraordinarily vague; and for all
> I know, there may be many propositions which may be properly called
> features in 'the Common Sense view of the world' or 'Common Sense beliefs',
> which are not true, and which deserve to mentioned with the contempt with
> which some philosophers speak of 'Common Sense beliefs'.[15]

Moore clearly does not want to defend as true or even reasonable everything that might be called a common sense belief. I assume that the same is true of Chisholm. It seems clear that Moore and Chisholm do not believe that a belief is true, justified, or an instance of knowledge *because* it is a common sense belief. They do not accept a general criterion of the form, "If a belief B is a common sense belief, then B is justified or an instance of knowledge." Second, Moore and Chisholm do not claim that their knowledge of particular epistemic beliefs is based on their knowing such a criterion. Such a view would be incompatible with their being common sense *particularists*. They do not accept the proposition, it is reasonable to believe that one was alive yesterday, because that proposition is a common sense proposition. Third, while Moore and Chisholm do not want to defend all common sense beliefs, it is clear that they think they *do* know *some* propositions, and that *some* of the propositions they know are also common sense propositions

[14] Paul Moser, "Epistemological Fission," *The Monist*, 81 (1998), 364.
[15] G. E. Moore, "A Defence of Common Sense," *Philosophical Papers* (London: George Allen and Unwin, 1959), p. 45.

insofar as they are widely believed and known by almost everyone. These include propositions such as there are other people, other people think and feel, and there were many people alive in the past. Chisholm and Moore would take themselves to know these propositions and to know that they know them. But clearly to accept these propositions is *not* to accept any proposition that is at odds with our best available evidence from the sciences or ordinary perception. So, while Moser might be right to criticize some common sense beliefs, it is not clear that there is any good reason to claim that common sense particularism is committed to accepting propositions that are contrary to the best available evidence of the sciences or sense perception.

Moser also raises a question about the epistemic status of our particular epistemic judgments. He writes,

> It is often left unclear what the epistemic status of the relevant preanalytic epistemic data is supposed to be. Such data, we hear, are accessed by "intuitions" or by "common sense." We thus have some epistemologists talking as follows: "Intuitively (or commonsensically), justification resides in a particular case like *this*, and does not reside in a case like *that*." A statement of this sort aims to guide our formulation of a notion of justification or at least a general explanatory principle concerning justification. A simple question arises: is such a statement *self*-justifying, with no need of independent epistemic support? If so, what notion of self-justification can sanction the deliverances of intuition or common sense, but exclude spontaneous judgments no better, epistemically, than mere prejudice or guesswork?[16]

Moser suggests that the common sense tradition holds that these epistemic facts are accessed *via* "intuition" or "common sense." If this means that the common sense tradition holds that we have knowledge of epistemic facts on the basis of a faculty of common sense or intuition, as we have knowledge of the past on the basis of a faculty of memory, there seems to be no reason to accept this claim. There is no reason to think that Moore and Chisholm hold that particular epistemic propositions are known through a faculty of intuition or common sense. Does the common sense particularist hold that particular epistemic propositions are "self-justifying"? Moser wonders what a self-justifying proposition is supposed to be and finds the

---

[16] *Ibid.*, p. 363.

notion of self-justification troublesome. Perhaps it is troublesome. How could a belief or a proposition justify itself? Still, there is no reason to think that Moore or Chisholm holds that particular epistemic propositions are self-justifying.

But what *does* make particular epistemic beliefs justified? That, of course, is an interesting problem for epistemology. Perhaps they are justified in virtue of belonging to a (sufficiently broad and comprehensive) coherent body of beliefs or because they are the product of a reliable faculty or intellectual virtue or because they are appropriately related to what is given in experience. While it is not clear what justifies particular epistemic beliefs, particularists like Moore and Chisholm claim that we should distinguish between knowing *that* some particular belief is true and knowing *how* we know it or knowing *what* justifies that belief. One can have the former sort of knowledge without the latter. Just as one might know that some act is wrong without knowing what makes it wrong, so too one might know that one's belief is knowledge or justified without knowing what makes it so. So, in one respect, Moser is right that the epistemic status of these epistemic beliefs is unclear or problematic. It is hard to say, even for the common sense philosopher, *what* makes these epistemic beliefs justified. But from the fact that it is unclear what justifies these beliefs it does not follow that one cannot know that they are justified. So the common sense philosopher may ask, with Moser, "What justifies particular epistemic propositions?" But we have seen no reason why he cannot answer that question by using his particular epistemic beliefs as data.

Many critics have charged that Chisholm's defense of particularism is "question-begging." Chisholm is aware that his defense of particularism is open to the charge of begging the question. What is his response? Well, he admits it. He holds that his defense of particularism *does* beg the question against those opposing views:

> But in all this I have presupposed the approach I have called "particularism." The "methodist" and the "skeptic" will tell us that we have started in the wrong place. If we now try to reason with them, then, I am afraid we will be back on the wheel.

> What few philosophers have had the courage to realize is this: we can deal with the problem only by begging the question. It seems to me that, if we do

recognize this fact, as we should, then it is unseemly for us to pretend that it isn't so.

One may object: "Doesn't this mean that the skeptic is right after all?" I would answer: "Not at all. His view is only one of the three possibilities and in itself has no more to recommend it than the others do. And in favor of our approach is the fact that we *do* know many things after all."[17]

But what is the sort of question-begging that Chisholm admits to here? I think Chisholm admits that his defense of particularism begs the question in the sense that it assumes to be true what others have denied. Chisholm assumes that we do know some particular epistemic facts without knowing the relevant general epistemic principles. But this is what the methodist and skeptic deny. The same, of course, is true of Argument A above. In assuming that we do know some particular epistemic facts without knowing the relevant criteria, we are assuming something the methodist and the skeptic deny. So, in that respect, Argument A is also question begging.[18] Still, Chisholm maintains that in spite of the fact that his defense of particularism begs the question against these opposing views, it is nevertheless more reasonable to accept particularism than the opposing views.

But is such a question-begging defense or response philosophically acceptable? Consider the following opposing view expressed by Moser:

If we allow such question begging in general, we can support *any* disputed position we prefer. Simply beg the key question in any dispute regarding the preferred position. Given that strategy, argument becomes superfluous in the way that circular argument is typically pointless. Question-begging strategies promote an undesirable arbitrariness in philosophical debate. They are thus rationally inconclusive relative to the questions under dispute.[19]

---

[17] Roderick Chisholm, *Theory of Knowledge*, 2nd edn., p. 121.

[18] The sort of begging the question that Chisholm admits is that he assumes what the methodist and skeptic denies. Note that this is not a matter of "circular" reasoning in which one's knowledge of the premises is epistemically dependent upon knowledge of the conclusion. In Argument A, for example, one's knowledge of the premises is not epistemically dependent upon knowledge of the conclusion. It is not as though one's knowledge of the premises is epistemically dependent upon knowing that methodism is false.

[19] Paul Moser and Arnold vander Nat, *Human Knowledge: Classical and Contemporary Approaches*, 2nd edn., ed. Moser and vander Nat (Oxford: Oxford University Press, 1995), p. 27.

Moser assumes that if we allow question-begging arguments, then *any* position can be supported and argument in general becomes pointless. But is this true? Perhaps it is true if one thinks that supporting a position involves nothing more than giving an argument for it. But, of course, we might hold that there is more to supporting a position than simply giving an argument for it. We might hold that supporting a position involves giving an argument for it that has premises that one knows or that one is justified in believing. In this stronger, "epistemic," sense of supporting a position, it does not follow that one can support every position even if we allow question-begging arguments. For some question-begging arguments will have premises that are not known and which one is not episte- mically justified in believing. We need not hold, therefore, that if we allow question-begging arguments, then every position can be supported in this stronger epistemic sense. Consequently, we need not hold that if we allow question-begging arguments, then all question-begging arguments are epi- stemically on a par in terms of the strength of epistemic support that they provide their conclusions.

Must a question-begging strategy such as Chisholm's defense of parti- cularism or a question-begging argument such as Argument A involve an intellectually unsatisfactory procedure and must it be "rationally incon- clusive"? Suppose we take an argument that has premises that are known and that imply the conclusion to be a rationally conclusive argument. It then seems that an argument could be *both* question-begging insofar as it assumes some premise denied by someone *and* rationally conclusive insofar as the argument is valid and the premises are known. If "begging the question" and "rationally conclusive" are understood in this way, then it is false that no question-begging arguments are rationally conclusive. One might say that Chisholm's defense of particularism and Argument A *are* rationally conclusive and question-begging, since the arguments are valid and many people know the premises and yet they involve premises that some have denied.

If some question-begging arguments are rationally conclusive, it does not follow that they all are. Some are rationally conclusive and some aren't. So, endorsing some question-begging arguments as rationally conclusive does not commit us to endorsing them all or to regarding argument as pointless. Furthermore, I would say that if our aim is to reach the truth about the philosophical questions which concern us, then such "question-begging" is not always intellectually vicious. There is nothing intellectually vicious or unsound in reasoning from premises one knows or taking as data what one knows, even if someone has denied it. On the contrary, reasoning from what one knows would seem to be intellectually sound.

Still, I think that one might admit that Chisholm's defense of particularism and Argument A are in another sense "inconclusive." They are inconclusive in the sense that they will not *settle* or *conclude* the debate between the particularist, the methodist, and the skeptic. They might not be rhetorically or dialectically conclusive. But why must we judge the merits of Chisholm's defense of particularism or Argument A by how well it settles that debate? Why not judge it instead by its appeal to a rational, yet uncommitted, audience – to a thoughtful and open-minded jury who consider the plausibility of the premises? More importantly, why must we judge the merits of Chisholm's defense or Argument A by how well it settles a dispute? After all, how many good philosophical arguments really enjoy that feature? Indeed, how many good philosophical arguments *don't* beg the question against some other position? In any case, the settlement of disputes is but one possible aim of philosophical reflection and reasoning and resolving a dispute but one merit or virtue of an argument. Surely there are other aims, such as extending our knowledge and understanding, and other merits or virtues, such as yielding knowledge of the conclusion. From the fact that an argument does not settle the debate between the various parties it does not follow that it yields no knowledge of the conclusion. So, perhaps we should not see Moore and Chisholm engaged in the project of trying to refute or convince the skeptic or methodist by arguing from mutually accepted premises. Chisholm and Moore take as data what they take themselves to know, and we should view them, not as attempting to carry on a debate within the rules of rhetoric, but as attempting to know the answers to the philosophical questions with which they and others are concerned.

Is common sense particularism dogmatic?

Chisholm writes, "We reject the sceptical view according to which there is no reason to believe that the premises of an inductive argument ever confer evidence upon the conclusion. If the sceptical view were true, then we would know next to nothing about the world around us."[20] Being a good particularist, Chisholm holds that since we do know such things, we know that this skeptical view is false. Panayot Butchvarov cites this passage and warns, "We must guard against intemperate and dogmatic attitudes such as those expressed [by Chisholm]."[21] But why is Chisholm's attitude toward skepticism intemperate or dogmatic? Unfortunately, Butchvarov doesn't tell us. It is not as though Chisholm gives no reasons for rejecting skepticism. On the contrary, his reasons seem quite clear – skepticism implies that we know next to nothing about the world around us, but since that's false, it follows that skepticism is false. Perhaps Butchvarov thinks it is intemperate and dogmatic to claim that it is false that we know next to nothing about the world around us. But is such a claim really intemperate? That seems rather overstated. Indeed, perhaps itself a bit intemperate. Perhaps the claim is dogmatic? Dogmatic in the sense of an arrogant assertion? That seems rather harsh. Would it *really* be an arrogant assertion to claim one does know that there are other people? Perhaps it is dogmatic in the sense that Chisholm doesn't give any reasons in the passage cited for claiming that it is false that we know next to nothing about the world around us. But then wouldn't Butchvarov's charge that Chisholm's attitude is dogmatic be just as dogmatic, since he gives no reason for claiming that it is? And, in any case, the mere fact that one asserts something without giving a reason for it does not imply that it is dogmatic. People nondogmatically assert things everyday without actually giving reasons for them. Maybe the idea is that Chisholm asserts things without being able to give any reasons for his claims. But that's just false. Though they won't impress the skeptic, Chisholm can give reasons for thinking that he knows many things about the world around him, reasons having to do with his perceptual takings and what he seems to remember. It is hard to know why Butchvarov thinks Chisholm's attitude is dogmatic or intemperate.

The debate between particularists, methodists, and skeptics is a very old debate and surely there are more objections to each view that we might consider. Indeed, we might wonder whether particularism, methodism, and

---

[20] Roderick Chisholm, "On the Nature of Empirical Evidence," in *Empirical Knowledge: Readings from Contemporary Sources*, ed. Roderick M. Chisholm and Robert J. Swartz (Englewood Cliffs, NJ: Prentice-Hall, 1973), p. 232.

[21] Panayot Butchvarov, *Skepticism about the External World* (Oxford: Oxford University Press, 1998), p. 8.

skepticism are our only options. We might wonder, for example, whether one could have *some* justification for believing particular epistemic propositions that does not depend on one's knowing some general epistemic principle, but hold that this degree of justification does not amount to *knowledge* unless one knows the relevant epistemic principle. Similarly, we might wonder whether our knowledge of particular epistemic principles depends on our knowledge of general epistemic principles and *vice versa*. In other words, might these two types of knowledge be *mutually dependent*? These are possible views. Of course, if Argument A is sound, then neither of these views is correct. For Argument A implies that we know some epistemic propositions without knowing the relevant general principle. As with so many philosophical issues, there is much more one could say. Perhaps, however, we might end with Chisholm's observation, "'The problem of the criterion' seems to be one of the most difficult of all the problems of philosophy. I am tempted to say that one has not yet begun to philosophize until one has faced this problem and has recognized how unappealing, in the end, each of the proposed solutions is."[22]

---

[22] Chisholm, *The Foundations of Knowing*, p. 61.

9   The *a priori*

In this chapter we shall explore some views about *a priori* knowledge and justification. Many philosophers are convinced that we are justified in believing some things *a priori*, but, as we shall see, there are different views about how we might explain or define the concept of *a priori* justification. Moreover, philosophers disagree about the scope or extent of our *a priori* knowledge and justification. In the first section, we shall consider different views about what it is for a proposition to be justified *a priori*. In the second section, we shall consider some views about basic *a priori* justification. Must beliefs that enjoy basic *a priori* justification be certain, indefeasible, and true? Those who answer "yes" favor a "strong" account of *a priori* knowledge and justification. Others favor a more modest account. In the final section, we shall examine some views about what it is for a proposition to be analytic and we will consider briefly whether our *a priori* knowledge is confined to propositions that are analytic.

A priori justification

We know some propositions because we infer them from other things we know. A man might know, for example, that his wife is home because he infers it from the facts that her car is in the driveway, her coat is on the back of the chair, and he hears footsteps upstairs. Or, one might infer from various propositions of geometry that the Pythagorean Theorem is true. Reason or reasoning plays some role in our inferential knowledge. According to one venerable philosophical tradition, however, reason has an additional epistemic role. According to this view, reason itself furnishes us with basically justified beliefs and noninferential knowledge. Consider the following propositions:

(1) All swans are swans.
(2) All squares are rectangles.
(3) Whatever is red is colored.
(4) $7 + 5 = 12$.
(5) If some men are Greeks, then some Greeks are men.

We know these propositions. Indeed, they are among our clearest examples of knowledge. It seems that these propositions are basically justified for us and that our knowledge of them is immediate or noninferential. In order to know them it seems that all we need to do is think about them. We need only consider them and we can "see" intellectually that they are true. Concerning such propositions, Leibniz wrote, "You will find in a hundred places that the Scholastics have said that these propositions are evident *ex terminis*, as soon as the terms are understood..."[1] Similarly, Thomas Reid wrote, "There are...propositions which are no sooner understood than they are believed. The judgment follows the apprehension of them necessarily...There is no searching for evidence; no weighing of arguments; the proposition is not deduced or inferred from another; it has the light of truth in itself, and no occasion to borrow it from another."[2]

We may contrast the way we know (1)–(5) with the way we know the following propositions:

(6) All swans weigh under 40 pounds.
(7) There are at least six red things on the desk.
(8) Nick is a Greek.
(9) I have a headache.

Unlike (1)–(5), we cannot know or be justified in believing these propositions simply by considering or reflecting upon them. Our justification, if any, for believing them seems to be based on our having certain sorts of experience, such as perceptual or introspective experience. Our

---

[1] G. W. Leibniz, *New Essays Concerning Human Understanding*, trans. by Alfred Gideon Langley (La Salle, IL: Open Court, 1949), book IV, chapter 7, p. 462.

[2] Thomas Reid, *Essays on the Intellectual Powers of Man* (Cambridge, MA: The MIT Press, 1969), essay IV, chapter 4, p. 593.

knowledge and justification for believing these propositions is traditionally called *a posteriori* or *empirical*. Again, our knowledge of (1)–(5) seems different in an important way. In such cases, our knowledge and justified belief is not based on what we know through sources such as perception, memory, or introspection. Again, some hold that we know (1)–(5) on the basis of reason alone. When we know something in this way, on the basis of reason alone, our knowledge and justification are said to be *a priori*.

Many philosophers distinguish between *basic* or *immediate a priori* justification and *nonbasic* or *mediate a priori* justification. For most of us, our beliefs in (1)–(5) would seem to enjoy basic *a priori* justification. Our justification does not depend on our inferring them from other propositions we are justified in believing. As Reid would say, each has "the light of truth" in itself and no need to borrow it from another. Not all *a priori* justification, however, is basic. Some of what we are justified in believing *a priori* depends for its justification on other things we are justified in believing *a priori*. Suppose, for example, that you do not have basic *a priori* justification in believing *p*. One way to acquire *a priori* justification for believing *p* is by deducing it from other things you are justified in believing *a priori*. If you acquire *a priori* justification for believing *p* in this way, your belief that *p* enjoys nonbasic or mediate *a priori* justification. For most of us, the Pythagorean Theorem is not basically justified, but we can be justified in believing it *a priori* by deducing or inferring it from other propositions that *are* justified for us *a priori*. In this way, we can acquire nonbasic *a priori* justification in believing it.

Typically, philosophers sympathetic to *a priori* justification claim that it has a foundational structure. The foundation consists of those beliefs that enjoy basic *a priori* justification. Beliefs that enjoy nonbasic *a priori* justification are supported ultimately by one or more beliefs that have basic *a priori* justification.

Many philosophers are convinced that we are justified in believing some things *a priori*. Perhaps what we have said so far conveys a rough sense of the concept. But how might we define or more carefully explicate the concept of *a priori* justification? Let us consider briefly some of the main attempts.

One traditional way of explaining *a priori* knowledge and justification is that it is knowledge or justification that is *independent* of experience. This is the approach that Immanuel Kant takes in his Introduction to *The Critique of Pure Reason*. There Kant defines *a priori* knowledge as knowledge that is absolutely independent of all experience.[3] Kant is concerned with *a priori* knowledge, but we may take a similar view with respect to the concept of *a priori* justification and hold that it is justification that is independent of experience. Such an approach seems promising since it seems plausible that our knowledge and justified belief that, for example, all swans are swans is not dependent on experience. Suppose, then, we consider the following definition:

D15   S is justified *a priori* in believing that $p =$ Df. S's belief that
               p has some degree of justification that does not depend on
               any experience.

We may take D15 to imply that S is justified *a priori* in believing that p just in case S has some justification for believing that p that is not based on any experience. We shall understand the relevant sense of "experience" in D15 very broadly. It includes such things as sense experience, memory experience, and introspective experience. Propositions (1)–(5) do not seem to be justified on the basis of such experience.

According to D15, if your justification for believing p depends essentially on some proposition that is justified for you empirically, or *a posteriori*, then you are *not* justified in believing p *a priori*. In that case, your justification for believing p depends on your experience. You do not have some degree of justification that is independent of experience. Thus, if my justification for believing p depends on my deducing it from q and r, and r is justified for me empirically, then I am not justified *a priori* in believing p.

It is important to note, however, that D15 does not rule out the possibility that one might have *both* an *a priori* and an empirical justification for believing a proposition. One's justification for believing a proposition can be over-determined in the sense that one has two distinct ways in which the proposition can be justified. One way might be *a priori* and the other might be empirical. A child might, for example, accept the proposition that all squares are rectangles on the testimony of her teacher. Her belief that this is so might be rooted in testimony which is in turn based on experience. Still, at some point the child might come to "see" intellectually for herself that all squares are rectangles and thus her belief will also be justified

---

[3] Immanuel Kant, *Critique of Pure Reason*, trans. Norman Kemp Smith (New York: St. Martin's Press, 1929), p. 43.

a priori. Similarly, a student in a logic class might accept de Morgan's laws on the basis of the teacher's testimony and thus be justified in believing them empirically. Still, he might come to be justified in believing them *a priori*.

One objection to D15 might be put this way: "(1) One needs some experience in order to form the concepts of a square, a rectangle, or a swan. (2) One needs some experience in order to grasp the propositions all squares are rectangles and all swans are swans. Therefore, (3) one's belief is justified on the basis of some experience. And, therefore, (4) according to D15, one cannot be justified in believing them *a priori*." In response, the proponent of D15 might point out that D15 does not imply that one can be justified *a priori* without having any experience at all. He might concede that one does need some experience to form the concepts of a square, a rectangle, and a swan and to understand the proposition that all squares are rectangles or all swans are swans. Still, even if some experience is needed to grasp a proposition, it does not follow that the proposition is justified *by* that experience or on the basis of any experience at all. If some experience is needed to grasp the proposition that all swans are swans, it does not follow that one's belief in that proposition is justified on the basis of that experience. Consequently, the proponent of D15 will hold that (1) and (2) do not imply that either (3) or (4) is true.

A proponent of D15 might concede, for example, that some experience is needed to grasp the proposition that all swans are under forty pounds. But again, from the fact that some experience enables you to grasp that proposition it does not follow that the proposition is justified for you *by* that experience. Let's assume that various experiences enable me to grasp the proposition that all swans are under forty pounds. Still, I am not justified in believing it. I haven't the faintest idea whether it is true. None of my experiences provide me with any reason to believe it. What would justify me in believing it is some experience I don't yet have. So, again, from the fact that one has some experience that enables one to grasp a proposition, *p*, it does not follow that one is justified in believing that *p* on the basis of that experience or that one's experience provides any reason to believe it is true.

D15 seems quite promising. Still, it does face some objections. One objection concerns the connection between justification and experience. Consider, for example, certain forms of the coherence theory of justification. Pure coherence theories hold that *all* beliefs are justified solely in virtue of their relations to other beliefs, and that *no* beliefs are justified on the basis of experience. Suppose that this view were true. If it were true, then all justified beliefs would have some degree of justification which is not dependent on any experience. It would then follow, according to D15, that *all* justified beliefs are justified *a priori*. Such a result would seem to be a mistake, since it seems that some justified beliefs are not justified *a priori*. It seems that D15 is correct only if such coherence theories of justification are false. Of course, a proponent of D15 might hold that we have good reasons to think that coherence theories of justification are false.

Another objection also concerns the connection between justification and experience. Consider reliabilist theories of justification and the case of Norman the clairvoyant. Suppose that Norman forms the belief that the President is in New York on the basis of his reliable power of clairvoyance. Suppose further that his belief is not based on any experience. According to some versions of reliabilism, Norman's belief is justified. If this is so, then D15 implies that Norman's belief is justified *a priori*. But that does not seem right. Though not dependent on any experience for its justification, Norman's belief does not seem to be justified *a priori*. Similarly, suppose that Cassandra forms lots of true beliefs about the future on the basis of a reliable faculty of precognition. According to some versions of reliabilism, Cassandra's beliefs are justified. But they do not seem to be justified *a priori*. So, a proponent of reliabilism or a virtue approach to justification might hold that D15 is mistaken. Again, a proponent of D15 might argue that we have good reasons to think that reliabilist and virtue theories of justification are mistaken.

Some critics object that D15 is an unsatisfactory negative account. It tells us what *a priori* justification does *not* depend on. Some of these critics would suggest that D15 ignores the central role of reason as a source of *a priori* justification. *A priori* justification is more than simply justification that does not depend on experience. It is justification that depends on reason alone. According to these critics, Norman's clairvoyant belief and Cassandra's precognition aren't justified *a priori* because they aren't based on reason. So, these critics object, D15 is unsatisfactory because it ignores the role of reason.

Finally some philosophers object that, contrary to D15, *a priori* justification *does* depend on experience. One might hold that *a priori* justification is based on a certain sort of "purely intellectual" experience. One might hold that there is some phenomenologically distinctive nondoxastic state which justifies or serves as evidence for our *a priori* beliefs. Consider, for example, the following passage by George Bealer:

> By intuition, we do not mean a magical power or inner voice or a mysterious "faculty" or anything of that sort. For you to have an intuition that A is just for it to *seem* to you that A. Here 'seems' is understood, not as a cautionary or "hedging" term, but in its first use as a term for a conscious episode. For example, when you first consider de Morgan's laws, often it neither seems to be true nor seems to be false; after a moment's reflection, however, something new happens: suddenly it just *seems* true. Of course, this kind of seeming is *intellectual*, not sensory or introspective (or imaginative).[4]

Bealer distinguishes intellectual seemings from beliefs. He holds that one can believe that *p* without its seeming to one that *p* and *vice versa*. For example, someone who accepts de Morgan's laws on the basis of testimony might believe them without their seeming true to him. More importantly, he holds that these intellectual seemings are reasons or evidence for beliefs. They are a kind of intellectual experience that justify our *a priori* beliefs. If Bealer is correct, then, contrary to D15, beliefs that are justified *a priori* are based on experience–they are based on a kind of intellectual experience.

If we follow this line of thought, should we say that S has a justified *a priori* belief that *p* just in case it intellectually seems to S that *p*? No. S might have nonbasic or mediate *a priori* justification for believing *p* without its intellectually seeming to him that *p*. One might be justified *a priori*, for example, in accepting the Pythagorean Theorem without its seeming intellectually to be true. Perhaps, however, we may say,

D16   S is basically justified *a priori* in believing that *p* = Df. S's belief that *p* has some degree of justification on the basis of its intellectually seeming to S that *p*.

D16 is, of course, controversial. Whether beliefs are justified *a priori* on the basis of intellectual experiences or intellectual seemings is a difficult question. Some philosophers doubt that there are the sorts of purely intellectual experiences that Bealer describes. Others concede that such experiences might *accompany* our basically justified *a priori* beliefs without being what justifies them.

---

[4] George Bealer, "A Theory of the A Priori," *Philosophical Perspectives*, 13 (1999), 30.

Reflection on D15 and D16 illustrates one problem in trying to define *a priori* justification. We begin with what we take to be clear examples of propositions, such as (1)–(5), that we are justified in believing in a special way, that we are justified in believing *a priori*. Suppose we then try to define *a priori* justification in terms of the source of such justification. We might say, as in the case of D15, that *a priori* justification is justification that does *not* have a certain source, i.e. experience. Or we might say, as in the case of D16, that it is justification that *does* have a certain kind of source, e.g. a sort of intellectual experience. But since it is a matter of debate whether *any* beliefs in general are justified by experience and whether *these* beliefs in particular are justified by experience, these definitions are bound to be controversial. Of course, this does not imply that either D15 or D16 is false. Still we might wonder if there is an alternative approach.

Let's consider one further account of the *a priori*. Suppose we say:

D17   *p* is an axiom for S = Df. (i) Necessarily, if S accepts *p*, then *p* is certain for S, and (ii) *p* is necessarily true.[5]

According to D17, a proposition is an axiom for a person just in case it is impossible for him to accept it without being certain of it. So, consider again (1)–(5). We might say that these propositions are axioms for us insofar as they are necessarily true and it is impossible for us to accept them without being certain that they are true. Given D17, we might then say:

D18   *p* is axiomatic for S = Df. (i) *p* is an axiom for S, and (ii) S accepts *p*.

According to D18, a proposition is axiomatic for a person just in case it is an axiom for him and he actually does accept it. So, if (1)–(5) are axioms for you, and you *do* accept them, then we may say that they are also axiomatic for you. It seems plausible to say that if a proposition is axiomatic for a person, then he is justified in believing it *a priori*. But note that this account does not take a stand on whether *a priori* justification is based on a purely intellectual experience or whether it is independent of all experience. It seems to leave open what justifies our basic *a priori* beliefs. To many philosophers this seems to be a virtue of the account.

[5] Compare Roderick Chisholm's account of axioms and the *a priori* in *Theory of Knowledge*, 2nd edn. (Englewood Cliffs, NJ: Prentice-Hall, Inc., 1977), pp. 42–43. D17–D18 are very similar, though not identical to the account that Chisholm develops and defends.

Still, we cannot say that a proposition is justified *a priori* for S just in case it is axiomatic for S. This is because there are some propositions, such as the Pythagorean Theorem, that we are justified in a believing *a priori* but which are not axiomatic for us. Our *a priori* justification goes beyond what is axiomatic for us. Perhaps, however, we might say,

D19   S is justified *a priori* in believing that *p*=Df. Either (i) *p* is axiomatic for S or (ii) there is a proposition, *h*, that is axiomatic for S and it is axiomatic for S that *h* implies *p*.

According to D19, you are justified in believing a proposition *a priori* just in case it is axiomatic for you or there is some *other* proposition that is axiomatic for you and it is axiomatic that this other proposition implies *p*. The account of *a priori* justification that we find in D17–D19 is a foundational model. The foundation consists of those propositions that are axiomatic for a person. In order to be justified *a priori* in believing something outside the foundation, one must "see" that it is logically implied by something in the foundation.

Is the account of *a priori* justification we find in D17–D19 a satisfactory account? There are reasons to think it is not. Some philosophers would hold that it requires too much for *a priori* justification, that it is too "strong." We shall consider why this is so in the next section.

Strong and modest *a priori* justification

Must beliefs that enjoy basic *a priori* justification be certain? Must they be indefeasible? Some philosophers favor a "strong" account of *a priori* justification. Such an account holds that the immediate testimony of reason enjoys a very privileged and special status. A strong account holds that basically justified *a priori* beliefs must be, for example, certain, indefeasible, or true. As we shall see, there are reasons to doubt that *a priori* justification must meet these high standards. Some philosophers reject those high standards and favor instead what we may call "modest" accounts of *a priori* justification.

The account of *a priori* justification we find in D17–D19 is a strong account of *a priori* justification. According to that view, S is basically justified *a priori* in believing that *p* if and only if *p* is axiomatic for S. If this is so, then all basically justified *a priori* beliefs are certain. Second, this account implies that all basically justified *a priori* beliefs are *indefeasible*. If a proposition is axiomatic for you, then as long as you accept it you are maximally justified in believing it. This means that as long as you accept what is an axiom for you, you can never be unjustified in believing it. As long as you accept it, you can have no evidence that defeats your justification for believing it. Finally, this account implies that whatever we are justified in believing *a priori* is *true*.

Whether a strong or modest view of *a priori* knowledge and justification is true is relevant to the scope or extent of such knowledge and justification. Some philosophers have claimed to be justified *a priori* in believing various sorts of philosophically interesting propositions. Kant, for example, thought he was justified *a priori* in believing the metaphysical proposition:

(C) Every event has a cause.

Other philosophers have claimed to be justified *a priori* in believing various ethical claims, such as

(P) If someone has made a promise to do an act, then he has a *prima facie* duty to do it.

(G) Someone's having a pleasure is intrinsically good.

Still others have suggested that one can be justified *a priori* in believing various epistemic principles. For example,

(S) If someone seems to see that something is F, then S is *prima facie* justified in believing that something is F.

(I) If you know that there are 1,000 marbles in a jar, 999 are black, 1 is white, and 1 has been randomly selected (and you have no other relevant information), then it is reasonable for you to believe that the one selected is black.[6]

Consider these philosophically interesting propositions. Do we have basic *a priori* justification in believing these claims? If the strong account is correct, then it seems the answer is "no." This is because these propositions do not seem to be certain for us or maximally justified. They are not as justified for us as $2 = 2$ or all swans are swans. Moreover, we typically do not think of them as indefeasible. Even if we accept them, we remain open to the

---

[6] Richard Feldman, *Epistemology* (Upper Saddle River, NJ: Prentice-Hall Inc., 2003), p. 138.

possibility of counter-examples or defeating evidence. It seems, then, that if a strong account of basic *a priori* justification is correct, then we don't have basic *a priori* justification for believing these propositions. It also seems that none of these propositions enjoys nonbasic *a priori* justification since it seems that we cannot deduce them from any propositions that are axiomatic for us. If the account of *a priori* justification we find in D17–D19 is correct, then it is hard to see how any of these claims could be justified for us *a priori*. Indeed, it is hard to see how many philosophically interesting claims could be justified *a priori*. If D17–D19 is correct, then the scope or extent of our basic *a priori* is much narrower than some philosophers would claim.

Some philosophers find strong accounts of *a priori* justification, such as that represented by D17–D19, unsatisfactory. They hold that basically justified *a priori* beliefs need not be certain, indefeasible, or true. To see why this is so let's begin with the claim that all beliefs that have basic *a priori* justification are certain.

First, critics point out that the fact that a belief is basic does not imply that it is certain. There is no reason to think that basic *a priori* justification must be certain just because it is basic. As we saw in chapter 3, modest foundationalists hold that perceptual and memory beliefs can be basic without being certain. If some of the basic beliefs that issue from perception and memory are not certain, then there is no obvious reason to assume that all basic beliefs that issue from reason must be.

Second, if everything that has basic *a priori* justification is certain, then everything that has it has the same degree of justification. But that does not seem right. Consider the propositions (a) if some men are Greeks, then some Greeks are men, (b) no horse is both four-legged and a nonanimal, (c) there are no things that do not exist, (d) if it is more reasonable to believe *p* than withhold *p*, then it is more reasonable to believe *p* than *not-p*. It seems plausible that these propositions enjoy basic *a priori* justification, but it does not seem that they all must have the same degree of justification. It does not seem that they are all as highly justified as $2 = 2$ or that they are maximally justified. On this point, we may also consider the following observation by Bertrand Russell:

> It should be observed that, in all cases of general principles, particular instances dealing with familiar things, are more evident than the general

principle. For example, the law of contradiction states that nothing can both have a certain property and not have it. This is evident as soon as it is understood, but it is not so evident as that a particular rose which we see cannot be both red and not red.[7]

The law of contradiction, presumably, has basic *a priori* justification. But if, as Russell claims, that general principle is less evident than the particular instance, then the general principle is not *maximally* justified or certain. Indeed, if the law of contradiction is less evident than *some* other proposition, such as $2 = 2$, then it is not certain.[8]

Must basic *a priori* justification be indefeasible? Again, some philosophers would say "no." In arguing that basic *a priori* justification need not be indefeasible several writers have pointed out that sometimes we find ourselves in the following situation. Sometimes we find that we believe several propositions and it seems reasonable to us to believe each of them. Indeed, it seems that each of them is justified *a priori*. But then we find on further reflection that they cannot all be true. We realize that some things that seem intuitively plausible to us cannot all be true. When this happens our justification for at least some of our initial beliefs is defeated. To illustrate this point, Matthias Steup calls our attention to "the paradox of the heap."[9] Consider the proposition:

(H)   If two collections of sand differ in number by just one grain, then either both collections are heaps of sand or neither is.

(H) seems quite reasonable. It seems plausible to hold that one could be justified *a priori* in believing that (H) is true. Our justification for believing it is not based on empirical investigation into heaps. On reflection, however, (H) seems to lead to absurdity. It seems to imply that a single grain

---

[7] Bertrand Russell, *The Problems of Philosophy* (Oxford: Oxford University Press, 1912), pp. 112–13.

[8] Other philosophers have held that basic *a priori* justification need not be certain. Alvin Plantinga, *Warrant and Proper Function* (Oxford: Oxford University Press, 1993), p. 112; Laurence BonJour, *The Structure of Empirical Knowledge* (Cambridge, MA: Harvard University Press, 1985), p. 208; Donna Summerfield, "Modest A Priori Knowledge," *Philosophy and Phenomenological Research*, 51 (March 1991), 49–50.

[9] Matthias Steup, *An Introduction to Contemporary Epistemology* (Upper Saddle River, NJ: Prentice-Hall Publishing, 1996), p. 54.

of sand is a heap.[10] But that's clearly false. Steup points out that once one sees that (H) leads to absurdity one is no longer justified in believing it. One's justification for believing (H) has been defeated by seeing its paradoxical implications.

Similarly, consider the various assumptions that led to Russell's paradoxes. Consider, for example, the propositions (1) every property has a complement, and (2) there is a property of self-exemplification. When we think about these propositions they might seem true to us. One might be justified *a priori* in believing them. But let's consider (1) and (2) more closely. If (1) and (2) are true, then there is a property of non-self-exemplification. But now consider the property of non-self-exemplification. Does it exemplify itself? If it does, then it doesn't. If it doesn't, then it does. Accepting both (1) and (2), then, leads to an absurd conclusion. But once we see that our initial assumptions imply something absurd, it is reasonable for us to reject one or more of these assumptions. Our justification for believing both of these propositions is undercut by seeing what they imply. The German philosopher Frege accepted propositions very similar to (1) and (2) until Bertrand Russell pointed out to him the paradoxical implications of his assumptions. Still, until Russell pointed out their paradoxical consequences, it seems that Frege was justified in accepting his initial assumptions. Alvin Plantinga notes, "No doubt Frege was rational in believing *a priori* that for every condition there is a set of just those things that satisfy that condition; but no doubt he was equally rational in rejecting that proposition later on, upon seeing where it led."[11] If the preceding considerations are correct, then basic *a priori* justification is not indefeasible. Seeing that a set of propositions we believe implies something absurd can defeat our justification for believing one or all of those propositions.

---

[10] To see this suppose we start with a large pile of sand that qualifies as a heap. Create a second collection by removing exactly one grain of sand. Given (H), the remaining pile is also a heap. Now repeat the process over and over again until you are left with exactly one grain of sand. (H) implies that the remaining grain is also a heap. But that seems absurd.

[11] Alvin Plantinga, *Warrant and Proper Function* (Oxford: Oxford University Press, 1993), p. 112.

Some philosophers hold that *a priori* justification can be defeated by other sorts of considerations. Thomas Reid asks us to consider the case of a mathematician having completed a demonstration. Reid writes,

> He commits his demonstration to the examination of a mathematical friend, who he esteems a competent judge, and waits with impatience the issue of his judgment. Here I would ask again, Whether the verdict of his friend, according as it has been favorable or unfavorable, will greatly increase or diminish his confidence in his own judgment? Most certainly it will and it ought.[12]

According to Reid, the level of justification the man's belief enjoys can be affected by the testimony of his friend. Even though he might be justified *a priori* in believing his conclusion, his justification can be defeated or undercut by the testimony of his friend. In this example, Reid deals with the nonbasic *a priori* justification one has for accepting the conclusion of an argument. But similar considerations apply to basic *a priori* beliefs. Reid says that men can disagree about "first principles" and when they do: "A man of candour and humility will, in such a case, very naturally suspect his own judgment, so far as to be desirous to enter into a serious examination, even of what he has long held to be a first principle."[13] Reid suggests that when we disagree with someone else about a first principle, knowledge of such disagreement can sometimes lower or even defeat our justification. Plantinga suggests a similar view: "I am a philosophical tyro and you a distinguished practioner of the art; you tell me that those who think about such things are unanimous in...rejecting the view that there aren't things that don't exist: then too, I should think my view would no longer have warrant (or *much* warrant) for me."[14] Both Reid and Plantinga suggest that knowing that an expert rejects what seems true to you can sometimes lower or defeat one's justification even in the case of a basically justified *a priori* belief. If this is right, then basic *a priori* justification need not be certain or indefeasible.

Finally, if the preceding considerations are right, then it seems clear that one could have basic *a priori* justification in believing a false proposition. It seems that one could be justified *a priori* in believing (H) or be justified

---

[12] Thomas Reid, *Essays on the Intellectual Powers of Man* (Cambridge, MA: The MIT Press, 1969), essay VI, chapter 4, pp. 49–50.

[13] *Ibid.*, pp. 603–4.

[14] Alvin Plantinga, *Warrant and Proper Function*, p. 112.

a priori in believing some false proposition that leads to Russell's paradox. If this is right, then we should not regard the basic beliefs of reason as infallible.

The debate between those who favor a strong view of *a priori* justification and those who favor a more modest view resembles the debate between classical and modest foundationalists. As we noted in chapter 3, classical foundationalists hold that basic beliefs must be infallible. Classical foundationalists hold that basic beliefs must have some sort of special epistemic privilege. Similarly, those who favor a strong view of *a priori* justification hold that basically justified *a priori* beliefs must have some special epistemic status. Moreover, if classical foundationalism is true, then the scope or extent of our knowledge is much narrower than it is according to modest foundationalism. Similarly, if strong views of *a priori* justification are correct, then the scope of *a priori* knowledge and justification is much narrower than it is according to more modest views of *a priori* justification.

Still, if the arguments we have considered in this section are sound, then we should reject the strong view in favor of a more modest view that does not insist that what has basic *a priori* justification must be certain, indefeasible, or true. The basic testimony of reason, like that of perception and memory, comes in degrees of epistemic justification. Like the testimony of perception and memory, it can sometimes be defeated by other considerations.

The analytic–synthetic distinction

In this section we shall focus on the analytic–synthetic distinction. Traditionally, it has been characteristic of *empiricism* to hold that our *a priori* knowledge and justification is confined to *analytic* propositions. In contrast, *rationalism* holds that there are some nonanalytic, or *synthetic*, propositions that we can know or be justified in believing *a priori*. Empiricists thus hold that the scope of our *a priori* knowledge and justification is narrower than rationalists take it to be. Assessing the debate between them is difficult and complicated. This is due in part to the fact that there are different ways of understanding the technical terms "analytic" and "synthetic." In this section, we shall consider briefly some ways philosophers have understood these concepts and whether our *a priori* knowledge and justified belief is confined to what is analytic.

How are we to understand the analytic/synthetic distinction? One of the most important suggestions was made by Kant. Roughly, we may take Kant's view to be:

A1   Proposition *p* is analytic = Df. Either (a) *p*'s subject is identical to its predicate, or (b) *p*'s predicate is conceptually contained in its subject.

In a proposition of the form, "All S is P," "S" is the subject and "P" is the predicate. So, in the proposition "All men are mortal", the subject is "men" and the predicate is "mortal." Now consider the following propositions:

(1) All swans are swans.

(2) All squares are squares.

In both of these propositions the subject is identical to the predicate. So, according to A1, both (1) and (2) are analytic propositions. Identity of the subject and predicate is not the only way for a proposition to be analytic according to A1. Consider:

(3) All squares are rectangles.

(4) All bachelors are unmarried.

In these propositions, the subject is not identical to the predicate. Still, the predicate is said to be "conceptually contained" in the subject. But what does that mean? One way to think about conceptual containment is that a predicate, P, is conceptually contained in a subject, S, just in case P is part of the definition or analysis of S. Since "bachelor" can be defined or analyzed as "unmarried adult male" and "square" can be defined or analyzed as "equilateral rectangle," "unmarried" is conceptually contained in "bachelor" and "rectangle" is contained in "square." According to A1, then, both (3) and (4) are analytic propositions.

Given A1, a proposition such as "All swans are white", is not analytic, since the predicate "white" is neither identical to the subject nor conceptually contained in the subject. "White" is not part of the definition or analysis of "swans." We may say that any proposition that is not an analytic proposition is a synthetic proposition. Thus, the proposition that all swans are white is a synthetic proposition.

The view that our *a priori* knowledge and justification is confined to what is analytic is important. Consider the philosophically interesting proposition from the previous section. None of them appears to be analytic. Consider (C) for example. It is not part of the definition or analysis of "event" that it has a cause. Similarly, it is hard to see how the consequence of (I) is part of the definition or analysis of the antecedent of (I). Now, *if* none of these of philosophically interesting propositions is analytic, and *if* our *a priori* knowledge and justification is limited to analytic propositions, then none of these philosophically interesting propositions is known or justified *a priori*. This would mean that if one is to have *any* justification for believing such propositions it would have to be on the basis of something other than reason alone. In many cases, it is very hard to see what that alternative source of justification could be. The claim that our *a priori* knowledge and justification is confined to analytic propositions is important because it implies that the scope or extent of our *a priori* knowledge and justification is much less than some philosophers have thought.

But is it true that the only propositions we are justified in believing *a priori* are those which are analytic according to A1? The answer seems to be "no." This is so for at least two reasons. First, consider propositions such as,

(5) If some men are Greeks, then some Greeks are men.

(6) Either all men are mortal or it is not the case that all men are mortal.

It seems clear that we know (5) and (6) *a priori*, but neither of these is an analytic proposition according to A1. Neither has the subject–predicate form of "All S are P," and so in neither case is the predicate identical to the subject or contained in it.

A second problem concerns propositions such as,

(7) All red things are colored.

It seems clear that (7) is something that we know *a priori*. But is (7) an analytic proposition? In this case, the subject "red thing" is not identical with the predicate "colored." But is "colored" contained in "red thing"? Clearly, "colored" is not part of the definition or analysis of "thing." Is "colored" part of the analysis or definition of "red"? Many philosophers would hold that "red" is a *simple* concept. A simple concept is one that is indefinable or unanalyzable, one that cannot be broken down into logically independent concepts.[15] According to some, we cannot analyze the concept of "red" into logically independent concepts the way we can analyze "square" into the logically independent concepts of "equilateral" and "rectangle." Other allegedly simple concepts would be perceptual qualities such as "sweet," "sour," "salty," "C#," as well as other color concepts, such as "blue," "yellow," "green," etc. If "red" is a simple concept, then (7) is not an analytic proposition. If so, then our *a priori* knowledge and justification is not confined to what is, according to A1, analytic.

There are, however, other views about what it is for a proposition to be analytic. The German philosopher and logician Gottlob Frege suggested another approach. Roughly, Frege proposed the following:

A2   Proposition p is analytic $=$ Df. Either (a) p is a logical truth or (b) p is reducible to a truth of logic by substituting synonyms for synonyms.

In order to understand this account we need to know what it is for something to be a "logical truth." Consider the following propositions:

(8) If all men are mortal, then all men are mortal.

(6) Either all men are mortal or it is not the case that all men are mortal.

Each of these propositions has a certain "logical form." The logical form of (8) is "If p, then p" and the logical form of (6) is "Either p or not-p." Both of these logical forms are such that if we substitute *any* proposition for p, the result will be a true proposition. In other words, any of the "substitution instances" of these logical forms will result in a true proposition. What is a logical truth? Let us say that a proposition is a logical truth just in case its logical form is such that all of its substitution instances are true.

As we have seen, A1 implies that the following propositions are analytic:

(3) All squares are rectangles.

(4) All bachelors are unmarried.

---

[15] A and B are logically independent concepts just in case it is possible for something to have A without anything having B and *vice versa*. "Equilateral" and "rectangle" are logically independent concepts since it is possible for something to be equilateral without anything being a rectangle and *vice versa*.

Are these propositions analytic according to A2? Yes. Consider (3). If we substitute for "squares" the synonym "equilateral rectangles," then we get:

(3') All equilateral rectangles are rectangles.

(3') has a logical form. It has the logical form "All AB's are B's." If we substitute *any* properties or concepts for A and B, we will get a true proposition. Any proposition with that logical form is a logical truth. So, we may say that we can reduce (3) to a logical truth, (3'), by substituting synonyms for synonyms. According to clause (b) of A2, this makes (3) an analytic proposition. We can say something similar about (4).

One advantage that A2 enjoys over A1 is that A2 implies that some propositions are analytic that A1 does not. In this respect, the Fregean notion of analyticity is broader than the Kantian. As we have seen, A1 does not imply that (6) is an analytic proposition. But (6) is an analytic proposition according to A2 since (6) is a logical truth. Moreover, as we have seen, A1 does not imply that,

(5) If some men are Greeks, then some Greeks are men

is an analytic proposition. But note that (5) does have a logical form. Suppose we assume that it has the logical form "If some A's are B's, then some B's are A's." In this case, *any* properties or concepts we substitute for A or B will result in a true proposition. So, (5) is a logical truth. If so, then A2 implies that (5) is an analytic proposition.

A2 is a broader notion of analyticity than A1. It treats more propositions as analytic than the Kantian notion. Suppose we accept A2 as our account of analyticity. Is our *a priori* knowledge and justification confined to what is analytic in this sense? Many philosophers would say that the answer is "no." Consider the following two propositions:

(9) If x is larger than y and y is larger than z, then x is larger than z.

(10) Nothing can be both red all over and green all over.

Many philosophers would hold, plausibly, that they are justified *a priori* in believing (9) and (10). (9) tells us something about a certain relation, "is larger than," and (10) tells us something about the properties of being red all over and green all over. But are (9) and (10) *logical* truths? We have been assuming that a proposition is a logical truth just in case its logical form is such that all of its substitution instances are true. Suppose we take the logical form of (9) and (10) to be:

(9′) If xRy and yRz, then xRz.

(10′) Nothing can be both A and B.

Neither (9′) nor (10′) is such that all of its substitution instances are true. Consider (9′). There are some substitution instances of (9′) that would not yield true propositions. If we substitute some relations for R, e.g."fathers" or "is twice as large as," we do *not* get a true proposition. Similarly, there are some substitution instances in (10′) that do not yield a true proposition. If we substitute "red" and "square" for A and B, we do not get a true proposition. If this is right, then neither (9) nor (10) is a logical truth.[16] Neither satisfies the first clause of A2.

Could it be that (9) and (10) satisfy clause (b) in A2? Are (9) and (10) reducible to logical truths by substituting synonyms for synonyms? Perhaps, but it is not clear how this can be done. What would the relevant synonym be for "is larger than" that would reduce (9) to a logical truth? What relevant synonyms for "red all over" and "green all over" would reduce (10) to a logical truth?

One might suggest that "red all over" is synonymous with "is red all over and is not green all over" and "is green all over" is synonymous with "is green all over and is not red all over." If this is so, then we might say that we can replace (10) with,

(10″) Nothing can be both red all over and not green all over and green all over and not red all over.

(10″) seems to be a logical truth. It has the logical form "Nothing can be both A and not-B and B and not-A." In response, however, we might ask whether "red all over" is really synonymous with "is red all over and is not green all over." If two expressions are synonymous, then they have the same meaning. The one expression should mean no more and no less than the second. But it seems that "red all over and not green all over" means *more* than "red all over." It seems that the former concept is *richer* than the latter.

---

[16] Of course, in denying that (9) and (10) are logical truths in our technical sense of the term, we are *not* denying that they are necessarily true.

This is because the former involves two distinct color concepts, "red" and "green" and the latter only one – "red." If this is right, then, arguably, the two expressions are not synonymous.

None of the preceding remarks show that the Fregean definition of analyticity is false. The point is rather that even if we accept the Fregean account, it is far from clear that everything we know or are justified in believing *a priori* is analytic.

Finally, let us consider briefly one more approach to defining analyticity. According to this view, analyticity is a property of *sentences* rather than propositions. Sometimes it is suggested that a sentence is analytic just in case it is true simply in virtue of the way we use words or simply in virtue of the rules of our language.[17] This view is sometimes called *lingusiticism.* Perhaps we can formulate the view as:

A3   Sentence "p" is analytic = Df. "p" is true solely in virtue of the way people use words.

Alternatively, we might say that a sentence is analytic just in case it is true solely in virtue of its meaning. In order to understand this view, let's consider the sentence "snow is white." It seems clear that whether this sentence is true does depend in part on how we use words. If "snow" meant grass or "white" meant hot, then the sentence would be false. But it is clear that the truth of the sentence "snow is white" does not depend *solely* on how we use words or on its meaning. The truth of that sentence also depends upon the fact that snow is white. Its truth depends, in part, upon something other than language. So, according to A3, the sentence "snow is white" is not, therefore, an analytic proposition.

But now let's consider the sentence:

(11) Whatever is red is colored.

Some philosophers will suggest that (11) is true *solely* in virtue of the way people use the words "red" and "colored." They would suggest that (11) is true solely in virtue of the "rules of our language" and, thus, according to A3, it is an analytic sentence. Other philosophers, however, reject this view. They concede that the truth of this sentence depends in part on the

---

[17] Cf. Anthony Quinton, "The *A Priori* and the Analytic," in *Necessary Truth*, ed. Robert Sleigh (Englewood Cliffs, NJ: Prentice-Hall, Inc., 1972), pp. 89–109.

meaning of "red" and "colored." If people used the word "colored" to mean square, then (11) would be false. Still, they say that the truth of (11) also depends on the fact that whatever is red is colored. They hold that the truth of (11) also depends on certain facts about the properties of being red and being colored. In this respect, (11) and the sentence "snow is white" are similar. In neither case does the truth of the sentence depend *solely* on the way we use words.

Whether our *a priori* knowledge and justification are confined to what is analytic remains controversial. As we have seen, part of the difficulty is that philosophers use the terms "analytic" and "synthetic" in different senses. But even when we are operating with a reasonably clear account of analyticity, it often remains a matter of debate whether some proposition is both synthetic and known *a priori*.

10   Naturalized epistemology

There are many forms of naturalized epistemology and it is hard to say exactly what it is. The various forms have different views about the relations between natural science and traditional epistemology. In its most radical forms, naturalized epistemology holds that traditional epistemology should be abandoned or at least replaced by some empirical science, such as psychology. Other less radical forms of naturalized epistemology don't call for the abandonment of traditional epistemology but hold that the empirical sciences, especially psychology, can solve or help to resolve many of the problems confronting traditional epistemology. Others claim that there is "a continuity" between empirical science and epistemology. In general, proponents of naturalized epistemology stress the importance of the natural sciences for epistemological inquiry. In this chapter, we'll explore some arguments and claims made by the proponents of naturalized epistemology.

Quine and the replacement thesis

In his essay "Epistemology Naturalized" W. V. Quine offers one of the earliest defenses of naturalized epistemology. He argues that the traditional Cartesian epistemological project of deducing truths about the external world from infallible knowledge of our own mental states is a failure. Attempts to justify or to provide a rational reconstruction of our beliefs in that way are doomed. If knowledge did require such a justification, the result would be skepticism. (We discussed the difficulties with classical foundationalism in chapter 3.) Confronted with the failure of the traditional

Cartesian epistemological project, Quine seems to recommend that we abandon epistemology in favor of psychology:

> The stimulation of his sensory receptors is all the evidence anybody has had to go on, ultimately, in arriving at his picture of the world. Why not just see how this construction really proceeds? Why not settle for psychology?[1]

The traditional Cartesian epistemological project focused on how our sensory experiences justify our beliefs about the external world. But since that project has failed, Quine seems to suggest that we should rather focus on how we get our beliefs. He seems to suggest, for example, that we should focus on the psychological processes that lead us from our sensory stimulations to our beliefs about the external world. Instead of focusing on the *justification* of our beliefs, we should rather be seeking a *scientific explanation* of how we get those beliefs. Instead of being concerned with the *normative* or *evaluative* status of beliefs we would be concerned with a *descriptive* inquiry about the psychological processes that produce them. Quine elaborates on this view in the following passage:

> But I think that at this point it may be more useful to say that epistemology still goes on, though in a new setting and a clarified status. Epistemology, or something like it, simply falls into place as a chapter of psychology and hence of natural science. It studies a natural phenomenon, viz., a physical human subject. This human subject is accorded a certain experimentally controlled input – certain patterns of irradiation in assorted frequencies, for instance – and in the fullness of time the subject delivers as output a description of the three dimensional world and its history. The relationship between the meager input and the torrential output is a relationship we are prompted to study for somewhat the same reasons that always prompted epistemology; namely, in order to see how evidence relates to theory, and in what ways one's theory of nature transcends any available evidence.[2]

According to Quine's proposal, "Epistemology in its new setting...is contained in natural science, as a chapter of psychology."[3] The view

---

[1] W.V. Quine, "Epistemology Naturalized," *Ontological Relativity and Other Essays* (New York: Columbia University Press, 1969), p. 75.

[2] *Ibid.*, pp. 82–83.

[3] *Ibid.*, p. 83.

that traditional epistemology should be supplanted by natural science or, more specifically, psychology is sometimes called "the replacement thesis."

Not many philosophers have accepted the replacement thesis. First, suppose that classical foundationalism is false. Why would it follow that traditional normative epistemology with its focus on justification and reasonableness must be abandoned? If classical foundationalism is false, nothing follows about the truth or falsity of other traditional normative epistemic theories, such as moderate foundationalism, coherentism, or reliabilism. Even if classical foundationalism is mistaken, it does not follow that all other theories about what justifies beliefs are false. Second, suppose that Quine is right and Cartesian or classical foundationalism is false. Suppose that beliefs cannot be justified in the way classical foundationalism claims. Why would it follow that the normative epistemologist concerned with justification should turn to *psychology*? As Jaegwon Kim observes, "if normative epistemology is not a possible inquiry, why shouldn't the would-be epistemologist turn to, say, hydrodynamics or ornithology rather than psychology?"[4] Finally, some philosophers object that it is misleading to refer to the study of how our beliefs arise as epistemology.[5] Traditional episte-mology is concerned with normative or evaluative concepts such as justifi-cation, reasonableness, and knowledge. It asks, for example, how do our sensory experiences *justify* our beliefs about the external world. In contrast, Quine seems to propose that we set aside these normative or evaluative questions, and ask how our sensory experiences *cause* or *bring about* our beliefs. Traditional epistemology and the sort of inquiry Quine advocates are thus concerned with different relations between sensory experience and belief. As Richard Feldman puts it, "The original epistemological questions seem to be perfectly good questions, well worthy of our attention. It is difficult to see, then, why the availability of this other field of study, concerning how we reason, is a suitable replacement for the evaluative questions that are at the heart of epistemology."[6]

---

[4] Jaegwon Kim, "What is Naturalized Epistemology?" *Philosophical Perspectives*, 2, 391.

[5] Richard Feldman, *Epistemology* (Upper Saddle River, NJ: Prentice-Hall, Inc., 2003), pp. 167–68.

[6] *Ibid.*, p. 68.

Kornblith and the Darwinian argument

Hilary Kornblith defends a naturalistic approach to epistemology. Kornblith asks us to consider the following questions:

Q1   How ought we to arrive at beliefs?

Q2   How do we arrive at beliefs?

Q3   Are the processes by which we do arrive at beliefs the ones by which we ought to arrive at our beliefs?

Traditional epistemology has long been concerned with answering Q1. In asking Q1, we are asking a normative or evaluative question. In answering Q1, we want to distinguish between good and bad ways of forming beliefs, between the ways we ought to form beliefs and those we ought to avoid. According to Kornblith, in order to answer Q2 we need to consult empirical psychology. Empirical psychology is concerned to discover the actual processes we actually use to form beliefs.

According to Kornblith, thinking about these two questions and their relations gives us one way to understand naturalistic epistemology. Naturalistic epistemology, he suggests, holds that we cannot answer the traditional normative question independently of answering Q2. He writes, "I take the naturalistic approach to epistemology to consist in this: question 1 cannot be answered independently of question 2."[7] He suggests that in order to know how we ought to form beliefs we must know how we do actually form beliefs. In order to answer the traditional normative epistemological questions we must do empirical psychology.

But how would empirical psychology, which focuses on how we actually form beliefs, tell us how we *ought* to form beliefs? Kornblith makes the following suggestion. Consider Q3. Suppose that we know that the answer to Q3 is "yes." We would then know:

(1) The processes by which we do arrive at beliefs are the ones by which we ought to arrive at our beliefs.

Now, suppose that empirical psychology identifies some way of forming beliefs. Suppose, for example, it tells us that:

(2) Perceptual processes are one way in which we do arrive at beliefs.

[7] Hilary Kornblith, *Naturalizing Epistemology* (Cambridge, MA: The MIT Press, 1987), p. 3.

(1) and (2) imply:

(3) Perceptual processes are one way in which we ought to arrive at beliefs.

If we know that the answer to Q3 is "yes," in other words, if we know that (1) is true, then we can discover how we ought to form beliefs just by doing empirical psychology. As Kornblith says:

> If we know in advance, however, that we arrive at beliefs in just the way we ought, one way to approach question 1 is just by doing psychology. In discovering the processes by which we actually arrive at beliefs, we are thereby discovering the processes by which we ought to arrive at beliefs. The epistemological enterprise may be replaced by empirical psychology.[8]

Kornblith here defends a version of the replacement thesis. If we know that (1) is true, then we can answer the normative questions of traditional epistemology just by doing empirical psychology. Indeed, empirical psychology would seem much better suited to answering those questions than traditional epistemology.

This is an intriguing proposal. But what reason do we have to answer "yes" to Q3? Why should we think that premise (1) is true? Kornblith suggests that we might support (1) by appealing to evolutionary biology. Basically, the idea is that the cognitive processes of human beings have enabled us to survive and reproduce over tens of thousands of years. If our cognitive faculties did not have a bias in favor of true beliefs, then we would not have been able to successfully survive and reproduce. Having true beliefs has survival value. So, natural selection gives us a predisposition to form true beliefs. Kornblith claims that "If nature has so constructed us that our belief-generating processes are inevitably biased in favor of true beliefs, then it must be that the processes by which we arrive at beliefs just are those by which we ought to arrive at them."[9] We might take Kornblith to support premise (1) and a positive answer to Q3 with the following argument:

The Darwinian argument

(4) Nature has endowed our cognitive processes with a bias toward true beliefs.

---

[8] *Ibid.*, p. 5.
[9] *Ibid.*, p. 5.

(5) If nature has endowed our cognitive processes with a bias toward true beliefs, then the processes by which we do arrive at beliefs are the ones by which we ought to arrive at our beliefs.

Therefore,

(1) The processes by which we do arrive at beliefs are the ones by which we ought to arrive at our beliefs.[10]

The Darwinian argument is a valid argument. The conclusion follows from the premises. So, again, *if* we know that (1) is true, then it seems we can answer the traditional questions of normative epistemology by doing empirical psychology. Furthermore, it would seem that would could answer the traditional normative questions empirically or *a posteriori*.

There are a variety of objections to Kornblith's approach. First, consider premise (4) in the Darwinian Argument. Suppose we take (4) to mean:

(4′) Nature has endowed *all* of our cognitive processes with a bias toward true beliefs.

(4′) does not seem very plausible. Some of our cognitive processes seem woefully unreliable and not biased toward true belief. Consider such processes as hasty generalization and wishful thinking. Those processes do not seem biased toward the truth. The same is true of the common forms of logical fallacies, formal and informal, to which most of us seem prone. So, if we understand (4) in terms of (4′), then it seems that the Darwinian Argument is unsound. Suppose, however, we understand (4) in terms of:

(4″) Nature has endowed *some* of our cognitive processes with a bias toward true belief.

(4″) might well be true. But if we understand (4) in terms of (4′), then we should also modify (5):

(5′) If nature has endowed *some* of our cognitive processes with a bias toward true belief, then *some* of the processes by which we do arrive at beliefs are the ones by which we ought to arrive at our beliefs.

---

[10] I am indebted to Matthias Steup for this formulation of the argument. Matthias Steup, *An Introduction to Contemporary Epistemology* (Upper Saddle River, NJ: Prentice-Hall, Inc., 1996), p. 198.

But, now, from (4″) and (5′), we can only draw the more modest conclusion:

(1′) *Some* of the processes by which we form our beliefs are the ones by which we ought to form our beliefs.

(1′) is a much weaker claim than our original (1). It does not tell us which of our cognitive processes we ought to use. If we are simply entitled to (1′), then it is far from clear that we can answer the traditional epistemological question Q1 *simply* through empirical psychology. Since we cannot simply answer "yes" to Q3, then it seems we cannot answer Q1 simply by answering Q2. If some of our cognitive processes have a bias toward true beliefs and some do not, then in order to know how we *ought* to form beliefs it would not be enough to know *how* we actually form beliefs.

Second, let's consider premise (5′) in the Darwinian Argument. Premise (5′) is a normative premise. Basically, (5′) presupposes that *if* our cognitive processes have a bias toward the truth, then those are the processes we *ought* to use. This seems initially quite plausible. Still, we might wonder if it is true. Suppose that a cognitive process has a bias toward true belief if just slightly over half of the beliefs produced by that process are true. Now, suppose that some process, P, has such a slight or minimal bias toward the truth. Is it true that we ought to use P? Some might object that this is too permissive or too lax a standard. They might say, "Look, while it is admittedly a good thing to have true beliefs, it is *really* bad to form false beliefs." They might hold that we ought not to use such minimally truth-biased standards because it is really important to avoid error. We ought to use processes that are much more reliable. Still, others might insist that because error is so bad, we ought to use only infallible processes. Just how reliable or truth-biased should a process be in order for it to be the case that we *ought* to use it? The normative claim in (5) and (5′) is certainly debatable. Moreover, how should we answer this question? Is this normative question one that can be answered by empirical psychology, by studying the ways in which we actually form beliefs? Can it be answered by considering evolutionary biology? It is hard to see how our normative question can be answered by either of those disciplines. Indeed, whether these normative questions can be answered empirically, or *a posteriori*, is controversial.

A *posteriori* epistemology

While few philosophers have accepted the replacement thesis, naturalized epistemology remains attractive to many. In this section, we'll look at another way of understanding naturalized epistemology, or at least what some regard as a central theme in naturalized epistemology. James Maffie suggests that "Naturalists are united by a shared commitment to the continuity of epistemology and science."[11] But what exactly does a belief in the "continuity of epistemology and science" amount to? Quine suggests that epistemic questions are "scientific questions about a species of primates, and they are open to scientific investigation."[12] Following Quine, Maffie suggests that one way of understanding the naturalist's commitment to the continuity of epistemology and science is that "Epistemology, like science, is an a posteriori enterprise. Epistemic issues are empirical and resolvable a posteriori."[13] Understood in this way, naturalized epistemology holds that epistemological issues are to be resolved empirically *and* that empirical science is central to the resolution of these issues. Let us call this view "the empirical thesis." Naturalized epistemology, so understood, rejects the view that we can have significant epistemic knowledge *a priori*.

It seems quite plausible that some important epistemological questions are not resolvable *a priori*. Consider, for example, whether sense perception or memory are reliable. It seems clearly to be a contingent matter whether they are reliable. It seems logically possible that they are reliable and logically possible that they are not. But since *a priori* knowledge seems confined to what is necessarily true, it seems clear that we cannot know *a priori* that sense perception and memory are reliable. Further, it is a contingent fact that we have perceptual and memory knowledge. But, again, since it is a contingent fact, it seems clear that we cannot know *a priori* that we have perceptual or memory knowledge. Whether perception and memory are reliable and whether we have perceptual or memory knowledge

---

[11] James Maffie, "Recent Work in Naturalized Epistemology," *American Philosophical Quarterly*, 27, no. 4 (October 1990), 281.

[12] W. V, Quine, "The Nature of Natural Knowledge," in *Mind and Language*, ed. Samuel Guttenplan (Oxford: Clarendon Press, 1975), p. 68.

[13] *Ibid.*, p. 283.

are important questions. Thus, it seems clear that some important epistemological issues cannot be resolved *a priori*.

Moreover, suppose we are interested in what are *good* ways of forming beliefs, where good ways of forming beliefs are understood to be ways of forming beliefs which are reliably truth-conducive. Here again, it seems that knowing which are the good ways of forming beliefs would be an empirical or *a posteriori* matter. It seems clear that epistemologists would be interested in discovering which are the good ways of forming beliefs and which are not. This, too, seems to be an important philosophical issue that cannot be decided *a priori*.

While it seems clear that there are important epistemological issues that cannot be resolved *a priori*, some philosophers would deny that we can have no *a priori* grounds to believe some substantive epistemic principles. Consider the following epistemic principle about perception:

> (P) If you seem to perceive that there is an F, and if you have no ground for doubting that you do perceive something that is F, then it is beyond reasonable doubt for you that you are perceiving something that is F.[14]

Principle (P) is a principle about justification. Some philosophers have suggested that we have some degree of *a priori* justification for believing principles similar to (P).[15] Some have suggested that we might also have some degree of *a priori* justification for believing the following principles about induction and testimony:

> (I) If you know that there are 1,000 marbles in a jar, 999 are black, 1 is white, and 1 has been randomly selected (and you have no other relevant information), then it is reasonable for you to believe that the one selected is black.[16]

> (T) Knowledge that a particular source has been trustworthy with respect to a given topic in the past provides good reason to believe things that source testifies to on that topic in the future.[17]

---

[14] Cf. Roderick Chisholm, "The Status of Epistemic Principles," *Nous*, 24 (April 1990), 209.

[15] Roderick Chisholm suggests that a principle very similar to (P) is knowable *a priori*. Other philosophers have suggested similar views. See H. H. Price, *Perception* (New York: Robert McBride, 1933), pp. 185–86 and Robert Audi *Belief, Justification, and Knowledge* (Belmont, CA: Wadsworth Publishing, 1988), p. 154.

[16] Richard Feldman, *Epistemology* (Upper Saddle River, NJ: Prentice-Hall, Inc., 2003), p. 138.

[17] *Ibid.*, p. 172.

Principles (I) and (T) are also principles of evidence and justification. They tell us that if one satisfies the condition laid out in the antecedent, then it reasonable for one to believe, or one has reason to believe, some proposition.

Not surprisingly these claims are controversial. Consider, for example, principle (P). Suppose, for example, that one is a reliabilist or an externalist who holds that perception is a source of justified belief only if it is a reliable truth-conducive faculty. Since one cannot know *a priori* that perception is a reliable source of belief, it would seem that one cannot know *a priori* that (P) is true. A reliabilist might make similar claims about these other principles. He might hold, for example, that whether induction is a source of justification depends on whether induction is a reliable way of forming beliefs. Since we cannot know *a priori* that it is a reliable way of forming beliefs, we cannot know *a priori* that (I) is true. Our attitude toward some fundamental questions about the nature of epistemic justification, whether, for example, we favor an internalist or externalist view, will influence whether we think these principles are knowable or justified *a priori*.

Let us set aside the difficult issue of whether epistemic principles such as those considered above are knowable or justified *a priori*. Many philosophers would still hold that there are important objections to the empirical thesis. Let us consider two lines of objection.

First, many philosophers will note that some epistemological issues concern the analysis or definition of important or interesting concepts. Consider, for example, issues about the definition or analysis of knowledge such as those we considered in connection with the Gettier problem. In seeking an analysis or definition of knowledge we seek a set of necessary and sufficient conditions that hold true necessarily. A satisfactory analysis of knowledge must tell us what is true of all *possible* instances of knowledge. It is not clear that we can arrive at a satisfactory definition or analysis of knowledge *a posteriori* or that we can discover such an analysis through empirical investigation. Consequently, many philosophers would hold that the definition of knowledge is a conceptual issue that must be resolved *a priori*. Of course, knowledge is not the only important epistemic concept for which we would like an analysis or definition. Consider concepts such as *justified*, *reasonable*, and *evidence*. It is unclear how we would discover the definitions or analyses of these concepts *a posteriori*, or through empirical research.

Again, there seem to be important conceptual issues in epistemology that do not appear to be resolvable *a posteriori*, or through the methods of science. Consider, for example, the debate about what it is for a belief to be justified. As we have seen, some philosophers view epistemic justification as a matter of believing in a way that is epistemically responsible. Others take epistemic justification to be a matter of believing in a way that is reliably truth-conducive. Philosophers disagree about the concept of justification and what it involves. This is an important epistemological issue. But it is far from clear that this issue is resolvable *a posteriori*. It is not clear how this issue would be resolved through further empirical research. So, if naturalism is committed to the view that all important epistemological issues are to be resolved *a posteriori*, then such a view seems mistaken.

Second, the empirical thesis holds that natural science is central to the resolution of important epistemological issues. Some philosophers would hold that even if some important epistemological issues are to be resolved empirically, or on *a posteriori* grounds, naturalism tends to overstate the importance and necessity of the role of empirical science. Consider, for example, the claims that perception and memory are reliable. It seems that most people know that perception and memory are generally reliable. Most people know that perception and memory are more reliable than mere guessing or wishful thinking. Moreover, most people have some idea of the circumstances in which perception and memory are reliable. It seems that this common knowledge about the reliability of perception and memory is *a posteriori* knowledge. But even if it is *a posteriori* knowledge it is not the result of scientific investigation or empirical science. This is not to deny, however, that there is much that science can tell us about how reliable memory and perception are and how different conditions can affect the reliability of each. Surely, there is a great deal that science can tell us about the reliability of our faculties, but it would seem to be an overstatement to say that one needs empirical science to know that perception and memory are reliable. One can know, for example, that one's car or television set is reliable without being an engineer or a scientist. This is not to deny, of course, that the engineer or scientist can tell us a great deal about why one's car or television is reliable and what conditions will affect their performance.

Again, even if one believes that *a posteriori* or empirical considerations are important for resolving various epistemological issues, it is not so clear that natural science must play a central role. Consider, for example, G. E. Moore's response to skepticism. Moore claims to know the epistemic proposition "I know I have a hand". This epistemic proposition is a contingent proposition. It is not something that Moore knows *a priori*. It is known *a posteriori*. Moore rejects skepticism because it conflicts with this bit of *a posteriori* knowledge (and with a great many other bits of *a posteriori* knowledge). In this respect, Moore rejects skepticism on *a posteriori* grounds. Moore and his followers would reject a great many proposed epistemic principles on the same *a posteriori* grounds. But Moore's knowledge of the epistemic proposition "I know I have a hand," is not based on scientific inquiry. Almost everyone knows similar epistemic propositions where this knowledge is not the result of natural science. The point is that even if we think that it is reasonable to reject skepticism on *a posteriori* grounds, it is not clear that these grounds *must* be provided by natural science. To think that we must turn to cognitive science or natural science to respond to skepticism would seem to be a mistake.

Epistemic values and natural facts

Maffie suggests that there is another way of understanding naturalized epistemology's commitment to the continuity between epistemology and science. According to this second proposal, there is a "metaphysical continuity" between the kinds of facts studied by natural science and those studied by epistemology. Maffie writes:

> Naturalizing epistemology also typically involves establishing metaphysical continuity between the *object domains* of (i.e., objects studied by) epistemology and science. Epistemic properties, facts, or states of affairs are argued to be identical with, constituted by, or supervenient upon descriptive properties, facts, or states of affairs. Epistemic value is anchored to descriptive fact, no longer entering the world autonomously as brute, fundamental fact.[18]

According to this view, naturalized epistemology holds that epistemic properties or facts are identical with, constituted by, or supervenient on descriptive properties and facts. Naturalized epistemology rejects the view that epistemic properties and facts are "autonomous," that they are

---

[18] Maffie, "Recent work in Naturalized Epistemology," p. 284.

independent of or not determined by descriptive or natural facts. Let us consider this view more closely.

Let us consider the view that epistemic properties and facts are identical with descriptive or natural facts. What makes a property A identical to property B? That is hard to say. There is no widely accepted set of necessary and sufficient conditions of property identity. Still, it is widely accepted that property A is identical to property B only if it is necessarily the case that whatever has A also has B and *vice versa*. So, consider the properties of *being water* and *being H$_2$O*. We can say that *being water* is identical with *being H$_2$O* only if it is necessarily the case that whatever has the property of *being water* has the property of *being H$_2$O* and *vice versa*.

Suppose that the property of *being epistemically justified* is identical with some descriptive or natural property, perhaps with some rather complicated natural or descriptive property, e.g. *being the product of a reliable truth-conducive process*. Let's suppose, for the sake of argument, that *being epistemically justified* is identical with some natural property, *being F*. This would be a clear sense in which the property of epistemic justification is not independent of the natural or descriptive properties of things. According to this view, *being epistemically justified* just *is* the descriptive property of *being F*. Since the former property is identical to the latter, it is necessarily the case that if something has the property of *being F*, then it also has the property of *being epistemically justified*. If this view is right, epistemic properties are not autonomous or independent of descriptive properties.

This view about the relationship between the epistemic and the descriptive or natural has its analog in ethics. Some forms of *ethical naturalism* hold that moral and evaluative properties are identical with descriptive or natural properties. According to these views, moral properties are not independent of natural or descriptive properties. They just *are* natural or descriptive properties. Ethical naturalists of this sort will hold that the property of *being morally obligatory* is identical with some descriptive or natural property. Some ethical naturalists will hold, for example, that *being morally obligatory* is identical with the property of *bringing about more utility than any alternative act*. Other ethical naturalists might hold that it is identical with the property of *being approved by the agent's society*. Ethical naturalists often disagree about the natural or descriptive properties with which moral properties are identical.

Those who believe that epistemic properties are identical with descriptive properties face a similar sort of problem. The problem is that it is unclear which natural or descriptive properties the epistemic properties are identical to. Consider the property of *being epistemically justified*. Just what natural or descriptive property is it identical to? Perhaps it is identical with the property of *being the product of a reliable cognitive process*. Or perhaps it is identical with the property of *belonging to a coherent body of beliefs*. Unfortunately, it seems clear, for reasons we have considered in previous chapters, that being epistemically justified cannot be identical with either of those properties. It is fair to say that even among those naturalists who think epistemic properties are identical with some natural or descriptive property there is no consensus about which natural properties they are identical to.

According to Maffie, the proponent of naturalized epistemology need not hold that epistemic properties are identical with natural or descriptive properties. Maffie suggests that they might hold instead that epistemic properties *supervene* on natural or descriptive properties. In chapter 3 we discussed some general features of this view. According to this view, epistemic properties are had *in virtue of* descriptive or natural properties. So, just as the goodness of an apple depends on certain natural or descriptive properties of that apple, the epistemic properties of a belief, such as its being justified, will depend on its descriptive or natural properties. As we noted in chapter 3, many philosophers who accept the view that epistemic properties supervene on descriptive properties also accept the following thesis:

E   Necessarily, if two things share all of their descriptive properties, then they share all of their evaluative properties.

If this view is correct, then the evaluative properties of a thing are determined by its descriptive properties, at least in the sense that two things cannot differ in their evaluative properties without having some difference in their descriptive properties. In this respect, the evaluative properties of things are tied to their descriptive properties. If epistemic properties do supervene on descriptive or natural properties, then epistemic properties are not autonomous or independent of descriptive properties.

One can accept that evaluative or normative properties supervene on descriptive or natural properties without holding that evaluative properties are identical to the descriptive properties on which they supervene. To hold that an evaluative property supervenes on a descriptive property is not to imply that the properties are identical. To see why this is so, consider, for example, the property of being intrinsically good (G). One might hold that G is a property of various mental states. One might hold that some mental states have G in virtue of having different kinds of descriptive properties. For example, one might hold that a mental state can have G in virtue of being an instance of pleasure (P) or in virtue of being an instance of courage (C). According to this view, G supervenes on P and G supervenes on C. Both P and C are intrinsically good-making properties. But since P and C are not identical, it follows that G is not identical with either of them.

The view that epistemic properties supervene on descriptive or natural properties seems very plausible. But it is not clear that this view is incompatible with the claims of traditional epistemology. There is no reason to think that various traditional epistemological views must reject this claim. Consider, for example, coherence theories of justification. Coherence theories of justification might hold that justification supervenes on a belief's having the property of belonging to a coherent body of beliefs. Even classical foundationalists would seem able to accept supervenience. Classical foundationalists might hold that a belief is justified in virtue of either being infallibly produced or being deduced from beliefs that are infallibly produced. If this is right, then traditional epistemology, at least certain forms of it, is not committed to the view that epistemic values are autonomous or that they are not anchored to the natural world. If accepting the supervenience of the epistemic on the descriptive is a virtue of naturalized epistemology, it seems to be a virtue that can be shared by traditional epistemology. If metaphysical continuity is a virtue of naturalized epistemology, it would appear to be a virtue traditional epistemology can also enjoy.

Limited naturalism

As we noted at the beginning of this chapter there are a variety of forms of naturalism. The most radical forms advocate the abandonment of traditional epistemology in favor of some form of natural science. Still, there are less extreme forms of naturalism. Some philosophers advocate a view that is sometimes called "limited naturalism." According to limited naturalism, there is a legitimate role for traditional philosophical activity. The limited naturalist holds that defining or giving an analysis of central epistemic concepts such as knowledge, justification, or evidence is a properly philosophical activity. There are also normative questions and issues that are appropriate topics for philosophical investigation. Thus, it is the business of philosophy to discover what makes beliefs justified or reasonable, to discover criteria for justified belief. Such a criterion or standard might have the form: A belief is justified if and only if it has F (where is F is some natural or descriptive property). Similarly, philosophical reflection might tell us that in order to be an instance of knowledge a belief must issue from a cognitive process or epistemic virtue with a certain degree of reliability.

So far this sounds very much like traditional epistemology. But now suppose that we want to know, for example, whether a belief is an instance of knowledge. In order to know whether it was we would need to know whether it met our standard. We would need to know whether it did in fact come from a cognitive process with the appropriate degree of reliability. Presumably, empirical psychology would be relevant to telling us whether our beliefs did in fact meet that standard. Empirical psychology could identify what cognitive processes did in fact produce our beliefs and tell us whether those processes met the requisite standard of reliability. So, according to this view, empirical psychology can be relevant to whether some belief of ours counts as knowledge. Clearly, if being justified requires that a belief be the product of a cognitive process with a suitably high degree of reliability, then similar comments would apply. In that case, empirical psychology would be relevant to the issue of whether our beliefs met that standard of justification.

Alvin Goldman is a proponent of this sort of limited naturalism. Goldman writes, "To the extent that human epistemic achievements critically depend on human cognitive endowments, those endowments are relevant to epistemology. The nature and extent of those endowments are matters to be ascertained by psychological science, specifically, by psychology or cognitive science. Hence, cognitive science is relevant to certain epistemological questions."[19]

---

[19] Alvin Goldman, "The Sciences and Epistemology," in *The Oxford Handbook of Epistemology*, ed. Paul Moser (Oxford: Oxford University Press, 2002), p. 146.

The connection Goldman sees between traditional normative issues in epistemology and empirical science has an analog in ethics. Suppose, for example, that we want to know what makes right actions right? Discovering the appropriate standards or criteria of right action seems to be a traditional normative philosophical enterprise. It is the business of normative ethics to discover such criteria. Suppose, however, that philosophical reflection convinces us that act utilitarianism is true. Imagine, in other words, that philosophical reflection tells us that an act is right just in case it maximizes utility. Now, suppose we want to know whether a particular act *is* right. To know whether some particular act satisfies our utilitarian criterion we would need to know whether it did in fact maximize utility. This would require, in turn, that we know a great deal about the consequences of that act and the consequences of alternative acts. Knowledge of these things is not a matter of armchair philosophical speculation. To have knowledge of these things would require that we do some empirical research. In particular, we might expect that various social sciences could tell us much that was relevant concerning the consequences of certain types of actions, and in this respect they are relevant to certain ethical questions.

Of course, even if we do not accept a utilitarian standard of right action, we might think, nonetheless, that the moral rightness of a practice, policy, or decision depends at least in part on its consequences and those of the alternatives. So, we might think that whether the death penalty is a morally acceptable practice or whether a lowering of the tax rate is a morally correct decision depends in part on the consequences of those decisions. But, again, knowledge of the consequences of such policies and decisions is not to be determined through armchair philosophical investigation. We might expect that economics and other social sciences could tell us much that was relevant to determining the rightness of such practices and decisions.

According to this sort of limited naturalism, natural science does not replace epistemology, but instead it holds that epistemology should proceed in cooperation with natural science. Such cooperation *might* lead us to revise some of our epistemological views. To illustrate how this might happen, consider the following suggestion by Goldman. Suppose that an epistemologist holds that in order for a belief to be an instance of knowledge it has to meet standard S. Perhaps S requires that in order for a belief to be an instance of knowledge it must issue from a process with some high degree of reliability. But now suppose that our epistemologist "is told by science – at least by certain scientists – that human cognitive capacities are inadequate to realize standard S."[20] In this case, our epistemologist has three options. The first option is a skeptical conclusion. One might hold that since knowledge requires meeting standard S and since our beliefs do not meet that standard – at least according to some scientists – it follows that our beliefs do not amount to knowledge. A second option would be to revise or reject this particular standard of knowledge. She might hold that since we really do have knowledge, standard S must not be the right standard for knowledge after all. A third option would be to question the initial scientific claims. As Goldman notes, scientists sometimes differ among themselves concerning issues in their field. It might be that other scientists reject the claim that human beings cannot meet standard S. If this competing scientific story looks better, then our epistemologist might keep standard S and still reject the skeptical conclusion. According to Goldman, "Any of these upshots would certainly be important to epistemology, but they depend on what science has to offer. Thus, epistemology should proceed in *cooperation* with science."[21]

Whether cooperation between epistemology and science will prove fruitful and, indeed, what fruit it will bear, remains to be seen. In any case, it seems that traditional epistemology might welcome such cooperation. Why, after all, should it cut itself off from any avenue of investigation that could be relevant? Why should it shun anything that might be relevant? The view that epistemology should ignore the testimony of empirical science in evaluating some beliefs seems no more reasonable than the view that moral philosophy should ignore the testimony of the sciences in evaluating some actions and policies. The problems of epistemology are sufficiently perplexing that it would seem wise to seek illumination wherever it is to be found.

[20] *Ibid.*, p. 147.
[21] *Ibid.*, p. 147.

Select bibliography

Almeder, Robert, *Blind Realism* (Lanham, MD: Rowman and Littlefield, 1992).
  "On Naturalizing Epistemology," *American Philosophical Quarterly*, 27 (1990), 263–79.
Alston, William, *Epistemic Justification: Essays in the Theory of Knowledge* (Ithaca, NY: Cornell University Press, 1989).
  The Reliability of Sense Perception (Ithaca, NY: Cornell University Press, 1993).
  "Two Types of Foundationalism," *The Journal of Philosophy*, 73 (1976), 165–85.
  "Some Remarks on Chisholm's Epistemology," *Nous*, 14 (1980), 565–86.
  "How to Think About Reliability," *Philosophical Topics* (1995), 1–29.
  "A 'Doxastic Practice' Approach to Epistemology," *Empirical Knowledge*, 2nd edn., ed. Paul K. Moser (Lanham, MD: Rowman and Littlefield, 1996).
Amico, Robert P., *The Problem of the Criterion* (Lanham, MD: Rowman and Littlefield, 1993).
Audi, Robert, *Belief, Justification, and Knowledge* (Belmont, CA: Wadsworth Publishing, 1988).
  The Structure of Justification (Cambridge: Cambridge University Press, 1993).
  "The Sources of Knowledge," *The Oxford Handbook of Epistemology*, ed. Paul Moser (Oxford: Oxford University Press, 2002).
Aristotle, *Metaphysics*, trans. W. D. Ross in *The Basic Works of Aristotle*, ed. Richard McKeon (New York: Random House, 1941).
Armstrong, David, *Belief, Truth, and Knowledge* (Cambridge: Cambridge University Press, 1973).
Akins, Kathleen (ed.), *Perception* (Oxford: Oxford University Press, 1996).
St. Augustine, *On the Trinity* in *The Essential Augustine*, ed. Vernon J. Bourke (Indianapolis: Hackett, 1974).
Ayer, A. J., *The Problem of Knowledge* (New York: St. Martin's Press, Inc., 1955).
Baergen, Ralph, *Contemporary Epistemology* (Orlando, FL: Harcourt Brace and Co., 1995).
Bealer, George, "A Theory of the A Priori," *Philosophical Perspectives*, 13 (1999), 29–57.

Bender, John, W. (ed.), *The Current State of the Coherence Theory: Critical Essays on the Epistemic Theories of Keith Lehrer and Laurence BonJour, with Replies* (Dordrecht: Kluwer Academic Publishers, 1989).

Bergmann, Michael, *Justification without Awareness: A Defense of Epistemic Externalism* (Oxford: Oxford University Press, 2006).

Berkeley, George, *Three Dialogues between Hylas and Philonous*, ed. Robert Merrihew Adams (Indianapolis: Hackett, 1979).

A Treatise Concerning the Principles of Human Knowledge, ed. Colin M. Turbayne (Indianapolis: Bobbs-Merrill, 1957).

Blanshard, Brand, *The Nature of Thought* (New York: Macmillan, 1940).

BonJour, Laurence, *The Structure of Empirical Knowledge* (Cambridge, MA: Harvard University Press, 1985).

Epistemology (Lanham, MD: Rowman and Littlefield, 2002).

In Defense of Pure Reason (Cambridge: Cambridge University Press, 1997).

"Reply to Steup," *Philosophical Studies*, 55, 57–63.

"Internalism and Externalism," *The Oxford Handbook of Epistemology*, ed. Paul Moser (Oxford: Oxford University Press, 2002).

BonJour, Laurence and Sosa, Ernest, *Epistemic Justification* (Malden, MA: Blackwell, 2003).

Butchvarov, Panayot, *Skepticism about the External World* (Oxford: Oxford University Press, 1998).

Campbell, Donald, "Evolutionary Epistemology," *The Philosophy of Karl Popper*, ed. Paul Schillp (LaSalle, IL: Open Court, 1974).

Casullo, Albert, *A Priori Justification* (Oxford: Oxford University Press, 2003).

"A Priori Justification," *The Oxford Handbook of Epistemology*, ed. Paul Moser (Oxford: Oxford University Press, 2002).

Chisholm, Roderick, *Perceiving: A Philosophical Study* (Ithaca: Cornell University Press, 1957).

The Problem of the Criterion (Milwaukee: Marquette University Press, 1973).

Theory of Knowledge (Englewood Cliffs, NJ: Prentice-Hall, Inc., 1966); 2nd edn., 1977; 3rd edn., 1989.

The Foundations of Knowing (Minneapolis, MN: University of Minnesota Press, 1982).

"On the Nature of Empirical Evidence," *Empirical Knowledge: Readings from Contemporary Sources*, eds. Roderick M. Chisholm and Robert J. Swartz (Englewood Cliffs, NJ: Prentice-Hall, Inc., 1973).

"The Status of Epistemic Principles," *Nous*, 24 (1990), 209–15.

Clay, Marjorie and Lehrer, Keith, *Knowledge and Skepticism* (Boulder, CO: Westview Press, 1989).

Cohen, Stewart, "Justification and Truth," *Philosophical Studies*, 46 (1984), 279–95.

"Contextualism, Skepticism, and the Structure of Reasons," *Philosophical Perspectives*, 13 (1999), 57–89.

"Basic Knowledge and the Problem of Easy Knowledge," *Philosophy and Phenomenological Research*, 65 (2002), 209–329.

Conee, Earl, "The Basic Nature of Epistemic Justification," *The Monist*, 46 (1984), 279–95.

Conee, Earl and Feldman, Richard, *Evidentialism* (Oxford: Oxford University Press, 2004).

"Evidentialism," *Philosophical Studies*, 48, 15–44.

The Generality, et al., "The Generality Problem for Reliabilism," *Philosophical Studies*, 89 (1998), 1–29.

Cornman, James, *Perception, Common Sense, and Science* (New Haven, CT: Yale University Press, 1975).

Crumley, Jack S., *An Introduction to Epistemology* (Mountain View, CA: Mayfield, 1999).

Dancy, Jonathan, *Introduction to Contemporary Epistemology* (Oxford: Blackwell, 1985).

(ed.), *Perceptual Knowledge* (Oxford: Oxford University Press, 1988).

Dancy, Jonathan and Sosa, Ernest, *A Companion to Epistemology* (Oxford: Blackwell, 1992).

Davidson, Donald, "A Coherence Theory of Truth and Knowledge," in *Kant oder Hegel*, ed. Dieter Henrich (Stuttgart: Klein-Cotta, 1983).

DePaul, Michael (ed.), *Rethinking Intuition* (Lanham, MD: Rowman and Littlefield, 1999).

(ed.), *Resurrecting Old-Fashioned Foundationalism* (Lanham, MD: Rowman and Littlefield, 2001).

DePaul, Michael and Zagzebski, Linda (eds.), *Intellectual Virtue: Perspectives from Ethics and Epistemology* (Oxford: Oxford University Press, 2003).

Descartes, René, *Meditations* in *The Philosophical Works of Descartes*, vol. 2, eds. J. Cottingham, R. Stoothoff, and D. Murdoch (Cambridge: Cambridge University Press, 1991).

DeRose, Keith, "Solving the Skeptical Problem," *Philosophical Review*, 104 (1995), 1–52.

DeRose, Keith and Warfield, Ted A. (eds.), *Skepticism: A Contemporary Reader* (New York: Oxford University Press, 1999).

Dretske, Fred, *Knowledge and the Flow of Information* (Cambridge, MA: The MIT Press, 1981).

"Epistemic Operators," *Journal of Philosophy*, 67 (1970), 1007–23.

Elgin, Katherine, *Considered Judgment* (Princeton, NJ: Princeton University Press, 1996).

Feldman, Richard, *Epistemology* (Upper Saddle River, NJ: Prentice-Hall, 2003).

"An Alleged Defect in Gettier Counterexamples," *Australasian Journal of Philosophy*, 52 (1974), 68–69.

"Reliability and Justification," *Monist*, 68 (1985), 159–74.

"Skeptical Problems, Contextualist Solutions," *Philosophical Studies*, 103 (2001), 61–85.

Fogelin, Richard, *Pyrrhonian Reflections on Knowledge and Justification* (New York: Oxford University Press, 1994).

Foley, Richard, *The Theory of Epistemic Rationality* (Cambridge, MA: Harvard University Press, 1987).

Working Without a Net (Oxford: Oxford University Press, 1993).

"What's Wrong with Reliabilism," *The Monist*, 68 (1985), 188–202.

French, Peter, Uehling, Theodore E. and Wettstein, Howard K. (eds.), *Midwest Studies in Philosophy 5* (Minneapolis, MN: The University of Minnesota Press, 1980).

Fumerton, Richard, *Metaepistemology and Skepticism* (Lanham, MD: Rowman and Littlefield, 1995).

"Theories of Justification," *The Oxford Handbook of Epistemology*, ed. Paul Moser (Oxford: Oxford University Press, 2002).

Gettier, Edmund, "Is Justified True Belief Knowledge?" *Analysis*, 23 (1963), 121–23.

Goldman, Alan, *Empirical Knowledge* (Berkeley: University of California Press, 1988).

Goldman, Alvin, *Epistemology and Cognition* (Cambridge, MA: Harvard University Press, 1986).

Liaisons: Philosophy, the Cognitive and the Social Sciences (Cambridge, MA: The MIT Press, 1992).

"A Causal Theory of Knowing," *The Journal of Philosophy*, 64 (1967), 355–72.

"Discrimination and Perceptual Knowledge," *The Journal of Philosophy*, 73 (1976), 771–91.

"What is Justified Belief," *Justification and Knowledge*, ed. George Pappas (Dordrecht, Netherlands: D. Reidel, 1979), pp. 1–23.

"Strong and Weak Justification," *Philosophical Perspectives*, 2, 51–69.

"The Sciences and Epistemology," in *The Oxford Handbook of Epistemology*, ed. Paul Moser (Oxford: Oxford University Press, 2002).

Greco, John, *Putting Skeptics in Their Place: The Nature of Skeptical Arguments and their Role in Philosophical Inquiry* (Cambridge: Cambridge University Press, 2000).

(ed.), *Ernest Sosa and His Critics* (Oxford: Basil Blackwell, 2004).

"Virtues in Epistemology," *The Oxford Handbook of Epistemology*, ed. Paul Moser (Oxford: Oxford University Press, 2002).

Greco, John and Sosa, Ernest, *The Blackwell Guide to Epistemology* (Oxford: Basil Blackwell, 1998).

Haack, Susan, *Evidence and Inquiry: Towards Reconstruction in Epistemology* (Oxford: Blackwell, 1993).

Hare, R. M., *The Language of Morals* (Oxford: Oxford University Press, 1952).

Harman, Gilbert, *Thought* (Princeton: Princeton University Press, 1973).

   Change in View (Cambridge, MA: The MIT Press, 1986).

   "Inference to the Best Explanation," *The Theory of Knowledge: Classic and Contemporary Readings*, ed. Louis P. Pojman (Belmont, CA: Wadsworth Publishing Co., 1993).

Harris, James and Severens, Richard H. (eds.), *Analyticity* (Chicago: Quadrangle Books, 1970).

Hume, David, *An Enquiry Concerning Human Understanding*, ed. Charles W. Hendel (Indianapolis: Bobbs-Merrill, 1976).

James, William, *Essays in Pragmatism* (New York: Hafner Publishing Co., 1948).

Kant, Immanuel, *Critique of Pure Reason*, trans. Norman Kemp Smith (New York: St. Martin's Press, 1929).

Kim, Jaegwon, "What is Naturalized Epistemology?," *Philosophical Perspectives*, 2 (1988), 381–405.

Klein, Peter, "A Proposed Definition of Propositional Knowledge," *The Journal of Philosophy*, 68 (1971), 471–82.

   "Knowledge, Causality, and Defeasibility," *The Journal of Philosophy*, 73 (1976), 792–812.

   "Skepticism," *The Oxford Handbook of Skepticism*, ed. Paul Moser (Oxford: Oxford University Press, 2002).

Kornblith, Hilary (ed.), *Naturalizing Epistemology* (Cambridge, MA: The MIT Press, 1987); 2nd edn., 1994.

   "Beyond Foundationalism and the Coherence Theory," *The Journal of Philosophy*, 72 (1980), 597–612.

   "Justified Belief and Epistemically Responsible Action," *Philosophical Review*, 92 (1983), 33–48.

Kvanvig, Jonathan, *The Intellectual Virtues and the Life of the Mind* (Savage, MD: Rowman and Littlefield, 1992).

   (ed.), *Warrant in Contemporary Epistemology: Essays in Honor of Alvin Plantinga's Theory Knowledge* (Lanham, MD: Rowman and Littlefield, 1996).

   The Value of Knowledge and the Pursuit of Understanding (Cambridge: Cambridge University Press, 2003).

Leibniz, G.W., *New Essays Concerning Human Understanding*, trans. Alfred Gideon Langley (La Salle, IL: Open Court, 1949).

Lehrer, Keith, *Knowledge* (Oxford: Oxford University Press, 1974).

   "Knowledge, Truth, and Evidence," *Analysis*, 25 (1965), 168–75.

   "The Fourth Condition for Knowledge: A Defense," *The Review of Metaphysics*, 24 (1970), 122–28.

   Lehrer, Keith and Cohen, Stewart, "Justification, Truth and Coherence," *Synthese*, 55 (1983), 191–208.

Lemos, Noah, *Common Sense: A Contemporary Defense* (Cambridge: Cambridge University Press, 2004).

Lipton, Peter, *Inference to the Best Explanation* (London: Routledge, 1993).

Luper-Foy, Steven (ed.), *The Possibility of Knowledge* (Lanham, MD: Rowman and Littlefield, 1987).

Lycan, William, *Judgment and Justification* (Cambridge: Cambridge University Press, 1988).

"Moore Against the New Skeptics," *Philosophical Studies*, 103 (2001), 35–53.

Maffie, James, "Recent Work in Naturalized Epistemology," *American Philosophical Quarterly*, 27 (1990), 281–93.

Mill, John Stuart, *Utilitarianism* (Indianapolis: Hackett, 1979).

Montmarquet, James, *Epistemic Virtue and Doxastic Responsibility* (Lanham, MD: Rowman and Littlefield, 1993).

Moore, G. E., "Some Judgments of Perception," *Philosophical Studies* (London: Routledge and Kegan Paul, 1960).

"Proof of an External World," *Philosophical Papers* (New York: Macmillan, 1959).

"Hume's Philosophy Examined," *Some Main Problems of Philosophy* (New York: Macmillan, 1953).

"A Defence of Common Sense," *Philosophical Papers* (New York: Macmillan, 1959).

Moser, Paul, *Empirical Justification* (Dordrecht: Reidel, 1985).

Knowledge and Evidence (Cambridge: Cambridge University Press, 1989).

Philosophy After Objectivity (New York: Oxford University Press, 1993).

(ed.), *A Priori Knowledge* (Oxford: Oxford University Press, 1987).

(ed.), *The Oxford Handbook of Epistemology* (Oxford: Oxford University Press, 2002).

"Epistemological Fission," *The Monist*, 81 (1998), 353–70.

Moser, Paul and vander Nat, Arnold (eds.), *Human Knowledge: Classical and Contemporary Approaches* (Oxford: Oxford University Press, 1995); 2nd edn., 1995; 3rd edn., 2002.

Moser, Paul, Mulder, Dwayne, H., and Trout, J. D. (eds.), *The Theory of Knowledge: A Thematic Introduction* (Oxford: Oxford University Press, 1998).

Nozick, Robert, *Philosophical Explanations* (Cambridge, MA: Harvard University Press, 1981).

The Nature of Rationality (Princeton, NJ: Princeton University Press, 1993).

Pappas, George (ed.), *Justification and Knowledge* (Dordrecht: Reidel, 1979).

Pappas, George and Swain, Marshall (eds.), *Essays on Knowledge and Justification* (Ithaca, NY: Cornell University Press, 1978).

Plantinga, Alvin, *Warrant: The Current Debate* (New York: Oxford University Press, 1993).

Warrant and Proper Function (Oxford: Oxford University Press, 1993).

Plato, *Meno*, trans. G. M. A. Grube (Indianapolis: Hackett Publishing, 1976).

Pojman, Louis P., *What Can We Know?*, 2nd edn. (Belmont, CA: Wadsworth, 2001).

Pollock, John and Cruz, Joseph, *Contemporary Theories of Knowledge*, 2nd edn. (Lanham, MD: Rowman and Littlefield, 1999).

Price, H. H., *Perception* (New York: Robert McBride, 1933).

Pryor, James, "The Skeptic and the Dogmatist," *Nous*, 34 (2000), 517–249.

"What's Wrong with Moore's Argument?," *Philosophical Issues*, 14 (Oxford: Basil Blackwell, 2004).

Quine, W. V., *Word and Object* (Cambridge, MA: MIT Press, 1960).

"Two Dogmas of Empiricism," in *From a Logical Point of View* (New York: Harper and Row, 1953), pp. 20–46.

"Epistemology Naturalized," *Ontological Relativity and Other Essays* (New York: Columbia University Press, 1969), pp. 69–90.

"The Nature of Natural Knowledge," *Mind and Language*, ed. Samuel Guttenplan (Oxford: Clarendon Press, 1975).

Quinton, Anthony, "The *A Priori* and the Analytic," *Necessary Truth*, ed. Robert Sleigh (Englewood Cliffs, NJ: Prentice-Hall, Inc., 1972).

Rawls, John, *A Theory of Justice* (Cambridge, MA: Harvard University Press, 1971).

Reid, Thomas, *Essays on the Intellectual Powers of Man* (Cambridge, MA: The MIT Press, 1969).

Inquiry and Essays, eds. Ronald E. Beanblossom and Keith Lehrer (Indianapolis: Hackett, 1983).

Rescher, Nicolas, *Scepticism* (Oxford: Blackwell, 1980).

Rorty, Richard, *Philosophy and the Mirror of Nature* (Princeton, NJ: Princeton University Press, 1979).

Roth, Michael and Galis, Leon, *Knowing: Essays in the Analysis of Knowledge* (New York: Random House, 1970).

Russell, Bertrand, *The Problems of Philosophy* (Oxford: Oxford University Press, 1912).

Human Knowledge: Its Scope and Limits (New York: Allen and Unwin, 1948).

Schmitt, Frederick, *Knowledge and Belief* (London: Routledge, 1990).

Shope, Robert, *The Analysis of Knowing: A Decade of Research* (Princeton, NJ: Princeton University Press, 1983).

"The Conditional Fallacy in Contemporary Philosophy," *The Journal of Philosophy*, 75 (1978), 397–413.

"Conditions and Analyses of Knowing," in *The Oxford Handbook of Epistemology*, ed. Paul K. Moser (Oxford: Oxford University Press, 2002).

Skyrms, Brian, "The Explication of 'X knows that p'," *The Journal of Philosophy*, 64 (1967), 373–89.

Sosa, Ernest, *Knowledge in Perspective* (Cambridge: Cambridge University Press, 1991).

"The Foundations of Foundationalism," *Nous*, 14 (1980), 547–65.

"The Raft and the Pyramid: Coherence versus Foundations in the Theory of Knowledge," *Midwest Studies in Philosophy, Volume V* (Minneapolis, MN: The University of Minnesota Press, 1980), pp. 3–26.

"Philosophical Scepticism and Epistemic Circularity," *Empirical Knowledge*, 2nd edn., ed. Paul K. Moser (Lanham, MD: Rowman and Littlefield, 1996), pp. 303–29.

"How to Defeat Opposition to Moore," *Philosophical Perspectives*, 13 (1999), 141–53.

Sosa, Ernest and Kim, Jaegwon (eds.), *Epistemology* (Malden, MA: Blackwell, 2004).

Sosa, Ernest and Villanueva, Enrique (eds.), *Philosophical Issues*, 14 Epistemology (Oxford: Basil Blackwell, 2004).

Steup, Matthias, *An Introduction to Contemporary Epistemology* (Upper Saddle River, NJ: Prentice-Hall, 1996).

  Knowledge, Truth, and Duty (Oxford: Oxford University Press, 2001).

Stich, Stephen, *The Fragmentation of Reason* (Cambridge, MA: The MIT Press, 1990).

Stine, Gail, "Dretske on Knowing the Logical Consequences," *Journal of Philosophy*, 68 (1971), 296–99.

Strawson, P. F., *Skepticism and Naturalism: Some Varieties* (New York: Columbia University Press, 1985).

Stroud, Barry, *The Significance of Philosophical Skepticism* (Oxford: Oxford University Press, 1984).

Summerfield, Donna, "Modest A Priori Knowledge," *Philosophy and Phenomenological Research*, 51 (1991), 39–66.

Tienson, John, "On Analyzing Knowledge," *Philosophical Studies*, 25 (1974), 289–93.

Tomberlin, James (ed.), *Philosophical Perspectives*, 2 Epistemology (Atascadero, CA: Ridgeview, 1988).

  (ed.), *Philosophical Perspectives*, 13 Epistemology (Cambridge, MA: Blackwell, 1999).

Van Cleve, James, "Foundationalism, Epistemic Principles, and the Cartesian Circle," *Philosophical Review*, 88 (1979), 55–91.

  "Epistemic Supervenience and the Circle of Beliefs," *Monist*, 68 (1985), 90–104.

  "Supervenience and Closure," *Philosophical Studies*, 58 (1990), 225–38.

Vogel, Jonathan, "Cartesian Skepticism and Inference to the Best Explanation," *The Journal of Philosophy*, 87 (1990), 658–66.

  "Reliabilism Leveled," *The Journal of Philosophy*, 97 (2000), 602–25.

Williams, Michael, *Problems of Knowledge: A Critical Introduction to Epistemology* (Oxford: Oxford University Press, 2001).

Williamson, Timothy, *Knowledge and its Limits* (Oxford: Oxford University Press, 2002).

Zagzebski, Linda, *Virtues of the Mind* (Cambridge: Cambridge University Press, 1996).

  "What is Knowledge?," *The Blackwell Guide to Epistemology*, eds. Ernest Sosa and John Greco (Oxford: Blackwell, 1999).

Zagzebski, Linda and Fairweather, A. (eds.), *Virtue Epistemology: Essays on Epistemic Virtue and Responsibility* (Oxford: Oxford University Press, 2000).

Index